History of Greene County
[N E W   Y O R K]

Volume 1
1651–1800

J. Van Vechten Vedder
County Historian

TOWN HISTORIANS

Ashland	Mrs. Hattie C. Munson
Athens	Andrew D. Peloubet
Cairo	Mrs. Jennie W. Mangam
Catskill	Mrs. J. V. V. Vedder
Coxsackie	Edwin C. Hallenbeck
Durham	William S. Borthwick
Greenville	Miss Ellen M. Baker
Halcott	Mrs. James C. Johnson
Hunter	Samuel E. Rusk
Jewett	Mrs. John Towner
Lexington	Robert S. Tuttle
New Baltimore	Miss Julia Carhart
Prattsville	Arthur A. Disbrow
Windham	*No Historian*

COMMITTEE
William S. Borthwick * Edward A. Webb * Corwin B. Bronson (deceased) * Orin Q. Flint * Floyd L. Ives (1927)

HERITAGE BOOKS
2013

HERITAGE BOOKS
AN IMPRINT OF HERITAGE BOOKS, INC.

Books, CDs, and more—Worldwide

For our listing of thousands of titles see our website
at
www.HeritageBooks.com

A Facsimile Reprint
Published 2013 by
HERITAGE BOOKS, INC.
Publishing Division
100 Railroad Ave. #104
Westminster, Maryland 21157

Originally published 1927

— Publisher's Notice —
In reprints such as this, it is often not possible to remove blemishes from the original. We feel the contents of this book warrant its reissue despite these blemishes and hope you will agree and read it with pleasure.

International Standard Book Numbers
Paperbound: 978-0-7884-2794-7
Clothbound: 978-0-7884-6961-9

IN COMPILING this History of Greene County it has been thought best, because of length of such history and consequent expense, to touch only on the earliest events of importance in the settlement of each town in the county, adding to it from time to time, should the book prove of enough practical value to warrant its continuance. Much of the county's history has been written before, but is not in available form. Accuracy of statement has been the first consideration. Care has been taken to designate doubtful statements as such.

To this early history has been added the most important events of 1925-26-27, together with a limited directory of each town as decided upon by the committee. At least one of the following subjects will be found in each volume under separate heading:

    Indians
    Pioneers and Their Homes
    Highways
    Churches and Schools
    Public Buildings
    Newspapers
    Soldiers and Sailors
    Physicians and Druggists
    Attorneys
    Fire Protection
    Lodges and Associations

FOREWORD

Mrs. Vedder, the talented County Historian of Greene County, having requested that I supply copy for the first Report of the County Historian, it is my bounden duty and great pleasure to do so. I take it that whatever is to grace these pages must be pronouncedly historic in character. Not yet has there been written a comprehensive history of this County, though certain very valuable publications detailing local historic fact and fancy, intermingled, have appeared. It is exceedingly difficult to measure or appreciate the true value of recorded incidents of to-day in the light of their significance to-morrow.

The broadmindedness of the Board of Supervisors of Greene County in establishing the office of County Historian, as was done in the session of 1924; and, also, to provide for binding the maps and records of the County in substantial and accessible form, should be a subject of pride and gratification to everyone. Interest in these matters should not cease, but increase as the years go by, and these worthy projects sustained.

In the space allotted me, it may be well to record here for permanent reference some facts relating to the County, its political units, and a few references to early settlers and land titles.

In accordance with the spirit of the times fightings within and fightings without marked the earliest history of this section, as elsewhere. Both the English and the Dutch claimed the territory. The English based their claim upon Cabot's discovery (1497) under Commission from Henry VII. In 1501 Henry VII issued a Patent to colonize the new world. But no colony was planted. Both the French and the English had colonies before the coming of the Dutch. The Dutch based their claim upon the discoveries of Hendrick Hudson (1609). Probably the first white settlement in the present State of New York was on Manhattan Island in the year 1612, by the Dutch. It has been contended that the first Dutch colonization was when the Walloons were brought over from Holland in 1623. The conflicting claims between the Dutch and the English as to the right to the territory of what is now Long Island and eastern New York, including what is now Greene County, brought about bitter controversies and hostilities.

In 1664 the English, by conquest, obtained possession of all the Hudson Valley and the lands claimed by the Dutch; and, while the Dutch for a brief time regained possession, it was soon forcibly repossessed by the English and ever remained under their rule until the present government of the United States was instituted following the Declaration of Independence.

It may be noted that while religious persecutions and adventure led to the settlements of New England and the English colonies, as they became known, the desire for gain by trade, and nothing else, led to the founding of New Netherland by the Dutch, under the Dutch West India Company.

The manorial idea of settlement was favored, and the original patroon was Kilian van Rensselaer, but who never left Holland for this country. He sent a few settlers over in 1630. His manorial possessions included very extensive areas on both sides of the Hudson river. He claimed as far south as to include the present town of Catskill. This part of his title to lands was disputed by the Dutch governors and governor generals, and eventually was released to them. When New Netherland passed to the English in 1664, the Van Rensselaer estates were confirmed to the family and not confiscated, as the then patroon (Jeremias Van Rensselaer) took oath of allegiance to the English Crown, and he renewed his patent under the Duke of York.

In 1632 a Judicial system consisting of a schout and a court of schepens was laid out for Rensselaerwick. It was the first local court established in New Netherlands. The first schout was Jacob Albertsen Planck, followed by Adraen van der Donck.

There were clashings and quarrels as to authority between the patroons and the director generals and the governors under the Dutch, creating, among other things, disputes as to earliest land titles.

Under the English, and the Duke's Laws, so-called (The Duke of York's laws) no purchase of land from the Indians should be valid without a license from the governor, and the purchaser must bring the sachem or right owner before him to confess satisfaction. See Chester's "Legal and Judicial History of New York," vol. I, 158-163.

Nov. 1st, 1683, the Colony of New York was divided into twelve original counties. Those having direct relation to the present county of Greene were Albany and Ulster. The dividing line on Hudson's river, between these two counties appears to have been Murderer's Creek, in the village of Athens.

It is interesting to learn that in 1797 the then town of Freehold had 20 schools, principally log huts, with 949 children attending school in that year. Compare this with the attendance in district schools to-day. See Land Papers, Vol. No. 5, Office State Engineer and Surveyor, Albany.

In 1795 the first attempt was made to establish a system of common schools by legislative enactment. See Laws of 1795, Chap. 75.

The County was named in honor of General Nathaniel Greene of Revolutionary War fame. Its area is scarcely appreciated. It contains 643 square miles of territory as given by the Federal census of 1920. Some of the very wildest territory in the Catskill Mountains is within its confines, as, for instance, Platau Mountain, extending westwardly from Overlook Mountain to the Stony Clove. It is an absolute safe statement to make that no one person in the County has as yet fished in all its several streams. The Catskills, formerly often called the Blue Mountains, how they conjure eerie thoughts, with their legends and but half told tales of early settlers

HISTORY OF GREENE COUNTY

and hunters, striving against nature and wild beasts! Halsey in his Old New York Frontier refers to Akra (Acra) as a settled place as early as 1754 mentioning a settler by name Beach; and that to stand off the wolves at night, on the slow journey from the Hudson to the Susquehanna through an unbroken wilderness, was a fearsome daily experience.

A reference to the political organization of the County, and of the several towns, discloses the following:

The County was erected by Chapter 59 of the Laws of 1800, passed March 25, 1800, entitled, "An act to erect parts of the county of Ulster and Albany into a separate county." There appear to have been taken two entire towns from Ulster County, and two from Albany County. These towns were Catskill and Windham (and a portion of Woodstock) from Ulster County; and Coxsackie and Freehold from Albany County. The act provides as follows:

"Be it enacted by the people of the State of New York, represented in the Senate and Assembly, That all those parts of the counties of Albany and Ulster, beginning at Hudson river, on the line between the towns of Kingston and Catskill, running along the southeast bounds of the town of Catskill, to the northeast corner of the town of Kingston, thence along the town of Kingston opposite to the southeast corner of the town of Windham, thence to the southeast corner of the said town of Windham, thence along the southerly bounds thereof, to the southwest corner thereof, adjoining the county of Delaware, thence along the division line between the town and county aforesaid, to the northwest corner of said town, and to the southerly boundary of the town of Freehold, thence westerly to the most westerly extremity of the said town of Freehold, thence easterly along the northerly bounds of said town of Freehold and Coxsackie, to the northeast corner thereof, thence to the middle of Hudson's river aforesaid, thence down the middle of said river to the intersection of a line drawn from the place of beginning easterly on the course of the line first mentioned, and thence to the place of beginning, shall be and hereby is erected into a distinct county by the name of Green."

"And be it further enacted, That all that part of Woodstock included in said county of Green, shall be, and is hereby declared to be a part of the town of Cattskill."

By Chapter 123 of the laws of 1801 the state was divided into counties and the counties were bounded. The boundaries of the county of Greene are as follows:

"The county of Green to contain all that part of this State bounded southerly by the county of Ulster and part of the county of Delaware, as hereafter described; easterly by the middle of Hudson's river; north and northwesterly by a line drawn west from the southernmost part of Bearen island in said river to the southwest corner of the manor of Rensselaerwyck, and a line drawn from thence to the place where the line formerly run from the head of Katters creek issuing out of the southerly side or end of a certain lake or pond lying in the Blue mountains to a small lake called Utsayantho intersects the Schoharie creek and westerly by the said county of Delaware."

By Chapter 163 of the laws of 1801 the counties were divided into towns and bounded. The county of Green was composed of four towns, Catskill, Windham, Freehold and Coxsackie and are bounded as follows:

"And that all that part of the county of Green bounded southerly and westerly by the county of Ulster and by a line continued from the northwest corner of the town of Kingston in the county of Ulster to the head of Katterskill creek where the same issues out of the southerly side or end of a certain lake or pond lying in the Blue mountains and from thence in a direct course towards the small lake Utsyantho till it intersects a line beginning at the south bank of the mouth of the Murderer's kill at Lunenburgh and running from thence north eighty degrees west to the said intersection and northerly by the said last mentioned line shall be and continue a town by the name of Catskill.

And all that part of the said county of Green bounded southeasterly, southerly and westerly by the bounds of the county easterly by a line running from the northwest corner of Kingston in the county of Ulster, northerly by Catskill and by the southwesterly line of Catskill continued in the same direction to the bounds of the county shall be and continue a town by the name of Windham.

And all that part of the said county of Green bounded northerly by the county of Albany, westerly by Windham and the west bounds of the county, southerly by Catskill and easterly by Coeymans confirmation and a south line to be drawn from the southwest corner thereof to the town of Catskill shall be and continue a town by the name of Freehold.

And that all that part of the said county of Green bounded westerly by Freehold, southerly by Catskill, northerly by the county of Albany and easterly by the county of Columbia shall be and continue a town by the name of Coxsackie."

Chapter 52 Laws of 1803.

Town of Canton formed from parts of towns of Catskill, Coxsackie and Freehold.

Town of Greenfield formed from parts of towns of Coxsackie and Freehold.

All those several parts of the towns of Catskill and Freehold lying west and southerly of the summit of Catskill Mountains shall be and are hereby annexed to the town of Windham.

By Chapter 57 of the laws of 1805 it was provided: "That the town of Freehold in the county of Greene shall hereafter be called and known by the name of Durham."

By Chapter 127 of the laws of 1808 the name of the town of Canton in the county of Greene was changed to Cairo. The name of the town of Greenfield in the county of Greene was changed to Freehold.

By Chapter 78 of the laws of 1809 the name of the town of Freehold was changed to the town of Greenville.

By Chapter 46 of the laws of 1812 entitled "An Act to alter the division line between the counties of Ulster and Greene" it was provided:

"Whereas it appears that ever since the erection of the county of Greene the division line between that county and the county of Ulster has been supposed to run from the northeasterly bounds of great lot number eight in the Hardenburgh patent then easterly to the north end of Shens lake and the same line continued to the west bounds of the town of Kingston in the said county of Ulster: And whereas it also appears that by the act entitled "an act to divide the State into counties" the division line between said counties runs from the southwest bounds of said lot number eight to the north end of Shens lake which if adhered to would produce great inconvenience to the freeholders and inhabitants residing between the lines aforesaid, for remedy whereof,

I: Be it enacted by the people of the state of New York represented in senate and assembly That from and after the passing of this act the division line between the counties of Ulster and Greene shall begin at the point where the division line between the counties of Ulster and Delaware intersects the line run from the northeasterly bounds of great lot number eight in the Hardenburgh's patent, thence southeasterly along the said line until it intersects the line run by Jacob Trombour junior in the year one thousand eight hundred and eleven for the division between the counties of Ulster and Greene thence along the last mentioned line easterly to the west bounds of the town of Kingston in Ulster County."

By Chapter 45 of the laws of 1811 the town of New Baltimore was erected from the town of Coxsackie.

Chapter 15 of the laws of 1813 entitled An Act for dividing the town of Windham into three towns is as follows:

"Be it enacted by the people of the state of New York represented in Senate and Assembly That all that part of the town of Windham in the county of Greene lying east of the easterly line of great lot number twenty two in the Hardenburgh patent and south of the height of land between the east kill and the great hollow be erected into a separate town by the name of Greenland and that the first town meeting in the said town of Greenland be held at the house of Daniel Bloomer in said town; That all that part of the said town of Windham lying northwardly of the last mentioned line and of the height of land between Batavia and the south mountain settlement crossing the highway leading from John Tuttle's to Abel Holcomb's at a hemlock sapling standing on the east side of said road marked R. D. and crossing the Schoharie kill on the south line of lot number eighteen in the subdivision of lot number twenty in said Hardenburgh patent and running from thence westerly to the county of Delaware be erected into a separate town by the name of Windham; and that the first town meeting in the said town of Windham shall be held at the house of John Tuttle in said town; and that all the remaining part of the said town of Windham shall be erected into a separate town by the name of New Goshen and that the first town meeting in the said town of New Goshen shall be held at the house of Abel Holcomb in said town."

By Chapter 66 of the laws of 1813 the town of New Goshen in the county of Greene was changed to the name of Lexington.

By Chapter 211 of the laws of 1814 all that part of the town of Greenland in the county of Greene lying to the eastward of a certain line beginning in the south bounds of said town of Greenland eighty chains south eighty degrees west from the southeast corner thereof and to run from thence north twenty four degrees east to the Caderskill thence down the same to the east bounds of said town be annexed to and from and after the passing of this act shall form a part of the town of Saugerties in the county of Ulster and that the remaining part of said town of Greenland shall be a town by the name of Hunter.

By Chapter 43 of the laws of 1815 the town of Athens was erected from the towns of Catskill and Coxsackie.

Chapter 66 of the laws of 1816 perfects the boundaries of the town of Athens.

By Chapter 243 of the laws of 1822 part of the town of Saugerties was annexed to the town of Catskill.

By Chapter 251 of the laws of 1823 it was provided that the islands in the Hudson river or so much thereof as belongs to any of the inhabitants of the county of Greene known by the name of Scutters Island, Little Island, and Willow Island being parts of the town of Kinderhook in the county of Columbia county be and the same hereby are annexed to the town of New Baltimore, Greene County.

By Chapter 138 of the laws of 1822 it is reported "Whereas the town clerk's office of the said town (Durham) and the records therein were consumed by fire on the 24th day of February last and whereas great inconvenience and loss may arise therefrom unless legislative aid be given, therefore," provision is made for certified copy of the records.

By Chapter 54 of the laws of 1833 the town of Prattsville was formed from the town of Windham.

By Chapter 31 of the laws of 1836 a part of the town of Durham was annexed to the town of Broome in the County of Schoharie.

By an Act on Page 150 of the laws of 1848 the town of Ashland was erected.

By an Act on Page 208 of the laws of 1848 a part of the town of Hunter was annexed to the town of Lexington. Chap. 125 passed Mch. 25, 1848.

By an Act on page 808 of the laws of 1850 the town of Jewett was erected.

By an Act on Page 705 of the laws of 1852 the town of Halcott was erected.

By an act on Page 722 of the laws of 1852 a part of the town of Jewett was annexed to the town of Lexington.

By Chapter 911 of the laws of 1866 the line between the town of Hunter and Jewett was changed.

In passing, it may not be amiss to call attention to a very curious situation that arose when the town of Jewett was erected. That is, a portion of the town of Hunter, lying westerly of South Jewett settlement, and against the mountain southerly of the Schoharie Kill, *was not included* in the new town of Jewett. This leaves a portion of the town of Hunter, in the location to which reference is here made, surrounded by the towns of Lexington and Jewett, like an island. This came to my attention in the process of my work as title examiner, and may be clearly demonstrated. It is a condition that should be corrected.

Space will scarcely permit reference to the grants of land and patents, conveying land to individuals or companies. The history of certain patents alone would take space sufficient to make a good size book, if fully written. Some of the principal patents are: Certain Great Lots of the Hardenburgh Patent, as Nos. 20, 21, 22, 23, 24, 25, 26, 48 and 49, The State Land Tract, The Catskill Patent (so-called generally) Loveridge's Patent, Treat and McLean's Patent, Loonenberg Patent, and others.

I judge it will be of special interest here to give the names of the original owners of the tract known as the Greene's Patent in the town of Cairo. Some residents of the County may trace back their ancestry to certain of these patentees.

The tract was granted to twelve officers and privates of the French and Indian Wars by the Colony of New York as follows:

Gabriel Woods, 50 acres, Lot No. 9,
James Smith, Lot No. 8,
Jas. S. Johnson, Lot No. 7,
Matthew Holland, 350 acres, date of conveyance Apr. 18,1769,
Thomas More, 350 acres, date of conveyance, 1769,
James Scott, 200 acres, Lot No. 6, date of conveyance August 11, 1768,
T. Millett, 350 acres, date of conveyance March 10, 1772,
Thos. Cowans, Lot No. 5,
Henry Green Shields, Lot No. 4,
John Black, Lot No. 3,
James Barker, Lot No. 2,
James Coleman, Lot No. 1.

It may well be that there are original maps and surveys of tracts or lots of land in the homes of residents of the County that never have been filed with the County Clerk. It is suggested that this be done, for the benefit of all landowners. It is an important matter.

How changed on every hand are conditions in living from those earlier days of the County's organization. When the first town meeting was held in the new town of Freehold, the inhabitants were given a week to come and deposit their ballots for the election of the town officers, while to-day the voting machine quickly registers the individual vote and quickly tells the result. In passing, it may not be amiss to note that the first voting machine in this section for many years was installed in the town of Athens, Nov. 5, 1901; Henry I. Van Loan, Supervisor.

In conclusion let me urge upon all to confer with your town historian and the county historian relative to any subject deemed to be of interest. Preserve ancient documents and records, and refer them to someone qualified to advise relative to their worth. It is needless to remind that accuracy and fairness in statement are above all things to be faithfully observed. In this way permanent records of incalculable value will be preserved.

Just at present these things may not be well appreciated. But there is an awakening, and the day is not far distant when it shall be said of all who have aided this local history undertaking—right well did they serve us—we of coming generations—and such meed of praise as we may give, and unbounded appreciation, shall be our laurel wreath to them.

January 15, 1927.

ORIN Q. FLINT.

GREENE COUNTY COURT HOUSE, ERECTED 1813.

PRESENT COURT HOUSE, ERECTED 1908.

GREENE COUNTY

When the first pioneer came to what is now Greene County, whether along Indian trails, on horseback through the forest, by canoe or sloop, looking for furs, mill-sites or a home, he found it all a wilderness, its streams well stocked with fish, the forest filled with fur-bearing animals, and the soil of the valleys only waiting to be cleared of trees to produce, with little cultivation, large crops of corn and grain.

Here and there along the streams he found villages of peaceful Indians of the Mohican tribe, willing to trade rich furs for trinkets and beads.

Settlements were first made along the Hudson, for the mountain region was practically an impassable wilderness, with only here and there the log cabin of some adventurous trader or settler until after the Revolution, "when emigration from Connecticut and other eastern states began." The Dutch had taken possession of the lowland of the valley by right of purchase from the Indians. Grist and saw mills were the first industries, and rude mills were set up or built on nearly every stream as fast as trails opened, the Dutchmen securing and utilizing the many water privileges; for Greene County abounds in streams and specializes in natural dams, falls and cascades.

Timber was needed for the pioneer homes, the Dutch building chiefly of stone and the New Englander using rough boards, while grist mills furnished coarse meal and flour for the household, often carried for a score of miles along narrow forest trails. The Kings Highway in 1703, and the Susquehanna Turnpike in 1801, opened up the country and from that time settlements grew rapidly into villages and towns.

Greene County contains 643 square miles and has a population of 28,207, of which 930 are aliens. "In the first organization of the Province of New York into shires and counties (Nov. 1, 1683) what is now Greene County was included in the wide scope of Albany County, and so remained until March 24, 1772, when by act of Legislature it was divided into fifteen districts." In 1718, the "inhabitants of the Precincts of Catskill and Coxsacky, and all the inhabitants dwelling to the southward of Rensselaerwyck, on the west side of the Hudson River as far as the county of Albany extends," were allowed to elect a Supervisor.

Of the fifteen districts formed in 1772 the principal were those two known as the "Coxsackie and Great Imboght Districts." In 1788 another change was made and the towns of "Cocksackie and Cats-Kill" formed. In the next few years these towns underwent various changes, until, after numerous petitions to the Legislature for and numerous petitions against a change, during which time meetings of the inhabitants of Catskill for the purpose had been held at Martin G. Schuneman's* (Madison), and Petrius Souser's

---

* Catskill Packet, October and November of 1792 (the meeting was held Nov. 20).

(Jefferson), an act was passed March 25, 1800,† erecting certain parts of the counties of Albany and Ulster into a distinct county "to be called Greene."

The county was named after General Nathaniel Greene of the Revolutionary Army,§ and was composed of the towns of Catskill, Coxsackie, Freehold and Windham, and, according to the late Judge Chase in his "Local History Gleanings," on "March 29, 1800, civil officers of the county were appointed by the council of appointment. * * * Immediately thereafter a struggle commenced between the people of the different settlements within the territory in regard to the location of the county buildings. It appears from old letters that there was a bitter feeling among the people growing out of the discussion that followed, and such feeling grew in intensity until it was settled that the county buildings should be located at Catskill."

Previous to this the location of the Surrogate's office had depended upon the residence of the man holding the office. The first Supervisors of the new county were: Garret Abeel, Catskill; Jonas Bronk, Coxsackie; James Thomson, Freehold; William Beach, Windham. James Pinckney was clerk of the Board for many years. The first County clerk was James Bill,‡ and according to the late Judge Chase the first meeting of the Board was held at the hotel of Terrence Donnely, "which was situated substantially in the center of the front of the present county lot facing Main street. It has, therefore, come about that the rooms designed for the use of the Board of Supervisors in the present Court House are located substantially at the same place where the meetings of the first Board of Supervisors were held."

The late James Pinckney states that James Bill, lawyer and County Clerk, "dressed in nankeen breeches, white stockings and buckled shoes, a perfect specimen of old school gentleman. He resided at the top of the hill on Thomson Street, afterward known as the Croswell house, rebuilt and enlarged by J. Joesbury."

The act erecting the new county provided that "until further legislative provision the Court of Common Pleas and General Sessions of the Peace should be held in the Academy in the town of Catskill, and in the dwelling house of John Vandenburgh, in the town of Coxsackie, alternately."

There was no gaol or jail at this time, and prisoners were taken to Hudson and confined in one of logs on Warren street. In 1804 the Legislature passed an act (Chap. 33) directing the

---

† Chapter 59, Laws of New York, 1800.

§ Occasionally the final e is left off in early records and at least on one map.

‡ From Catskill Packet: Notice.—The inhabitants of the county of Greene are hereby notified that the clerk's office for said county is kept in the Main street of Catskill Landing, nearly opposite the house of Captain T. Donnelly.

Catskill, June 12, 1800.   James Bill.

HISTORY OF GREENE COUNTY

Supervisors of Greene County to raise $1,000 for the completion of the jail on "what is now the corner of Clark and Broad streets," which seems to fix the date of its completion.§

"The first session of the Greene County Court of Common Pleas* was held May 6, 1800, with Leonard Bronk first judge, Samuel Van Vechten, Stephen Day and Thomas Barker, judges. The first Surrogate of the county was John H. Cuyler, and the first District Attorney" (called Attorney General) was Ebenezer Foote.

In 1807 Greene County had her first murder trial. The murder took place in a house of ill repute kept by Nancy McFall on the road to The Point. The murdered man was John Scott of Coxsackie, and the supposed murderer one John Williams. An angry crowd pulled down the house of Nancy to the foundation. Williams was tried and found guilty; Nicholas Stiles accessory. Williams was to have been executed Dec. 22, 1807, but the presiding judge recommended a respite to the Governor, who consulted with Chief Justice Kent. The outcome was a reprieve and a final sentence was afterward imposed of five years.

Town of Ashland

The town of Ashland was formed in 1848 from what was left of the western part of old Windham after Prattsville had been set off, and its history as a town is therefore largely of a later date than that of the present volume. The town is said to have been named from the home of Henry Clay, who had warm friends living there. John S. Ives was the first supervisor, serving ten years (1848-1858).

The highest mountains in the town are Huntersfield and Ashland Pinnacle; its principal streams the Batavia, Lewis creek and West Hollow brook. The "old Windham and Durham Turnpike, which, running nearly east across the north end of the town, entered Durham from below Mt. Pisgah, by way of Cornwallville, intersected the Cairo and Windham road near Acra. The Windham and Cairo turnpike was laid out and constructed about 1790, in part under the direction of Col. Stephen B. Simmons. Lacking a kettle large enough to cook for his workmen, he went to Catskill, bought one and carried it home on his back. One of the industries of that day was turnpike yeast made by a Mrs. Fowler, a soft yeast dried and cut

---

§ In 1801, Laws of New York, Chapter 40, Samuel Hale, Caleb Benton, Leonard Bronk and Stephen Simons were appointed commissioners to cause the gaol to be built. Different amounts authorized by Legislature to be raised for this purpose from 1801 to 1804 amounted to $6,167.34.

* A County Seal, which is described as a "sword erect supporting a balance," and the motto, "County of Greene," around the seal, was adopted, according to Justice Alden Chester in "Courts and Lawyers," at the first Court of Common Pleas. This is not the seal used to-day, on which is the date 1847.

OLD ASHLAND SEMINARY, BUILT 1854.

into cakes for convenience of transportation during the building of the turnpike."

Among the earliest industries were woolen factories or fulling mills of George Brainard and Bidwell; a brick yard and a rope walk. Foster Morse had a mill and tannery. Between the years 1850 and 1855 the tannery business failed, owing to the exhausting of the hemlock bark, and cotton and woolen mills also suffered severely from their inland location, which caused very high transportation charges. In 1860 Ashland had a further business depression by the closing of the hat-making industry.

The town of Ashland lies in the northwest part of Greene County, its north and south borders occupied by two parallel spurs of the Catskill mountains, 800 to 1,000 feet above the valley. Batavia Kill flows westward through the town at the foot of the south range. This stream is bordered upon the north by steep bluffs 150 to 200 feet high; and from their summits the surface gradually slopes upward to the foot of the north ridge near the northern border of the town.

The first public school house was of logs and stood on what is known as Argulus White's farm. Six others are known to have been in the town, some of which served the purpose of church as well as school.

As George Stimson was the first settler of Windham, so he was among the first at Ashland, coming there in 1785, when his family of four sons and five daughters came from Massachusetts. His son Henry became the first minister of the Presbyterian church.

Zachariah Cargill was early on the spot, and sold his land to Nicholas Martin, one of whose sons lived to be ninety-eight years old, dying in 1881. Dr Thomas Benham came in 1793, the first doctor in the town, and traveled the rough roads and trails for many years on horseback with medicine in his saddlebags, never refusing a call to a sick-bed. It has been written of him that "he could never be hurried, but he always went." Three of his sons became physicians, practicing in Greene and Schoharie counties. After many years his practice was shared by Dr. Harvey Camp.

Dr. Benham had for a neighbor (1793) Argulus White. Elisha Strong engaged in wood-chopping, and in 1787 brought his wife and seven children, purchasing the land now occupied by the village. Nathaniel Ormsbee was there in 1787, and was distinguished as having previously nearly lost his scalp in some Indian war, a ridge across his head testifying to the truth of the tale.

Samuel Ives came from Connecticut in 1789. Amos Cook settled at West Hollow six years later, and had for neighbors Asa Goodyear, Gilbert Ferris and the Munsons. There was a rough road into Schoharie county in 1794, and along this road lived Stephen Simmons, Jabez Barlow and Giles Lewis Sr. Beyond the house of Lewis the road was still a blazed trail. The next year Jacob Hitchcock settled between Barlow's and Lewis's, later moving from his log house to one of frame some distance away.

On the Batavia was Jedediah Hubbard, who, with his son Timothy, were deacons in the Presbyterian church. The Hunt tavern was beyond the church, and east of the Hunt house was the tavern of Jeheil Tuttle, who came to Ashland when there was but a blazed trail up the East Windham mountain, with his household goods fastened to two saplings drawn by oxen.

Jedediah Hubbard with his son Timothy, both deacons in the Presbyterian church, settled on the Batavia. Foster Morss came in 1799, his brother Benjamin about 1812. John Turney was owner of 365 acres in 1790.

The pioneers of this region were not greatly troubled by Indians after the Revolution, although Indians followed the trail from the Susquehanna to the Hudson, and a few are said to have lived a mile north of the village, but the whites were harrassed by the wild beasts of the forest, which killed their cattle and sheep. Wolves were the most numerous, and these were finally almost extinguished by wolf-hunts, when the men banded together, surrounding the mountains upon which wolves were known to gather in large numbers, when the men would close in on all sides and kill many of them.

The first homes were of logs until saw mills appeared on most of the streams, then frame houses were built, patterned after those of New England, with huge chimneys and a bakery of brick. The stone house of the Dutchman is seldom seen among the mountains.

NORTH SETTLEMENT

Solomon Munson came to this vicinity in 1800, and two years later was killed at a house-raising on the Spring place. Silas Lewis, who was a surveyor, came to North Settlement previous to Munson, afterward buying the grist mill of Marshall Munson.

Nathan Osborne with his family of eight children came to North Settlement in 1799. On their arrival he built a log house, and three years afterward a frame one which was burned in 1804. Returning to the log house, another was soon built. Nathan was a soldier of the Revolution. Colonel Simmons had a house there and was justice of the peace and elected to the Legislature.

ASHLAND VILLAGE

The village of Ashland was first Scienceville, then Windham (old Windham), and lies along the Batavia kill, the main street following the way of the state road, a somewhat different course than when a turnpike of early days. It was called "Scienceville" because of some families who settled there of more than ordinary education and who paid special attention to the establishment of schools of a high standing.

The early history is little different from that of other villages along this stream, and it is second to none in beauty of location. From its "city of the dead," on the mountainside, one looks down on the valley stream, where in summer is the perpetual green of grasslands and cornfields. In the early mornings herds of cattle pass through the "bar ways" to the mountain pastures, which year by year have crept farther and farther toward the summits, and the tinkle, tinkle of the cow-bells, which are no longer heard in the Hudson valley, is a pleasant thing to hear. The whole has been likened by travelers who know to a scene in Switzerland.

THE OLD INN.

It was in and around this village that the first pioneers made their homes, a few Dutchmen and their families coming down from Schoharie before the Revolution, lured by the lowlands. During the Revolution, Indian and Tory on the trail made safe and peaceful living impossible, and the prudent Dutchmen returned to more protected areas.

After the war, Elisha Strong and several brothers named Stimson made the first permanent settlement. In 1789 there was the store of Sandford Hunt and the inn of Medad Hunt. Dr. Thomas Benham (1793) was the first physician, and Deborah Stone the first baby to begin life here. Ex-Governor Washington Hunt, son of Sanford Hunt, was a native of Ashland. It was a village of patriotic families from New England. Jacob Hitchcock Jr. was a sergeant of the Revolution. Samuel Ives and Jabez Barlow, the brother of Joel Barlow, Revolutionary poet and statesman, were among them. Jacob Tiel was a soldier of the war of 1812, and so were John and Philip Frayer, and George Denton, "who never returned to their homes."

On the walls of Woodchuck Lodge, the home in Roxbury of the late John Burroughs, hangs a school-bag in which he carried his books when a student at the Ashland Collegiate Institute.

This institute opened on May 6, 1854, and burned in 1860. The main building had a front of over two hundred feet and was five and a half stories high, with a wing of one hundred feet which contained a chapel, recitation rooms, laboratory, etc. It had a library of 1,500 books. Its course of study included music, painting, trigonometry (plain and spherical), surveying, civil engineering, astronomy and the more common branches of learning.

There were Biblical lectures, and students were to attend church in the village on Sunday mornings and at the institute chapel in the afternoon. The associate principals were Rev. Henry J. Fox and C. Rutherford, A. M. In a lot back of the building was a rock, where I am told John Burroughs wrote his first essay. Students came from Catskill, Albany and New York.

A few days ago I was up where the building stood, looking down on the village, valley, creek and mountains beyond, with Tower Mountain where there is a beautiful little spring hidden from strangers, and this verse of Burroughs' poem "Waiting" came to mind:

"The waters know their own, and drew
The brook that springs in yonder heights.
So flows the good with equal law
Unto the soul of pure delights."

(The County Historian is indebted to Mrs. Peter Rucka of Ashland for drawing and description of Ashland Seminary.)

PIONEERS AND THEIR HOMES

DR. THOMAS BENHAM

Dr. Thomas Benham was the first doctor in the town. He traveled over the country from one farm to the other on horseback with his medicine in his saddlebags. He is said to have been slow and sure, never permitting himself to be hurried but always ready to answer any call. He would never see a patient until he had a smoke. He was of a cheerful disposition and his presence acted as medicine upon his patients. Three sons followed his profession. The roads at first were little better than paths with blazed trees to show the way.

HENRY STIMSON

George Stimson, after his family came, removed from Windham to Ashland, and Henry his son became the first minister of the Presbyterian church, marrying Rebecca Pond. Henry had studied theology with Rev. M. Thomson of Oak Hill and Rev. Samuel Fuller of Rensselaerville. The Rev. O. B. Hitchcock has described him as "wielding a potent influence over the mature and rising generation. His appearance was commanding even in extreme age, fully six feet in height, erect, spare and muscular. He had strongly marked features, nose, brow, chin and cheek bones all prominent; the whole contour of his face expressing intelligence, strength of will and decision of character. He was sincere, devoted and self-denying." He was pastor of the Presbyterian flock at Ashland for 24 years; his only charge.

ELISHA STRONG

Elisha Strong made the first permanent settlement after the war by West Hollow brook and owned the land upon which the village now stands, about 1785. He engaged in wood chopping and two years later brought his wife and seven children. He built a house which stood near where his son Elijah afterward built a tavern. Another son Jarius had a brick store and dwelling. Houses

STRONG HOUSE (1805).

were first of logs then as saw mills were built, frame houses became the fashion, and the brick yards in turn furnished bricks for homes.

Among the earliest settlers was Nathaniel Ormsbee, who came in 1787 and married Sally Hull. In some Indian war he had nearly lost his scalp. He was a tavern keeper.

Foster Morss came in 1799. He was the father of Burton G., founder of the Red Falls Manufactory. John Prout came the same year. In 1790 Jacob Hitchcock, and in 1795 Amos Cook settled in West Hollow. Gilbert Ferris was one of the earliest settlers. Peter Brandow and sons came from Leeds after the Revolution. The Hunts, Whites, Mallorys, Munsons, Hubbards, Tuttles and Lewises had a part in the first settlement. Abram Dudley was the first miller.

Town of Athens

By Andrew D. Peloubet.

The Town of Athens was erected by Act of the Legislature by Chapter 43 of Laws of 1815, and passed February 25th, 1815. It was formed from the towns of Coxsackie and Catskill. The Village of Athens had been erected in 1805.

The line that separated these two towns began at the mouth of the Murderer's Creek, where it empties into the Hudson River, on its south bank, and ran diagonally across the town, to near its present southwest corner.

The project of erecting a new town had been agitated for some time previous to the enactment of the Statute (by the Legislature of New York State) erecting the new town, and undoubtedly came from the desire of the inhabitants of what is now the Town of Athens, to have a local town government. The following is an extract of the Act as entered on the Town Minute Book:

"Beginning on the west bounds of the Hudson River, in the Town of Coxsackie, near the southerly point of an island called Paddocks Island, at a Buttonwood tree, and from thence running north seventy-three degrees, west four hundred and four chains, intersecting the Schoharie Turnpike Road, near what is called the Hoogeberg, or High Hill, then along the northerly side of said Turnpike, to a creek called Potick Creek, then down said stream to the corner of the Town of Catskill, Coxsackie and Canton (now Cairo), near where a fulling mill formerly stood, owned by Ezekiel Benton.

"From said corner, south sixty degrees, west along the Canton line sixty-four chains to the Catskill Creek, then down along the said Creek, one hundred and ninety-six chains to a small buttonwood tree standing on the east bank of Catskill Creek, thirty chains above or northerly of the dwelling house of Martin G. Schuneman.

"From said tree, south sixty-three degrees, east thirty-seven chains to the Athenian Turnpike Road, and South fifty-five degrees and thirty minutes, east one hundred and ninety-eight chains to what is called the Corlear's Kill, crossing the said stream, then along the said Kill, forty-seven chains to the aforesaid Hudson River, near the dwelling house of Garret Pierse, and from thence to the place of beginning.

"The first town meeting to be held at the house of Joseph Seeley, in the village."

The house here referred to was built by Joseph Seeley, and herein he kept a Tavern. This house is a part of the present Howland & So store building on Second Street, and said town meeting was held i the east part of the present store, on the ground floor.

At the meeting, Isaac Northrup, the founder of the Village of Athens, was elected the first supervisor of the new town, and the first town clerk was Henry Wells.

Athens has an historical event that is not generally known. but which is a matter of record. The land upon which our beautiful village is built, is one of the first places in this state upon which the foot of white man trod. In the Journal of the Voyage of the Half-Moon, the vessel in which Henry Hudson discovered the noble river that bears his name, this record is given, and I want to quote the Journal as far as it relates to that event.

On the night of September 15th, 1609, and during the day of the 16th, the Half-Moon lay at anchor just above the present site

HISTORY OF GREENE COUNTY

of Athens. Here they were visited by the Indians, and the crew bought corn, tobacco and squashes from them, and in return gave the Indians glass beads, and other trifling articles.

On the 23rd, Hudson, having sailed to above the present site of Albany, and explored the river as far as the rapids, in a small boat, became convinced that he had not discovered the coveted Northwest route to India, set sail and proceeded down the river. On the 24th they had fair weather and northwest wind. Sailing down the river the Half-Moon ran aground on a Flat in the middle of the river. While the ship lay aground the men went ashore and gathered chestnuts. About ten o'clock at night, the tide being at flood, they were able to get off the mud and anchor in deep water.

On the 25th they had a south wind, so they rode at anchor and went on shore to look at the land on the west side of the river. There they found good ground for corn, and other garden vegetables, "and with a great store of goodly oakes, walnut trees, Chestnut Trees, and Ewe trees, and a great store of slate for houses."

In my humble opinion, it is an undisputable fact, that the Flat mentioned here is the Flat that lies in the middle of the river between our village and the City of Hudson. In those days there was no vegetation on the Flats, as I have been informed by very old residents, and when the tide was at its flood point, this Flat was invisible, being entirely covered with water. The wild rice we see growing and flourishing each September, and that warns the inexperienced mariner of our time, is an importation of recent years. I have been told that the late Dr. A. H. Getty's father imported the seed, and sowed it on the flats and bays, and to-day it has multiplied until it is growing on all the bays and flats in this vicinity.

The spot on the Flats where the Half-Moon grounded is undoubtedly opposite that which we at the present time, call the "Oil Dock." In support of this opinion, and, I might add, in positive proof of it, are the ledges of slate rock at this point, where the Indians had a large encampment. The soil for many acres thereabout is a sandy loam, and it was here that Hudson found the "good ground" on which the Indians raised the corn and tobacco that they gave to the explorers.

I have been a collector of Indian relics for a number of years, and the arrows and other stone implements found on this camp site are the most beautiful in form and the finest in workmanship that I have found anywhere in our town. Archaeologists tell us that the prehistoric inhabitants here were the Algonquin Indians. It is thought that the period at which they first occupied this territory was about three thousand years ago.

The largest Indian flint quarry in eastern United States is situated in the Town of Coxsackie, just over the Athens town line, and it was from flint quarried there that the tribes of local Indians produced their flint arrows and other flint implements which they used. The only records we have of the existence of the Algonquins here are the stone relics they left behind them and which are occasionally found on the various camp sites they occupied. The polished stone axes that are found here and elsewhere in this State were all produced by the Algonquins.

Morgan, the Historian, tells us that the Indians of the other nations did not produce or use these axes, and there are other men contemporary with the early history of the colonization of our State who have left the same written record.

At the time of the discovery and colonization of this territory, it was occupied by the Mohicans, and the Delaware Indians. The Mohicans owned the land from Coxsackie Creek west to the mountains and north to the Adirondacks, and all the lands east of the river, from New York to Champlain Lake. The Delaware Indians owned the lands on the west bank of the river to the Catskill Mountains, and from the Catskill Creek south. It appears that the lands between the Catskill and Coxsackie Creeks was neutral property, where the hunting and fishing were free to both tribes.

How long ago the Delawares and the Mohicans came into possession of this land is not known. From Indian traditions it appears that a few years previous to the coming of the white man, the Mohawks, a tribe of six nations, conquered the combined forces of the Mohicans and Delawares, in war; and Indian tradition also tells us that the decisive battle of this war was fought on Rogers Island, a short distance below our village, on the opposite side of the river.

Before this war, the Delawares were a warlike people, but from then on to the time of their migration and disappearance from our land, they never again put on war-paint and gave battle to their enemies in this section. It appears that the Mohawks made no effort to expel the Mohicans and the Delawares from their lands, but on the contrary their hunting and fishing parties made frequent peaceful excursions into this part of the country to fish and hunt, and part of them made this their permanent home.

The Black Rock farm, situated in the southern part of our village, on the bank of the river, in prehistoric times was the site of a large Indian encampment. This place was called Makawomuc, a reputed name of one of the early Delaware chiefs. The soil for about ten or twelve acres about this camp is black. This is caused by camp fires having been burning there for a great number of years. This camp site in later years was occupied by the Mohawks, as nearly all the relics found there are of Mohawk manufacture.

To the student collector of Indian relics, the arrow point or other stone implements of the Red Man has its individuality. It is in many cases possible, by its shape and characteristics, to identify the tribe to which its maker belonged. The pieces of broken pottery found on this site (in all cases that have come under my observation) have embossed decorations that are characteristic of the Mohawks; and the arrow heads, in a large percentage of cases, are the war points as made by them. This is the only Indian camp site in our town where this kind of relics may be found in large numbers.

At the time of the granting of the Loonenburgh Patent, the land here was claimed by the Catskill Indians, and by them was called Caniskek. The Catskill Indians were a sub-tribe of the Delawares. The Black Rock camp, and the camp on the Harmon Van Woert farm, at the Oil Dock, were undoubtedly fortified camps, as each one is situated for defense, and covered six or more acres of land; and they are the largest sites in our town. There are many other places in our town where one or a dozen families have camped, and where a few relics have been found. The last appearance of descendants of the Indian owners of the land in our village was about the year 1852.

For many years previous to this date, each Spring there would come to Athens a very old Indian and his squaw.* They would camp on the bank of a small stream that ran parallel with and about two hundred feet north of Union Street. In those days there were very old willow trees standing there, and this old Indian couple would build a shack in the shade of one of these trees, living there about six months of the year. My mother (whose maiden name was Isabelle Briggs) has often told me that when a little girl she and other children would go there to see them make willow baskets, and the old Indian would boast of his Delaware ancestors, and say that his great-grandfathers owned the land upon which our village is built.

The original purchase of the land by the white man was made in 1665, and the following is a copy of the original deed, on file in Albany:

"Inasmuch as Jan Clute and Jan Hendrickson Bruyn, and Jurian Tunise (Glazemaker) have shown at the sessions of the Court of Albany, the consent at their request of the Governor of New York, and the Indians, to purchase a certain parcel of land lying on the west side of the North River, over against the Claverack, near Fort Albany,

"So them having appeared before him, the underwritten Sec. of Albany, five Indians; namely, Sackamoes, Mauriata, alias Schermerhorn; Keisie Way, Papeuna, Masseha, owners, who declared in the presence of the afternamed witnesses, that they sold, granted, and conveyed as by these presents they do grant and convey, in real and actual possession to the aforesaid Jan Clute, and Jan Hendrickson Bruyn, the said land, called Caniskek, in magnitude stretching along the river side of and from the land of Peter Bronk to the fly which lies on the point of said land, behind Berren Island, and so running into the woods on the south, and on the north, even to Katskill Path, and that for a certain sum in goods which the grantors acknowledge that they have received from the buyers, and therewith are completely paid, and said grantors waive their former title and declare Jan Clute and Jan Hendrickson Bruyn to be the rightful owners thereof,

"And promise to free said lands from all actions, claims and demands, of the other Indians who lay claim to some portion of said land or the right to set deer traps.

"Done at Albany, this 20th day of April, A. D. 1665."

---

* Indian's name was Nelse and that of his squaw Till.

This title to the land was confirmed by a patent granted by Governor Richard Nicolls.

When the first patent for the land here was granted in 1667, by Governor Nicolls, there was no name given to the land in the Patent. In the confirmation Patent obtained by Jan Van Loon and others, July 28, 1688, and given by Governor Thomas Dongan, the name "Loonenburgh" was applied to the recited tract of land. In the interval between the granting of these Patents, the name Loonenburgh had been given to the land embraced in the original Patent, and may have been given to honor and perpetuate the name of Van Loon, but this is not positive.

The Loonenburgh has often been confused with the name Lunenburgh (a city in Holland), and some people have advanced the theory that this place was named in honor of that city, but this theory can be discounted by the fact that other places in this vicinity have taken their names from those of the first settlers in that particular vicinity. I will recite only two such instances, to wit —Spoornburgh Road, and Jacksonville; familiar names to our generation, and given in the honor of those two family names—Spoor, and Jackson.

JAN VAN LOON HOUSE, ERECTED 1706.

The history of Loonenburgh for the first hundred years of its existence is the history of a very few families. Jan Van Loon and his descendants have occupied a very prominent place in the life of the community, from the granting of the Loonenburgh Patent to the present time. The first house of which there is an authentic record was built by Jan Van Loon on the ground now occupied by

Richard Lenahan's shipyard. We can still see, in the foundation of the dwelling house there, a stone taken from the original dwelling, and bearing the following inscription: "1731. J. V. L."* Undoubtedly there were other houses built here previous to this one, but their location and by whom they were built has been lost in the passing of time, as deeds to the parcels of land along the river were given by the original patentees following the original grant to them in 1665.

Christianity, the vital factor in making this the greatest country in the world to-day, was early manifested by the founders of our town, in the erection of a house of worship. The Records of Zion Lutheran Church of our village show that as early as the year 1703 the Reverend Justus Faulkner was officiating as Pastor to this congregation; and we can claim, even in the absence of any written record to confirm it, that this congregation had its beginning previous to the year 1700 A. D. We know, from the experience in organizing other churches in our Village, that it takes several years of preliminary work before the actual organization is effected and a minister installed.

Of the events that go to make up history of an exciting nature, very few indeed are recorded. The geography of Loonenburgh was not in the scope of the thrilling history-making events that are found in the annals of our neighboring counties, and the struggles incident to the founding of our national government. The lives of the Dutch burghers and their descendants, who founded and inhabited Loonenburgh, were not ones of excitement and enterprise. William S. Pelletrau, A. M., in his History of Athens, as published in Beers' History of Greene County, likens the life of the Dutch burghers to the inhabitants of the world before the flood—"they married wives, they planted, they builded," and that living on their Bowery farms, the family and servants composed a man's social world, except when on Sundays he met with the Dominie of the church and the few neighbors scattered at wide intervals from each other.

To me, this appears to be too much of a strait-jacket definition of their lives; it is too confining. We know that the Dominie mentioned here traveled between New York and Albany in his Pastorate, and incidentally he brought news of the outside world, which is so necessary to every people, no matter how remote may be their habitation—and the Dutch were not different from other nationalities in this respect.

The Dutch had settled here over a hundred years before the Yankees came. The number of families residing in Loonenburgh just previous to the founding of the Village of Esperanza, in 1794, was approximately fifty. With the coming of the Yankees, the whole order of things changed. The Dutch settlers were forced to compete with the shrewd incoming Yankees in the struggle for a

---

*Another stone, bearing the date 1706, is shown in Beers Greene County History but cannot be located at the present time.

livelihood and wealth, and we at this distant date are able to judge that the Dutch did not come off second-best in the struggle!

The founding of the "town" of Esperanza was purely a speculation. The success of the founding of the City of Hudson caused a company of men to plan to establish a city on the west bank of the river that would not only be a rival of the City of Hudson but would be the connecting link between the upper and central part of the state with New York City, and also the terminus of the present Erie Canal, even at that early date anticipated. At that particular time there happened to be a celebrated French engineer and surveyor by the name of Pharmix, who was making a tour of the Hudson River valley. This man the company of speculators employed to survey the tract of land purchased from Albert Van Loon. (This tract of land formed what is now the Upper Village.) A large map was engraved, and the following legend appears thereon:

"A PLAN—of the Town of Esperanza, situated on the West Bank of the North River, opposite Hudson, laid down in lots, 25 feet in front, and 100 deep. This place is situated nearly at the head of Deep Navigation of the Hudson River. It is directly East from the Military lands, and is supposed to possess more important commercial and local advantages than any other point on the River, the road for some hundred miles west passing through a fine and improving country to which this is the nearest port.

P. Pharmix."

These maps were circulated for the purpose of attracting to the new village men who would purchase lots and build their homes and business places thereon. These maps are now very rare. I have seen but two copies; one, Mr. Charles W. Stranahan presented to the county, and is now in the Greene County Clerk's Office, and the other is in the possession of Counselor O. Gates Porter.

The success of this enterprise was shortlived; the grandiose expectations of its founders did not materialize, and the speculators soon found themselves in financial straits and were forced to make partitions of their holdings in the company. And so ended the dreams and hopes for a great city of Esperanza.

About this time another speculator was attracted by the advantages of the natural situation of the land forming what is now the lower Village, for the establishment of a large city. Thus, on April 30th, 1800, Isaac Northrup purchased the farm of John M. Van Loon, containing about two hundred acres, and in 1801 had a survey made and a map drawn by John D. Spoor. The success of this enterprise was immediate, and attracted men of superior class to build on the new purchase.

The Village had increased in population to such a great extent that it was thought necessary and advisable to be incorporated as a Village. Therefore, on April 2nd, 1805, the Legislature passed an Act incorporating Athens as a Village. In the incorporation, the Village of Esperanza was merged with the lower Village, and the combined settlement was named Athens.

There has been quite some controversy as to how and why the Village was named Athens, and it has never to my mind been satisfactorily explained just why it was so named.

FERRYBOAT USED BETWEEN ATHENS AND HUDSON PRIOR TO 1850.

For the first years of its existence, the Village had a rapid development and growth, as the following extract copied from Spofford's Gazetteer for the year 1813 indicates:

"Athens, a flourishing Post-Village on the West bank of the Hudson, opposite Hudson City, five miles above the Village of Catskill, principally in the Township of Catskill, Greene Co., and 28 miles South of Albany. It is incorporated as a Village under the government of a Board of Trustees, and embraces an extent of one and a half miles along the river, and about the same distance back. The site of this place is pleasant, on a gentle slope toward the river, and the situation is very eligible for trade. This is within four miles of the head of ship-navigation; the shore of the Hudson is bold, its channel inshore, and the soil principally a light sand or sandy loam or gravelly loam, very excellent for the site of a large town. A small part of the area as incorporated is within the Township of Coxsackie. Its intercourse with the surrounding country is facilitated by numerous roads, and its trade is of auspicious promise.

"Athens has now one hundred and fifty houses, and contains near one thousand persons, including all descriptions. It has one Lutheran church, three school-houses, and a market-place, an extensive ropewalk, a large distillery, a pottery of stone-ware, a tallow-chandlery, and some other small manufactories. There are eight vessels employed in the trade on the Hudson, and considerable shipping is annually built here. This place was formerly called Loonenburgh, Esperanza and finally Athens, by act of incorporation.

"The very great extent of back country that must always pour its surplus products into the trading towns, in this vicinity, will produce in time a great city near the head of ship-navigation, and Athens has a commanding position.

(signed) C. S. & J. A."

Note: C. S. undoubtedly refers to Castle Seeley.

INDIAN IMPLEMENTS.
By Andrew D. Pelouhet, in Collaboration with Albert Van Loan.

The Indian implements shown in the illustration were collected by the above-named collaborators from various States of the Union, particularly Florida, Missouri and New York.

No. 1, Sinus Stones—These stones were used by the Indian for removing fat and rounding strips of skin to be used as bow-strings. The original grooves in these stones may be plainly observed.

No. 2, Knives—As crude as these may seem, they were used in a most efficient way in removing skins from animals and for almost any purpose for which our present-day knives are used.

No. 3, Tomahawk or Axe—These were used for the same purpose as our modern axe. Also in war or massacre the Indian always used this death-dealing implement. It is believed that the axe or tomahawk together with his bow and arrows were always carried by the Indians as "standard equipment."

No. 4, Spud—This implement was used mainly for peeling bark from trees, also removing skins from animals. This is a well-made implement and shows that the Indian could create tools of symmetrical design for efficient use.

Nos. 5 and 5A, Arrow-Heads—These are fine specimens of their choicest creation. No. 5A is a "spiral" arrow-head which was so constructed that as it sped through the air it assumed a twirling motion and when it hit its object it had a boring effect. This is quite similar to the present-day system of rifling, which gives a bullet a "twirl" and keeps it on a straight course. To make death a sure thing, the Indian often dipped his arrow heads in poison snake venom.

No. 6, Spear Points—These were used on larger shafts than the arrow for the purpose of throwing or fighting in close quarters.

As small a field as this collection covers, it is sufficient to show us that the Indian had a well-developed brain and used it.

Town of Cairo

The town of Cairo was formed from Coxsackie, Catskill and Freehold (now Durham), March 26, 1803.* It was at this time called "Canton," and so remained until April 1808, when it became Cairo. The name Cairo is said to have been given by Asabel Stanley.

OLD TURNPIKE, NOW MOHICAN TRAIL.

Its principal streams are the Catskill, Shingle-kill, Plattekill, Jan-de-Bakker‡ and Potick creeks. The town contains 36,109 acres. The land included in this town was a part of the Salisbury-Van Bergen Patent, the Barker Patent and others, most of which were subdivisions. The log cabin of the Stropes is supposed to have been the first dwelling in the town. Ebenezer Beach settled near by in 1778. The first settlement of any size was at Woodstock by James Barker, known as the "Patroon."

The first town officers were (1803):

Daniel Sayre	Supervisor	John L. Darby	Commissioner
James Gale	Town Clerk	Joseph Reed	Commissioner
Wessel Salisbury	Assessor	Edward Rundell	Commissioner
Samuel Foster	Assessor	Joseph Shepherd	Constable
Benjamin Hine	Assessor	Samuel J. Haight	Constable
Joseph Shepherd	Collector	Stephen Olmstead	Constable
Henry Persen	Poormaster	Oliver Palmer	Fence Viewer
Jonathan Nickerson	Poormaster	Jonathan Allerton	Fence Viewer
Stephen Bentley	Pound Master	Goodman Noble	Fence Viewer
Jonathan Allerton	Pound Master	Benjamin Foster	Fence Viewer
Warren Hamlin	Pound Master		

They were chosen at the house of Mary Carbine, April 5, 1803.
* Land paper at Secretary of State's office, Albany.
‡ After an Indian.

HISTORY OF GREENE COUNTY

WOODSTOCK

Woodstock started out with great promise for the future, being the oldest settlement of any size in the town of Cairo, when James Barker, known as "The Patroon," settled here with his tenantry of 23 families shortly before the Revolution. The Barker Patent covered 6,000 acres of land and extended from Woodstock nine miles north to the town of Durham, on both sides of the Katskill. In 1800 the Woodstock and Durham turnpike was built, passing through the little village, and a bridge built by the Canton Bridge Company. This bridge in 1810 broke down with a drove of cattle, 30 of which were killed. The bridge was rebuilt the same year, and twice washed away by high water. In 1806 there was a distillery (of Montgomery Stevens)* at this place, and it is claimed that the first grist and saw mill in the town was built here. Judge Moses Austin had a woolen mill in 1816, afterward owned by the Hon. Lyman Tremain. In later years a paper mill flourished, but to-day as a village the place is extinct. The Woodstock Light & Power Co. now furnishes light and power to much of the valley.

CAIRO VILLAGE

First Shingle-kill, then Canton, the present name of Cairo doubtless followed that of the town. The "great road to the western settlements," afterward the Susquehanna Turnpike, formed its principal street, stretching west toward the mountains. After 1800 Cairo was a place for changing horses, stretching cramped limbs, and tarrying for refreshments on the long and tedious journey to Unadilla. It knew the sound of the horn as the stage coach rocked and swayed behind the gaily tasseled horses, and drew up at the inn† of Major Dewey at the lower end of the village. It was the great weekly event which brought not only the mail but passengers from all parts of the country, and from foreign lands to their doors. These were ladies and gentlemen, rough men and youths, adventurers, business men, and all kinds of humanity, perhaps returned travelers, doubly welcome for the news they would bring from the outside world.

In the early days Cairo bade fair to become a manufacturing village, equipped as it was with considerable water power on the Catskill and Shingle-kill. Before 1808 Mr. Hyde of the Forge had a brick yard on what is now known as the Alden farm, but then included that of the late John Mower. The Mower house is said by an old resident of Cairo to be the oldest Alden house, and there were two brick yards at one time on the farm.

John Baylis lived in the house now occupied by Otto Pfordte,

---

* Montgomery Stevens seems to have lived and engaged in business at Catskill and Montgomeryville (Wolcotts Mills) also.

† Catskill Packet, February, 1796, states that the house of Herman Deyo, tavern keeper of Shingle-kill, **burned with all his** household goods. Adijah Dewey also lived at Cairo, in 1817.

and before Baylis it was owned by the Rouses. About 1809 there was a scythe factory, three years later the property of Pliny Barton and so remained for twenty years. A grist mill, built about 1790 by a Mr. Crooker, was taken down about 1824 or 1825, and re-erected became the property of Paul Raeder.

Daniel Sayre had a shoe factory, Alpheus Webster manufactured spinning wheels, and Captain Byington had a clock factory at the Forge on the Shingle-kill. The first frame house is said to have been built by a Mr. Carbine, and the second by Ira T. Day near the Episcopal Church.

PURLING.

Purling, its baptismal name "The Forge," lies one mile south of Cairo village, reached by one of Cairo's village-street highways along which one gets a view of the Catskills and the intervening country, most beautiful and satisfying. Below the road a short distance out lies the County Farm.*

SHINGLEKILL FALLS.

"The Forge" received its name from Enoch Hyde and Benjamin Hall of Litchfield, Conn., who, about 1788, built an iron forge on the bank of the Shingle-kill. This little stream runs through a beautiful glen in the center of the village. A little later another forge was built where the present grist mill stands. A few log houses were built around the forge, and two of them became the church and the school.

The iron for these forges is said to have come from Ancram.

---

* See Public Buildings.

Columbia Co., by boat on the Hudson and by mule power to the Shingle-kill. The iron was known as charcoal iron and was forged into bars to be used by blacksmiths. On the site of the forge at the top of the falls below the present bridge, Mr. Hyde built a grist mill which was carried away by a freshet in 1857. It was rebuilt by Jonathan B. Webster. The next year it was destroyed by fire and rebuilt by John A. Gallatin, afterward owned by ex-Assemblyman Frank S. Decker. At one time the Forge had a nail factory. In 1813 Rufus Byington built a tavern at Four Corners.

On the banks of the beautiful falls or cascades of the Shingle-kill at the Forge have been at various times grist and saw mills, a factory for the manufacture of grain-cradles, hand-rakes, and well-curbs, one for turning out furniture (A. Wright), and on the opposite bank in later years Porter and Akeley had a bucket-shop in which 5,000 buckets were made annually. A resident of Purling recently pointed out, at the foot of the first fall, the only thing remaining of the old forge. This was the stone upon which rested the trip-hammer.

ACRA

This village lies along the Mohican Trail to the northwest of Cairo village, and has a wide view of the surrounding country and the Catskills. The first church was the Presbyterian, a few years later sold to the Baptists. Its first inn or tavern was built by Moses Olmsted, and its first store by Joseph Lyon.

John Howell, a friend of Judge Daniel Sayre, and great-grandson of Edward Howell, founder of Southampton, came to Greene County in 1794, bought a farm and built the Howell homestead on the road from Acra to Centerville, and was founder of the First Presbyterian church in Acra, in 1795. He died in 1815, aged seventy-one years. His wife Mehitable died three years later.

SOUTH CAIRO.

South Cairo rambles along the Catskill, two and one-half miles below Cairo village on what was the Susquehanna Turnpike of 1800. In former years before the present bridge was built the creek was crossed by fording, and the ford was reached by the narrow road or street south of the Jones home. The Carman house (still standing) opposite the bridge was an inn where stage horses were changed.

William Barton (great-grandfather of Mrs. William Davis of Catskill), came to South Cairo in 1828 and established a bell-factory* where he manufactured bells of all kinds, and was the first to make

---

* There seems to be no doubt that the bell-factory stood at the foot of what is now known as "Aratoga Hill," where to-day there is a pond on a little stream called Myne kill, or Minorkill, and in the New York Magazine of 1797 (page 108) is the following: "At a meeting of the inhabitants, at Minor-kill, in the town of Catskill, Resolved: That the name of their settlement be known only by the name of Jay's Valley."

sleigh-bells in the country. Before coming here he served as a Revolutionary soldier, and had a bell-factory at East Hampton, Massachusetts, which is said to be still running. The first pension money he received was spent for a fine shawl for his wife, which Mrs. Davis still cherishes.

On the site of the old Catskill Creek House, Elisha Blackmar built an inn in 1816. Cattle were driven through this part of the country, and this was the stopping place for the drovers, where they spent the night. Later, Blackmar built the house on the Van Deusen homestead which is still standing, and retired from business.

SANDY PLAINS

Sandy Plains, rich in farm land, lies south-east of Cairo village and is composed of the scattered homes of prosperous farmers, and some of the earliest settlers located here. It was originally a part of the Salisbury Patent, and its early history is a history of its pioneers who came before 1800 and worshipped at Old Katskill.

Indian Ridge, north east of Sandy Plains, was the camping ground of the Indians. This is also a farming district and here was the Wicks homestead, the first house built in 1774, at an elevation of 1,200 feet.

ROUND TOP

Round Top was known to the Indians as Wa-wan-te-pe-kook, or "round head place," from the shape of this small mountain which seems to stand guard over the Catskills in the town of Cairo. The village of Round Top is not on the highest part, as one would be led to think by the name, but its eminence is such as to give a fine view of the surrounding country and the forest-covered sides of the Catskill Mountains. The village consists of a Methodist Episcopal church, a modern country school house, a few stores, and a number of boarding houses, with its city of the dead where rest many of those who made a way in the wilderness for the present generation.

Frederick Schermerhorn was but a lad of 17 when (1780) sent by his father from their home, on what is now the Barringer farm between Leeds and Cauterskill, to the vicinity of Round Top, where a brother Jacob lived, having married the daughter of Johannes Strope (Stroop), where they were living with her parents. It is said that Frederick's dog refused to go with him on this walk of ten or twelve miles through the forest, and the lad, although disliking to take the trip alone, continued on and reached the place in safety. His brother Jacob, who was to help him drive some sheep from the Shingle kill, had already gone to Wynkoop's mill on the Kaaterskill. Frederick remained over night and early next morning was awakened by his sister-in-law's screams, who called to him that the Indians were coming. She fled with her children to a field of rye near by and later escaped, reaching a neighbor's at Kiskatom.

The elder Stropes were both tomahawked and their bodies burned with the house, and Frederick taken captive to Canada (see Indians and Tories). Jacob came back later in the day to find his home in ruins. The father of the boys, becoming anxious about Frederick, started out and on the way met Jacob, who told him the sad news. It was not until a year later that word was sent him through a Tory that his son was living, but it was not until the close of the war that he returned home. He had been given the choice on reaching Fort Niagara of enlisting in the British Army or being turned over to the Indians. He chose the former, and although he made many efforts to escape was always unsuccessful. When ordered to fire the property of Americans he steadfastly refused. After spending some time with his parents he married and removed to Stockport, later to Round Top, where he bought a part of the Greene and Biddle Patent, building first a log and afterward a frame house about a mile from the church. He died in 1847, aged eighty-four, at the home of his son-in-law Miller Jones.

The picture shows Harrison Jones, father of County Clerk Floyd F. Jones, and grandson of Frederick Schermerhorn, as standing where the cabin of the Stropes was burned in 1780. Mr. Jones is now over eighty years of age, owns the Strope farm, and remembers when a boy hearing his grandfather tell of the tragedy and of his own captivity.

Among the earliest settlers at Round Top was Elias Dutcher, born in Dutchess County in 1755. He was among the first to volunteer in the war of the Revolution, and was with General Israel Putnam in several engagements. He married Mary Rose and had five children, removing to Cairo in 1790, not far from Round Top, near what was called Steuffel's Point. His son Seth was born here in 1796 and had what was called a liberal education in those days, of three months in a log school house. Seth married Mary, one of the

English Salisburys, and became one of the staunch supporters of the Round Top church, a loved and respected citizen. He died at Ellenville, Ulster County, in 1860.

PIONEERS AND THEIR HOMES
Before 1800
ISAAC ALLERTON*

Isaac Allerton, the ancestor of the Allertons of this vicinity, came over in the Mayflower, which sailed from Plymouth, September 6, 1620. He had with him his wife, three children and a servant, John Hooke by name.

When Isaac was born is not known, but it was between the years 1583 and 1585. Some time before removing to Holland he had resided in London. His business it has been stated was that of "farmer, seaman, and taylor," but he was more frequently called a merchant. As he was but twenty-four years old when he left England, it is quite possible he had no particular business or occupation, for he is generally admitted to have been the wealthiest of all the Pilgrims, and was always given the title of Mr., as was also Mr. Brewster. He was one of three upon whom the privilege of citizenship was conferred by the city of Leyden in 1614, the others being William Bradford, afterward Governor of the Colony, and Degory Priest, Isaac's brother-in-law.

Isaac Allerton married (Nov. 4, 1611) Mary Norris of Newbury, England, and had four children, all born in Holland. Bartholomew, Remember and Mary came to America with their parents, but Sarah came over later with her aunt, Sarah Priest. Isaac was the fifth signor of the famous compact made by the Pilgrims for self-government which has been styled the "first American Constitution."

He was assigned a "Garden Plote," and it is not known whether he built a house upon it or not, but in 1653 he lived at Rocky Nook, on Jones's River, in Kingston, which house he afterward sold to "my beloved sonne-in-law Thomas Cushman." The history of Isaac is bound up in that of the Colony, and for some time he held the position of Assistant Governor. His wife died in 1621, and five years later he married Fear Brewster, who had come over in the ship Ann (1623) with her sister Patience. Fear died in 1634.

Isaac was sent over to England in 1626 for supplies and on other business, and returned with a contract from the "Adventurers," the men who had advanced the money for the colony, by which contract they eventually sold their interest in the colony for 1800 pounds. He was immediately sent back to England to confirm the contract, and made several trips to that country on business for the colony. Being liberal-minded toward Roger Williams and the

---

* From Allerton Genealogy by Walter S. Allerton, loaned by Miss Betts of Catskill. When possible "Pioneers" have been given in alphabetical order.

Quakers, as well as toward religious beliefs in general, he finally had serious disagreements with Governor Bradford, and because of this he left Massachusetts in 1636 and went to New Amsterdam. His temper was quick and he was not easily reconciled. From 1634, when he lost his second wife, until 1644, he had a series of misfortunes. In 1644 he was wrecked at Scituate, and at that time there was reference to a third wife whose name was Johanna. Two years later he became a permanent resident of New Haven and built a "grand house on the creek, with four porches." He died early in the year 1659, about seventy-five years of age.

This Isaac Allerton was the direct ancestor of Jonathan Allerton, who bought with others in 1783 the Van Schaack Patent in the town of Cairo, N. Y. 'Jonathan was born at Plainfield, Connecticut, Sept. 15, 1746. He learned not only farming on his father's farm but his father's trade of builder and house-joiner. He taught school winters, and while at Amenia, Dutchess County, he married Bathsheba Mead, September 17, 1772. She was the daughter of Joshua Mead.

Jonathan Allerton was well educated and an excellent penman, always in demand to draw contracts, deeds and like documents. He was an ardent patriot and soldier of the Revolution, selling his homestead for $2,000 in Continental currency, losing nearly all he had of this world's goods. When he came to Cairo he taught school for several winters, and died August 10, 1806, his wife surviving him thirty-two years. His children were: Joshua, who was brought to Cairo by his parents in his childhood, and became a successful farmer, marrying in 1804 Polly Bassett. Isaac married Charlotte Townsend. John married Polly Andress, and they removed to Delaware County; Anna married Reuben Germain; Reuben married Maria Miller, was a soldier of 1812 and became a minister of the Christian Church. Lucy married Benjamin Bullock. Jonathan Allerton, the father, was buried near Cairo, and his grave was recently marked by the Sagtakoos Chapter, D. A. R., of Long Island, of which one of his descendants was a member.

JAMES BARKER

James Barker, who was known as "The Patroon," came from London, England, where he was born in 1727, and settled first at Catskill. His stay there was probably short. "He was a prominent member of the English Bar, and his wife a lineal descendant of the Tudors." She had married James Barker against her parents' wishes, left rank and friends and came to America with the husband of her choice to settle in a new country which was practically a wilderness.

Mr. Barker had forfeited his claim to a large estate in England to which he was heir. They brought with them 23 families, former tenants. He first purchased a tract of land in the town of Durham, and when his wife received a part of her mother's estate, they added land in the town of Cairo* (Woodstock). Soon dwellings were put up, the land was cleared for planting and sowing, and community life began under as excellent conditions as could exist in a new and unsettled country.

On Sundays his tenants were called together for divine service, which he conducted himself according to the form of the Church of England. A lawyer by profession, he found little time or perhaps inclination to follow it. Now and then he figured in a great criminal case, and defended his friend Salisbury in his famous murder case at Catskill, which never came to trial.‡ He took no part in the Revolutionary War, either for or against it. His life and property were often in danger from Indians and Tories, and he was obliged to bury his money and silver, much of which was never recovered. Mr. Barker lived to be ninety-three years of age; his wife Elizabeth Moore Barker died in 1796, aged fifty-eight years.

Town of Catskill

The district corresponding to that of the town of Catskill by act of March 24, 1772, was called the "Great Imboght District." Its boundaries are described as "All that part of the said county of Albany which lays on the west side of Hudson's River, and on the south of Coxsackie District."

This district was much larger than the present town, which was erected by the clause of the act of March 7, 1788, for dividing the county into towns. It was then bounded by Coxsackie on the north, Columbia County on the east, and Ulster on the south, and was to be called "Cats-Kill." By act of April 5, 1798, it was placed in the county of Ulster.

When Greene County was formed Catskill became one of four towns composing the county, and some territory from Woodstock, Ulster County, was added. It lost some of this territory when Canton or Cairo was formed, and some to the town of Windham. In 1812 the line bordering Saugerties was changed, still further reducing it, and in 1815 it again lost out to Athens.

The first town meeting was held April 8, 1789. The first officers: Egnatius Van Orden, Abraham Salisbury, Jurry Laman, John Fero and Egbert Bogardus, Assessors; Egnatius Van Orden, Samuel Van Vechten and Abraham Salisbury, Commissioners of Highways; Samuel Van Vechten and Frederick Smith, Overseers of the Poor; John Overbaugh Jr. and Marthagaritse (Martin Garretse) Schaneman (Schuneman), Collectors; Petrius Osterhoudt, John Overbagh Jr. and Arent Van Dyke, Constables; Petrius Souser, Johannes Saxe, Joseph Groom and Jurry Laman, Fence Viewers.

---

* Tagphkight and Magquamsasick, two plains along the Catskill, "between two creeks" (400 acres above Potick), was granted to Elizabeth Barker in 1791.

‡ A document at Catskill Public Library proves that the indictment was "quashed."

Hezekiah Van Orden was elected Supervisor, and William Van Orden Jr., clerk. For the purpose of keeping the highway in repair the town was divided into fourteen districts.

There were at least twenty-four taverns or inns in the town in 1789, and in 1803 fifteen schools. In 1795-97, pot and pearl ashes was a considerable article of trade, "brought to Katskill from a distance of about 150 miles." The potash sold for $175 a ton, and to produce a ton, from five to seven hundred bushels of ashes were required. The ashes sold for one shilling a bushel. "At this time workmen received $13 a month and were not easily procured."

The Rev. Clark Brown wrote in 1803 that the "principal timber was white and black oak, yellow and white pine, walnut and maple. About 1,000 bushel of walnuts are exported annually from the town. In the southwest part of the town black spruce grows in abundance, from which a large part of the essence is extracted for beer, the greater part of which is exported. There are between five and six thousand inhabitants in the town, 700 electors, between seven and eight hundred blacks, seven grist mills and about the same number of saw mills. In Madison a flouring mill lately erected by Ira Day and Company.

"Jefferson has ten dwellings, three stores and two public houses. The merchants trade in lumber which they receive for their goods. Catskill Landing forms a safe and convenient harbor for vessels. The creek is narrow and deep, but no vessels drawing more than ten feet of water can ascend it by reason of a sand bar near its junction with the Hudson River. There are twelve wharves built into the creek, twelve ware houses, 200 buildings, 31 mercantile stores, a court, a jail and a printing office, the remainder dwellings. Many of the buildings are of brick mostly two stories high, one large and handsome street, one dwelling* on the hill built the present year. A wharf might be built into the Hudson river as far as a small island a quarter of mile from shore at little expense. This is in contemplation.

"After October first next, a stage will start for Albany and for New York on every Tuesday and Friday. The mail goes to and returns from Hudson twice a week by water. There is also a mail from this place to Tioga-Point, Penn., which is commonly but one fortnight going and coming. Between three and four hundred thousand dollars worth of produce are exported to New York annually, more than three hundred thousand of which goes from Catskill Landing. The only bridge of any considerable magnitude is that over the Catskill creek; a toll bridge with a draw.

"Shad, bass, herring, sturgeon, pike, trout, perch etc. are caught in the Hudson. Wild geese and ducks are plentiful in spring and wild pigeons are the chief fowls which are killed for use. No restrictions to fishing and fowling. Land which sold for ten dollars an acre in 1786 now sells for $400. In Catskill village shipping to

---

* Stephen Day's.

the amount of 37,000 tons have been built in one year for foreign markets.

"There are fifteen schools in the town, three at the Landing. In the one languages are taught. There is a well regulated library of 672 volumes, four churches, two at the Landing, one Episcopal of which Mr. Bradford is minister, one Presbyterian at Lunenburg, one within two or three miles west, Mr. Labagh minister. The Presbyterian Society expect soon to build them a meeting house, also the Episcopals. There are eight licensed attorneys in town and several merchants who have received a public education, two of whom have been regular settled ministers in Connecticut, another a licensed candidate. These three are members of the Presbyterian church at Catskill Landing and gentlemen of reputable character."

OLD KATSKILL

Old Katskill was four miles from the present village of Catskill, about a half-mile southwest of Leeds, and entirely distinct from it. Here on the foothills overlooking the Leeds flats the first house and barn was built in 1680. By 1733, a church, a school house, six houses and a smithy had been built.

FIRST CHURCH AT OLD KATSKILL.

The name Katskill at that time probably covered most of the territory in the present town, but naturally centered around the church and houses mentioned. Why it was called Katskill is only conjecture. Undoubtedly it was first given to the creek as it was seen emptying into the Hudson, kill meaning creek. The most reasonable inference seems to be that the first Dutchman to look upon what is now Greene County named it after Jacob Kats, "Keeper of the Great Seal," in the homeland. The fact that in very early documents it is written Catskill means little, for at that time scant attention was paid to the spelling of either place or individual names. It has been most frequently written Kats-Kill, Kaatskill and Katskil by the pioneers.

Old Katskill was included in the patent of 35,000 acres of land purchased of the Indians July 8, 1768, by Silvester Salisbury,

Commander of Fort Frederick,‡ and Marte Gerritse Van Bergen, Commissarie General. (Jan Bronk's land, now Leeds, was excepted). The purchase price was 300 guilders in wampum, several hundred ells of woolen cloth (or duffels), ten blankets, ten fuses, ten axes and ten pair of stockings. This land is described as consisting of "five flats (vlaktens) lying on both sides of the kill, the name of the first flat being Wachachkeek, the second Wichguanachtikak, the third Pachquyak, the fourth Assiskowachkok, and the fifth Potick, with the wood land for a cattle range or otherwise, to wit, four English miles around said land."§   *   *   *   The first house and barn to be built at Old Katskill was that of Marte Gerretse Van Bergen in 1680. The house was small and of stone, the barn large, and it was necessary to procure help from Kingston and the neighboring settlers to raise it. There was also a stone smoke house.

Marte Gerretse Van Bergen* never lived there, and the farm was leased the same year to Teunissen Van Vechten, his wife's relative, and Johannes Volkertsen Douw for six years, "for twenty-

VAN BERGEN-VEDDER HOUSE, BUILT 1729.

two beavers yearly for the first three years, and twenty-five for the next three," and in addition to this "100 skipples of maize at market price. A house, barn, orchard, eight horses, six mares, one gelding, one stallion, a half worn wagon and plow, eight traces, four lines, four whiffletrees, four stirrups, two bits, one iron neck yoke, one fan, one iron chain, a harrow with iron teeth and a winnowing fan"

---

‡ Fort Frederick, called the "Fortress of the Crown," occupied the site of the present St. Peter's Church, Albany.
§ See map at Court House.
* Marte Gerretse Van Bergen was killed by Indians.

are mentioned as on the place, and in addition to these the lease goes on to state, "there is now fifty-one skipples of wheat in the ground, and the lessor promises to build a rick and have doors made for the barn.   *   *   *   In case of general war (from which God protect us), the loss shall fall upon the lessor, and in case of burning upon the lessees."

The house of 1680 was torn down about seventy years ago, having served as a kitchen and place for the slaves after a new house of brick was built in 1729† by Garret Van Bergen, the son of the first owner. The stone house was never occupied by the Van Bergens, but shortly after the new house was built Gerret came down from Albany (perhaps from Coxsackie) with his family, consisting of wife (Annetje Meyer) and seven children, to make their home there. The house was a story and a half high with roof of red tile (taken off in 1836 and the house raised a half story).

Martin, the brother of Garret, built a stone house the same year (1729) a few rods east, with interior arrangements much the

SALISBURY-VAN DEUSEN HOUSE, BUILT 1705.

same as his brother's. It was torn down in 1862 and replaced by the late Jeremiah Burgett with one of brick. Martin also built a large barn and had a smithy.

In 1733 the Reformed Dutch Church of "Katskill and Kocks-Hackie" was built on the rise of ground just above this house, and a parsonage on the hill across the flat to the east (June 12, 1733).‡

---

† The house of 1729 is still standing, the property of Henry M. Vedder Jr. The frame of the barn of 1680 is still doing duty.

‡ A stone bearing this date and taken from the old parsonage is in the possession of W. W. Van Vechten of Leeds.

A school house is spoken of in an old deed as being near the parsonage before 1787, and a little later one was built near the church.

Silvester Salisbury died sometime between 1679 and 1680. The formal division of the land was not made until 1721, but in 1682 the lands of Salisbury were leased by the trustees of the estate to Andreas and Hendrick Whitbeck. In lieu of rent they were to build a fence around certain portions of the land and orchard, "build a barn 52½ feet in length, and as broad as the barn Marte Gerretse (Van Bergen) has built." They were also to erect a dwelling 22½ feet square with roof of shingles and "a cellar of stone as large as the house." They were also to "plant an orchard of 200 fruit trees, and pay yearly rent of twenty-five pounds of butter." Whether the house was ever built is not known. The present house† was built in 1705, by Silvester's son Francis.

In 1730 Salisbury built two houses for his sons William and Abraham. The first, still standing;* the second, on the Elting farm, has long since been torn down.

(For continuation of Old Katskill history see Churches and Pioneers.)

CATSKILL VILLAGE
Incorporated 1806

Situated at the mouth of the Catskill Creek, in a swamp called Eckerson's Vly, where that stream joins the Hudson after a forty-mile journey from a little spring on the mountain-top, it was first called by the Dutch the "Het Strand" or Landing. Its rugged sloping hillsides "down which ran numerous brooks and rills" did not appeal as a permanent home to the early Hollander who purchased land farther up stream. Below the Hop-o'-Nose was an Indian village, and also at Mawignac, where the Kaaterskill enters the Catskill.

Very early in the history of the Landing the names Uylen Spiegel's Kill, Uylen-Vly and Uylen-Hoeck, had been given to what is now DuBois Creek and the land along it, and Uylen-Spiegel's (or Ulyenspeigel's) land is mentioned in an old deed, but little else is known of this probably earliest landowner of Catskill.

In 1653 Pieter Teunissen Van Brunswick was granted land on the north and south sides of the Catskill and his house is said to have been built in 1651, described as having been "only one story high of timbers," with a huge stone chimney, and roof thatched with rushes. The land granted to Van Brunswick in 1653 was the "plain which lies opposite the Van Vechten house, just below the second railway bridge. The house was built in 1651, just above the embankment of the railway." When the late Henry Brace was living the foundation could still be seen.

In 1686 Harme Gansefort and wife Maria deeded land on the west side of the Hudson River to William Loveridge for "200 good

---

† Now the Tiffany farm (Van Deusen's).
* George Y. Clements.

and merchantable beavers," which included "messuage, or dwelling house and barn, * * * near ye mouth of ye said kill or creek; where ye said Loveridge now dwells; which said land was purchased jointly by ye said Gansefort and Eldert Gerbertsen Cruyff, of Jan Andriese ye Yrishman; who married the widow and relict of Pieter Teunise Van Brunswick."

Harme Gansefort had sold this farm to Jan Conell, who was unable to pay for it and transferred his rights and title to William Loveridge. In 1682 the Indians released all claims to the land at the Hop-o'-Nose to William Loveridge, "felt maker and hat maker of Beverwyck."

Dirck Teunise Van Vechten had a mill 100 rods north of the mouth of the Vosenkill, which is mentioned in the deed of the Indians to Gysbert uyt Bogaert (Egbert Bogardus) in 1684, and account books in the possession of the family show entries from 1695 to 1741. He often received bear-skins in payment of accounts. In 1765 Petrius Souser lived in the house belonging to the mill. The stone of this mill is in the possession of William Van Dyke of Catskill. There is a grist mill permit dated 1675.

The lands which now compose the eastern side of Catskill village from the Hans Vosenkill to Boomptje's Hoeck (variously spelled), and northward to the little stream called "Stuck" or "Stuk," which enters the Hudson west of Roger's Island, cost Gysbert uyt den Bogaert "one coverlet, one gun, one kettle, one beaver in stocking, one beaver in rum, two shirts and two half casks of beer."

The deed "from Esopus Indians to William Loveridge" reads in part as follows: "Appeared before us the undersigned magistrates of Albany, colony of Rensselaerwyck and Schenectady, etc. the following Esopus Indians, owners of a certain parcel of land lying at Catskill viz, Wannachquatin, an old Indian; Mamanauchqua, a squaw, and her son Cunpwaen; and Usawanneek alias S( )heele (cross-eyed), Jacob, and Wanninmauwa, Taw-wequanis, Annaneke, and Naktemook, squaws, who declare they granted, conveyed and made over in true, rightful and free ownership to and for the behoof of William Loveridge senior, hatter," to certain lands from the kill at Loveridge's house to the Imbocht westward to falls on the Kaaterskill named Qwatawichnaak, and so along the east side of the Caaterskill, * * * (Early Records of Albany Deeds, Vol. 2, p. 161.)

Quoting the late Judge Chase, "Bogaert's house of logs was near the Catskill Creek, and the county property then constituted a part of the forest in the rear of his buildings. In 1688 he conveyed his lands in Catskill to his son-in-law Helmer Janse, who in 1703 obtained a patent of Confirmation thereof. Janse died in the house mentioned, without heirs, and in 1738 John Lindsay of Cherry Valley obtained what is known as the Lindsay Patent, covering a large tract of land between the Hudson River and the Catskill Creek. He sold the tract purchased by him to George Clarke and others. In 1741 the owners agreed upon a road from the Hans Vosenkill to the mouth of the Catskill sixty-six feet in width, which, except as to that part South of the present Greene street, is our Main street."

Hans Vos lived along the creek or brook which became known as Hans Vosen Kill, or John Fox's Creek.

In spite of its early beginnings, Catskill or the Landing was but a small and unattractive hamlet until 1792, when it began to wake up to commercial possibilities, acquired a newspaper—The Catskill Packet, published weekly and edited by Mackay Croswell—and its first settled physician, Dr Thomas O'Hara Croswell. It is not known when Dr. Elisha Camp came to Catskill, but he died there in 1793, and his wife turned to tavern-keeping to support her small children. In May of 1793 a post route was established "from Hudson through Catskill to the Painted Post in Tioga; there to meet the post from Reading, Pa."

Thomson and Greene streets were wood roads. There was no Long Dock, for an island called "Wanatonka" was what is now its eastern end, while between that and Boomptje's Hoeck or the main land was a stretch of water. "The Point," so called in those days, had reference to what is now known as DuBois Landing. There was a wharf at the mouth of the Vosenkill. The Long Dock was not filled in until 1820.

On the farm of William Loveridge, which had become that of Benjamin DuBois, a stone house was built. On the west bank of the Catskill Cornelius DuBois built a house in 1762, and the next year Madam Jane Goelet Dies commenced her mansion called by the prudent Dutchmen of the vicinity "Dies Folly." The ship yards turned out brigs, sloops and schooners, while from 1792 to 1802 dwellings increased from ten to 180 in the village.

The first post office was on the corner of Greene and Hill Streets. A house in the rear of William DuBois's drug store was occupied by Dr. Thomas Thomson, and in the remembrance of the late Abram Van Vechten's mother a peach orchard bordered on Main Street, and Peter Souser lived in the mill house on the Vosen kill, and Peter Meigs's house was a short distance north of Outhoudt's, (Jefferson), where Walter Palmatier later lived. Near the Corlaerskill was the stone house of Jacob Newkirk. It stood near a spring. The Corlaerskill was then known as Goetchius Creek.

The Van Orden house, which stood at the south end of Pruyn Park and a few years ago was removed to the east bank of the Vosenkill, was built by Captain Barent DuBois. What is now Upper Main Street, at that time (according to Brace) ran between this house and barn nearer the Catskill and from there to the Meigs house.*

In 1799 it was written of Catskill Landing that "from its eligible situation for trade and commerce and the excellent disposition of its roads, it may with propriety be termed, "a key to the Western

---

* The Meigs house is said by old residents to have been the house at the head of the street, the residence of the late George Warner.

Country" of prodigious extent, which bids fair to be the most rich, fertile and luxurious of any perhaps in the world." * * *

The article goes on to state that Catskill has four rivals but does not name them, and says that the principal rival of Catskill Landing "leaves no art unemployed to injure its reputation and prosperity, and spares no pains to monopolize the trade of the "Western Country." * * * One scarecrow argument employed by the enemies of the place is, that the land is in dispute, has no good title, and consequently there is no safety in settling upon it." Another accusation of this now unknown rival was that of "unfair dealing, which, should this prove true, the ruin of the place would be unavoidable."

Jack Croswell, then sixty-two, an illiterate but intelligent negro who was brought up by Dr. Croswell, told Brace in 1862 that he remembered a mill and dam on the Hans Vosen kill, and a house of two stories near by. Jack used to bathe in a brook which drained the Vosse gut, and which emptied into the Hans Vosen kill. It was eight or ten feet wide in many places; now it is only a foot or two wide and has water in it only in the spring, when the snows are melting.

In 1795 or 96,* Dr. Croswell opened a drug store in the building now occupied by William DuBois, and Dr. Brace was his successor.† William H. Wey married Dr. Croswell's adopted daughter and continued the business until his death, then Benjamin Wey kept it alone, having a partner for one year—Edward Lavelle. For thirteen years it was Wey and DuBois.

Dr. Croswell was the "Uncle Doctor" of Catskill, and Dr. Abel Brace studied with him, became partner and succeeded him, "not only in business but in the love of the community;" for sixty years a citizen, "one of the landmarks of a generation now passed away."

Harmony Lodge was the first Masonic association in Catskill, instituted in 1794. Among the first members was Samuel Haight, merchant and Brigadier General. Thomas Thomson, a great man who went to West Indies accompanied by two slaves, Josephus and Caesar, came home broken in health, a suspected leper, never going out without his head swathed in bandages. His mysterious West Indian experiences were never revealed by him or his faithful slaves. His mansion which he built was afterward the home of Thomas Cole. "He caused a vault to be built near his house, but later it was torn down and he rests in the village cemetery."

John Van der Speigle Scott was an able lawyer and politician respected by all. He was also Judge of Greene County. As a hobby he turned to horticulture and gained a reputation for raising choice fruits and vegetables which he sometimes protected from youngsters with a gun. It is recorded of Stephen and Ira Day that "they lived lives unblamable." Stephen Day "exchanged wares of Eastern Col-

---

* Copy of Dr. Croswell's certificate at Public Library, Catskill.
† See "Physicians."

onies and imports from West Indies for the grain of the farmers and dairy products of their vrouws." Before many years he became Judge Day. "By Captain Hale housewives used to set their clocks."

In 1773 the map of the Lindsay Patent shows only one road and that is Main Street, which was laid out as a road in 1741 and merged into the road which is now the main highway. At the Vosenkill the highway then followed the west bank of the stream back of the Allen house (now Elmer Davis's) and came out just below the Holcomb house on the top of the hill, where a little later there stood a tavern. This tavern site was pointed out by John Schuneman to William Van Dyke when the latter was a boy. The highway was surveyed and laid out in 1795 from Samuel Haight's (Allen house) to Martin Schuneman's at the stone bridge (Madison), "thence to the brew house of Francis Salisbury."

In 1795 Road District No. 6 was formed, "beginning at the south side of the Cauterskill bridge, running as the road now (1795) runs to the stone house or landing of Jacob Bogardus, from thence along the creek to Albertus DuBois'; from thence as it now runs, crossing the Catskill to the barn of Samuel Van Vechten, also beginning on the south side as it now runs up the hill to where it intersects the road as first mentioned, near the corner of Alburtus DuBois' fence. The above tracts shall be considered one road district numbered 6."

The store of Jacob Bogardus was at the west end of the bridge. The house* of Hubartus DuBois, built 1740, still stands on the Washburn brickyard property, and the barn of Samuel Van Vechten was near the ford of the King's Road, just across from the second railroad bridge. In 1799 Caleb Benton purchased from Jacob Bogardus and wife a large tract of land on the west side of the Catskill. He built the brick part of what is now best known as the Hopkins place, and planned for a large village. A map of 1807 is still in existence showing streets and building lots.

It was some time between 1795 and 1797 that Duke de la Rochefoucault Liancourt on a tour through the United States visited Catskill, the guest of Jacobus Bogardus, "an American Loyalist and son-in-law of Major Provost," who had purchased the house and lands of Cornelius DuBois. The duke was the guest of Mr. Bogardus for several days, and slept in the southwest corner room of what is now the home of Mr. and Mrs. William Palmatier.

In the Summer of 1797 Thomson and Grant established "a ferry across the North River at Catskill Landing with good, new, safe boats," and it was "hoped that no person will be induced in the future to lose several miles of travel by crossing at Hudson, as the price is here set at the same rate. Constant attendance will be given at the sign of the ferry landing, near Caleb Street's white house on the corner."

The winter of 1799 was severe, the river breaking up the last

---

* Afterward occupied by Benjamin P. DuBois.

HISTORY OF GREENE COUNTY

of March after having been closed for four months, and flocks and herds suffered from want of fodder.

In 1800 subscriptions to the Susquehanna Turnpike were open, the Commissioners being Henry Livingston of Ancram, Stephen Day, George Hale, Garret Abeel, Samuel Haight, Caleb Benton and Martin Schuneman of Catskill, Salmon Wattles of Franklyn, Solomon Martin of Unadilla. By the middle of August "2,500 shares had been taken and some distance laid out."‡

In 1801 Croswell notes "with pleasure the growth in population, and the flattering prospects of Catskill Landing." "In the year 1792," he says, "the village contained but ten buildings; a coasting sloop of 50 or 60 tons burthen was then the only vessel owned in the place, and this was more than sufficient to transport to New York, all the produce brought to market—no more than 624 bushels of wheat was purchased in the course of the year, during which time upwards of 700 bushels of corn was brought from New York and other places for the subsistence of the inhabitants at the westward, until their crops should come in. Now (1801) Catskill contains 156 buildings, two ships, and one schooner engaged in foreign trade, are owned here, besides 8 coasting sloops of 70 to 100 tons burthen, which are constantly employed in transporting the produce of the country to New York and the sea ports. Shipping to the amount of $37,000 was built here the season past. In 1792 there was brought to market 624 bushels of wheat, and in 1800 it had increased to 46,164 bushels. The prospect for 1801 is proportionately much greater, as in one day last week the quantity of wheat taken by the merchants of the place amounted to 4,108 bushels, and upward of 800 loaded sleighs entered the village on that day by the great western roads. The number from other quarters is not precisely known but was probably somewhat less. * * * Much more rapid growth may be calculated upon." That year the ice broke up in the creek and river the last week in April.

In 1802 the pride of Catskill was the new drawbridge, so much of a curiosity that people came miles to see it. It was opened with great ceremony. The fee for foot passengers was three cents, and of the bridge tenders "Old Batterson" tapped the pockets of the passers-by, knocking off their hats when they refused to pay, and Zacharias Dederick "tapped while they waited" the boots and shoes of the people in a little building at the end of the bridge.

The bridge across the Catskill was erected April 4, 1801, as a toll bridge; its incorporators, Joseph Graham, Gerritte Abeel, John M. Canfield, George Hall and Solomon Chandler. * * * Foot passengers paid 3 cents, two-horse carriages 25 cents, four-horse carriages 31 cents. It was open for traffic in 1802 and remained a toll bridge until 1870, when it was purchased by the town and toll

---

‡ "In 1804 high water carried off four valuable bridges on the Susquehanna Turnpike."

abolished. The present bridge was erected in 1881-82, at a cost of $52,000.

As early as 1803 Catskill had some kind of water system. The water ran through wooden troughs from Cold Spring on the lands of James Bogardus. Nearly every house in the village was supplied with water in this way. The Acqueduct Association was chartered in 1818, its name changed to Greene County Bank February 5, 1819, and a new charter was obtained. The institution failed in 1826, but the acqueduct continued to be used as late as 1837, when Elisha Meiggs was in possession of it.

The first public burial place in Catskill village is said to have been located on Broad and Livingston streets. Its occupants were moved to the present Thomson Street Cemetery. On Sept. 2, 1811, so the records run, it was "moved and carried that the trustees attend on the 2nd of October next, to point out a suitable lot for a burying ground." Land was purchased of John Bogardus and Sally his wife, April 16, 1812, and also of Garret Abeel. The cost of these lots was $125 each. In 1832, 1848 and 1859 it was added to; in 1859 a receiving vault was built.

Dr. Lee Ensign, who was most prominent and enthusiastic in enlarging the grounds, was the first to be buried in the new ground. His wife was the author of a poem of some length printed in The Examiner in 1860, from which I quote one verse:

"And let yon grand old mountains from afar
With their proud battlements fence in the scene
So vast and beautiful, that nought can mar
The symmetry and grace that intervene."

The real life of Catskill as a village began March 14, 1806, when it was incorporated. Its first Board of Trustees organized May 12th with Stephen Day president, Garret Abeel, James Pinckney, John Blanchard and Caleb Benton trustees, Hiland Hill, Stephen Root, Isaac Nichols, Orrin Day and John DuBois Jr. assessors, Isaac DuBois treasurer, and James Bennett collector. During the first year of village life William street was laid out, known as Jesse Brush street.

At the first meeting the Board adopted nine by-laws which in effect prohibited slaughtering of animals within the village limits, the "running at large to exceed 48 hours of unyoked and unrung swine, or of geese or ducks within the compact part of the village," for obstructing the street, neglecting to remove anything contrary to good health, for all of which fines were imposed, and also for willfully running or galloping a horse or horses through street or alley; and one dollar to be paid "by an inhabitant of the village who shall spend his time during the Sabbath at tavern or grocery and there purchase or drink any liquor on the Sabbath, or shall angle with hook or line or fish with nets in any creek, or shall swim or bathe in any creek or river within the limits of the village on the Sabbath." If horse or horses ran away through street or alley then the owner should "forfeit two dollars."

The history of Catskill village after this date is full of interest, but limited space forbids further recording at this time. In 1807 the future President of the United States, Martin Van Buren, was married by the Rev. Peter Labagh of the Dutch Church to Hanna Goes or Hoes in the Haxtun house in West Catskill. This house is said to be still standing. A few years later a "public supper was given Judge Cantine at Catskill, and among the guests was the Honorable Martin Van Buren."

LEEDS

The second village in size in the town of Catskill is Leeds, first called "Pasqoecq"* by the Indians, afterwards Madison, then Mill Village, and finally in 1827 it became Leeds in honor of Richard Hardwick, who came from Leeds, England. At this time a post office was established.

Jan Bronk, a trader among the Indians, who in 1675 invested in land along the Catskill upon which the village now stands, was its pioneer settler. Tradition says he "was the first man to make his home among the Indians" and sleep in their wigwams. That he actually lived with them as has been inferred is doubtful, for he is known to have had a log cabin before 1675 on the east bank of the Catskill just below the bridge, then a fording place. A trail led down what is now Green Lake Avenue and across the ford to the Indian village, and his nearest white neighbor was at the Landing four or five miles through an untraveled forest.

It is also doubtful if he lived in this cabin for long periods, as he was married and had children at Albany before 1686; very likely he occupied it only when gathering in the pelts which the Indians secured in this then great fur-bearing section. In 1711 Bronk gave Van Bergen and Salisbury the "privilege of building a mill or mills on the "Great Falls"† near his cabin, and around these mills were soon built a few rude houses. In 1731 he replaced the log cabin by a small house of stone, and it was in this house his second daughter Antje was married‡ to the Rev. George Michael Weiss, the first dominie of the Dutch church at Old Katskill. His eldest daughter became the wife of Jan Whitbeck, who built a third house which was of brick and "was finished inside with cherry panneling, with four fireplaces and considered very fine for the times." This house was sold in 1790 to Martin G. Schuneman, a son of the Rev. Johannes, for 1,187 pounds, 5 shillings and 6 pence and became a noted hostelry. Martin G. Schuneman had married a daughter of Jan A. Whitbeck and Agnietje Bronk (she died in 1800). Four years later Schuneman offers the house for sale with "large horse shed accommodating twenty horses, and opposite it a stone house, 42 by 21 feet,

---

* It has been written Pasqoecq, Pascakook, Pastakook and Pistakook in old deeds.
† Upper Falls.
‡ Nov. 25, 1733.

then occupied as a store." The brick house stood close to the road, with the first stone house attached at the back, and whether there was a stone house opposite or not is not known. There was, however, a large barn and an ashery directly opposite the house, and it is supposed that the stone building which once stood on the corner of what is now Duncan's is the one mentioned. This was a store in 1800 and occupied by James Brown; in 1824 by B. Demyer and Garret Schuneman as a grocery. It burned in 1883, and was then occupied by the late Benjamin T. White. The house of Bronk finally came into possession of John Van Vechten, whose second wife was Martin Schuneman's daughter, and it was burned in 1876 (now Elizabeth House).

A tree which stood back of this house and destroyed by the fire "measured 13 ft. 10 in. in girth, spreading out 74 feet. This tree was saved from cutting by a slave of the Van Bergen's, who told his companion, sent to clear the spot, that he must not cut the sapling for it was his. In his old age this slave, who could then only walk with two staves, used to spend most of his time sitting under the elm in a hickory arm-chair. Before him was a work-bench and a small tool-chest with which he amused himself making ladles and bowls out of wood brought by fellow-slaves from the forest. These things he sold for enough to keep him in tobacco and rum. When destroyed by fire this tree was over 160 years old."*

In the Catskill Packet of 1796, M. G. Schuneman is said to be building " a large and expensive house" at Madison, and in 1809 he offers for sale a brick house at the junction of the Athens and Susquehanna Turnpike at that place, then occupied as a tavern by Joel Bellamy (who before this occupied the stone store) and known as stand No. 2. This is undoubtedly the brick part of the house now owned by Louis J. Gelis and known as the "Madison." In 1805 M. G. Schuneman took into partnership at "his old stand No. 1" (near the bridge) Garret Persen Jr.

In 1805 Jonathan Kies or Kyes, who married Maria Van Bergen, kept a tavern on the east side of the Reformed Church where the chapel now stands. He was a surgeon in Colonel Abeel's regiment and had a son by the same name. He and his wife are buried in the cemetery at Leeds.

The Rev. Clark Brown in 1803 states that "Ira Day's flouring mill at Madison set in motion Feb. 1803 is a most curious and complicated piece of machinery. It daily manufactures between five and six hundred bushels of wheat into flour. * * * Madison consists of nine dwellings newly and neatly built at the mill, three stores, one public house and a few small buildings. There is also kept here a large store of West India and European goods."

A wooden bridge was built across the ford at "an early date and was washed away by the spring flood. About 1760† another

---

* From Henry Brace papers.
† From Van Vechten papers.

was commenced and the two eastern arches built, but for some reason now unknown the west end was finished with wood. This wooden part was set on fire by some malicious person in 1785, and it was not until Aug. 1792, that the western end of stone was added. This is proved conclusively by the "Catskill Packet" of Aug. sixth of that year."

OLD STONE BRIDGE AT LEEDS (1760-1792).

A one-arch bridge built 1804‡ by the Susquehanna Turnpike Company just below the Salisbury house, where the Kolk flows across the road in times of flood, is often confused with the first bridge. This small bridge was built across a gully of considerable depth which extended for some distance into the field, and on an old map a stream is shown running from it and crossing the Cauterskill road by Harry Vedder's hay-barn. The late Henry Brace says in his "Historical Memorandas" that the late Henry Vedder had told him this gully "was so deep at certain times of the year cattle had to swim in crossing it," and that the "Cripple Bush" was a thicket which extended along the north line of his (Henry's) father's land." The flats at that time had a number of these thickets and gullies dividing one field from another.

JEFFERSON

Jefferson was first known as the "Flats," then Jefferson Flats, and now as Jefferson Heights. When the Dutch first came to

---

‡ In 1804 sealed proposals were asked for building a bridge across the Catskill near Martin G. Schuneman's house. While this is not strictly across the Catskill, there is no other near his house excepting the larger bridge.

Catskill it was considered by them as a sandy waste and a portion was given away as "not worth fencing."

The first house to be built in this vicinity was on the Snake Road, and was built by Jan Van Bremen near the creek. This house was carried away by a flood. At this spot, just below the junction of the Kaaterskill with the Catskill, called "Mawignack" (or place where two rivers meet) by the Indians, Adrian Van der Donck in 1643 hoped to plant a colony, but the Patroon wanted this tract of land and objected to Van der Donck's taking it.

In 1646 "Cornelius Antonissen Van Slyck of Breucklen" obtained a grant of the lands at Catskill, but never claimed them. Three more years passed on and (1649) Brandt Van Slechtenhorst bought from Pewasck, an Indian squaw, and her son Supahoof, the "kill with the falls for 17½ ells of duffels, a beaver jacket and a knife." As this bargain had been made without the consent of the West India Company, Stuyvesant, the director general of New Netherlands, protested, and forbade any settlement being made there. Van Slectenhorst was arrested and became a prisoner at large in New Amsterdam for four months for trying to annex Catskill to his already large possessions. The conveyance was made void in 1652.

In the meantime (Jan. 14, 1650) Jan Van Bremen leased it for six years, agreeing to give a certain number of skipples of wheat, to "build a house, barn and barrack, that is furnish for the same stone, timber, and reeds for the thatch, dig the cellar, feed the carpenters, masons, thatchers and other laborers; the patroon to pay the wages and furnish various other necessities while Hans Vos should help the laborers for fourteen days." Van Bremen was to "reserve a room with a fireplace for the director of Rensselaerwyck and his family whenever he should need it, and on every Lord's day and holiday read to his christian neighbors the Holy Gospel, and according to the custom of the Reformed Church sing one or more Psalms before and after prayers." He was also enjoined "to live in peace with the Indians and his christian neighbors," or forfeit his lease.

In 1653 Van Bremen obtained a patent for his lands, and six years afterward purchased twelve acres of Jan Andriesen. Fourteen more years passed and he sold all his land to Eldert Gerbertsen Cruyff in exchange for a house in Beverwyck. In 1675 the land was conveyed to Stephanus Van Courtland, director of Rensselaerwyck, and Oct. 20, 1681, Van Courtland sold it to Dirck Teunis Van Vechten for "400 guilders in beaver skins and 256 guilders in patroons money; namely in wheat at ten guilders the muddle."

Van Vechten had a flour and saw-mill* on the bank of the Vosenkill. He also sold molasses (stroupe), rum and lumber. Sloops

---

* The deed of Curpuwaen to Gysbert uyt den Bogaert, July 26, 1684, mentions Van Vechten's mill. (Early Records of Albany. Bulletin 9, Vol. II, page 225.)

came up the Catskill as far as the mouth of that stream, where there was a wharf. The captain of the sloop took orders to New York for supplies and articles of trade not produced on the farms. A mill was built near the Van Vechten house in 1715, and the present one in 1830.

Neeltje Van Bergen Oothoudt and Anna Maria Van Bergen Schuneman inherited lands from their father, Martin Van Bergen of Old Katskill, and, as was the custom in those days, their husbands claimed to all intents and purposes, although not lawfully, their wives' property as their own, for why should a woman handle money, and of what use would land be to her?

Neeltje's husband, Henry Oothoudt, built a house in 1775 at the foot of the limestone hills called the "Kale Berg" (Brooks farm) and Rev. Johannes Schuneman (Dutch Dominie of the Catskills) about 1792 built one of brick on Anna Maria's portion of the land, which is still standing on Jefferson Avenue. Here he died in 1794. In 1783 Peter Mey lived near Henry Oothoudt's.

Before 1797 Petrius Souser had a tavern on or near the site of the house now owned by George Badeau, and many political meetings were held there. Near this tavern was the race track,† and the bend of the road just below this spot is attributed to the tavern.‡ An Indian trail ran from a fort on the southwest of the plain to the Kale Berg, and for a time in later years it was a wagon road.

The brick house recently owned by A. C. Fanchier was built in 1814 by Joseph Allen, a retired sea captain, and afterward owned by William Pullman, an Englishman. For thirty years it was the Jackson farm.

In Austin's Glen is the ruin of an old paper-mill, in 1800 that of Nathan Benjamin. This mill burned in 1807, almost impoverishing its owner, but was rebuilt the following year by Abner and Russel Austin, and when paper-making no longer proved profitable was suffered to fall into ruin. The warehouse of Abner Austin stood at the foot of the Salisbury hill and is now the home of L. Carlton Austin.

The first school house was of logs and before 1767§ stood on the Snake road just below the site of the Grant House. The second, also of logs, stood nearly opposite the present one and was used until 1832 or 1833. (See Schools and Libraries.)

THE IMBOGHT

The Imboght has no village center. It was a part of the

---

† The race track is located by a lease of land of 1797.

‡ The late Peter Van Vechten Jr. has stated that Souser's tavern was situated on the northwest corner of Jefferson Avenue and what is now the state road, but Wilhelmus Schuneman had a tavern there at that time, according to an advertisement in the Catskill Packet of that date.

§ Account book of Teunis Van Vechten of that date.

Loveridge Patent settled by a community of Dutch and Palatines of considerable importance, who in 1732 helped organize the church at Old Katskill and Kaatsban, and, like their distant neighbors at Kiskatom, traveled over the rough forest roads every other Sunday to Old Katskill, or with equal difficulty and courage to the latter church.

These settlers were also patriots, with now and then a Tory looked upon with disgust not unmixed with fear by his neighbors. Loyalists were no doubt watched closely, but many were respected as having an honest difference of opinion and keeping on their own side of the fence. When Kingston burned in 1777, the patriots drove their stock to the woods and packed their household goods for quick removal.

The "Kykuit"* or lookout, upon which in times of danger from Indian or Tory a signal fire was built, is but a short distance from West Catskill and on its side is the grave of Johan Pieter Overbagh, the stone of which is said to be "the oldest in the town" (Sept. 14, 1734). This hill rises abruptly on all sides to a considerable height, and on its summit Elias Lasher has built a bungalow very near if not on the exact spot of the signal fires of pioneer days. It commands one of the finest views in the county, taking in as it does the Hudson River from Hudson to Saugerties and beyond, with the broad sweep of Van Orden's Bay on the south, while to the west are the green fields of the Imboght, the rugged Kale bergs, with miles of mountains in the background.

From the Kykuit you motor down Burgett's Hill and strike the road which is a part of the dividing line between the Imboght and Kykuit districts, and turning to the east you come to the ancient stone house of Judge Wynkoop, built in 1792. (See Pioneers and Their Homes.)

Because of lapse of time and little but tradition and old deeds to depend upon for information, I can do no better for the earliest history of the Imboght than quote verbatim from the local sketches of the late Henry Brace, whose reliability as to local history is unquestioned, and to whom the town of Catskill owes much of patient untiring research along historic lines, and the recording of the same for future generations.

"The Loveridge Patent was divided from north to south by the precipitous face of an ancient coral reef, which bears in the county of Albany the name of Helderberg, and in the town of Catskill the name of Kale Berg.† In 1783 the region between the base of this cliff and the Kaaterskill, a few patches of land only were under cultivation. John Fiero had made a meadow of the intervale at the foot of the West berg; Petrius Overbagh was tilling a few acres in the lonely but picturesque glen of the Fuyk; Frederick Diedrich, a thrifty and industrious German, had established himself on the

---

* According to Brace, pronounced "Kakeout."
† This is said to be the proper spelling, by the State Archivist.

HISTORY OF GREENE COUNTY

Kaaterskill, above Loveridge's Valentje, or the rapids at the second bridge; farther down this river Benjamin DuBois had his wheat fields and an orchard of apple trees. The remainder of this rugged tract was covered by a dense forest, which for many years had been held as commons by the yeomen of the Imboght, with free access for timber, fuel, stone and pasturage. So late as 1860 a few of the larger trees of this primeval forest had escaped the axe. A white oak stood on the western side of the road to Saugerties, a short distance below the brick school house. Five feet from the ground this kingly tree when cut down measured fourteen feet in circumference, and I counted more than 200 rings of yearly growth in the stump.

"The southern boundary of Lot No. 2 in the Loveridge Patent began at the Hudson, one hundred and thirty-eight feet and six tenths of a foot below the mouth of the Grootekil or Plattekil, as Rams Horn Creek was once called, and extended upon a course north seventy-two degrees west to the Kaaterskill. In 1749, an old deed declares this boundary was a "line of marked trees now run by Jan Eltinge." The trees excepting one are all gone, but the line can still be traced by fences and stone walls of division. It lies between the lands of Burgett and Overbagh, crosses the road to Saugerties a few feet north of the stone cottage in which a negro woman, Sarah Person, once lived; crosses the King's Road a short distance north of the Mountain Turnpike and touches the Kaaterskil at a huge black oak (standing at this time).

"The land upon the north side of this line, between the Kalleberg and the Hudson, was bought by five Germans of the Lower Palatinate in the autumn of 1728. Johan Wilhelm Brandow became the owner of a hundred acres, which were afterward occupied by Paulus Schmidt and still later by Paulus Trumpbour; Jourya Overbagh became the owner of one hundred acres, which are now in the possession of James P. Overbagh; John Pieter Overbagh became the owner of one hundred and forty acres, which consisted of a strip of land nine chains wide extending westerly from the Hudson; Frederick Dederick, fifty-two acres adjoining Brandow on the north.
* * * These Palatines chose the uplands; if they had been Dutchmen they would have settled upon the flats or plains on the banks of the Catskill or Kaaterskill."

KISKATOM

Kiskatom is a small community of indefinite limits, and widespread flat lands. As Kisketon it was an Indian village, and in an old deed is designated as Kiskatominakauke, a purchase from the Indians by one William Beekman in 1708. It is described as "lying under the Blew Hills, and below where the Kiskatametie kill watereth the said Kaaterskill." In 1796 it is written Kiskadominatia. It finally settled down to Kiskatom, the meaning of which is disputed but is generally accepted as "Place of thin-shelled hickory nuts."

There is very little known of its history previous to the Revolutionary War, or until some time after that period, for the "beautiful vale," as it is then described, was almost deserted during the time when Indians and Tories were a menace to life and liberty in every unprotected community.

Becker, Rau, Jung, Schmidt and others lived there in 1727, and before the war the Timmerman family lived near the cross-roads on the way to Round Top. The house still stands and has heavy double doors and a well-sweep. The road formerly ran in front of the house, but this did not please the great-grandmother of the present owners, and a strip of ground was exchanged for it which brings the barn instead of the house facing the public road. Here Jacob Schermerhorn's wife and children found refuge when the Indians burned their dwelling and murdered the wife's parents.

In 1796 John Schepmouse died at "Kiskadominatia," a farmer and a captain in Colonel Abeel's regiment, and before 1804 John Freleigh owned 300 acres there. Rockwell, who wrote "The Catskill Mountains and the Region Around," says Wynkoop's mill was on the Kiskatom Creek, where Jacob Schermerhorn took his grist and so escaped death or captivity by the Indians, but Henry Brace says this mill was on the Kaaterskill near Drummond Falls.

Kiskatom was originally a tract of 370 acres, but in 1718 or 1720 the Patent was confirmed and enlarged to 2,000 acres, conveying the whole valley excepting such portions as had been previously covered by the Catskill Patent. It joined the Catskill Patent and was disputed land. The Van Bergens, part owners of this patent, retained an interest in the Kiskatom Patent, for their wills dispose of lands at that place.

Garret Van Bergen's will, dated July 5, 1758, says, "I leave to my daughter Ann, wife of Wilhelmus Van Bergen, all my right to a certain tract of land called Kiskatomachy," and an abstract appears in Albany County deeds whereby Ann Van Bergen conveys to John Moore land called Kiskatomachy, also privilege to cut wood from lots 2, 4, 6, 8, 16, etc., dated September 16, 1786.

John Moore married in 1767 Deborah, daughter of Ann and Wilhelmus Van Bergen, and must have built about 1786, the house on the farm lately owned by the late George Winans. This house has been added to and enlarged. The basement, built of stone, was the slave quarters and had a large bake oven at either end (this has been taken out). The beams overhead are of hard wood 10x12 inches thick and laid very close together. In 1796, or about that time, Henry, the son of John Moore, married Esther Ann Mallory. Esther for some reason left her husband, who in or about 1809 with his three children (John, Sarah Ann, and William) moved to Geneva, N. Y., and the farm was sold April 8, 1809. The first John Moore's oldest son Wilhelmus lived at Kiskatom for some years, in what is now best known as the Overbaugh house. The farm of Winans was owned by Jarvis Webster in 1828.

PALENVILLE

Palenville, the "Village of Falling Waters," is the namesake of Jonathan Palen, who had a large tannery at or near the entrance of the Kaaterskill Clove before 1817. Palenville, like her neighbor Kiskatom, has little but Indian history antedating the Revolution.

In the days when the Hudson valley settlements were slowly growing into villages, this particular spot was uninhabited. An Indian trail ran from the valley through the Clove to their fort on greater Round Top. Along this trail the Kaaterskill, a typical mountain stream, bounded over high ledges, travelled lightly and speedily to the valley among boulders and between laurel and fern-covered banks, overhung with the mammoth trees of the primeval forest.

PALENVILLE FROM SOUTH MOUNTAIN.

The winds of heaven swept down between cleft mountain sides, and the "old squaw of the mountains" from October until May had frequent spells of emptying her feather beds and sending the contents skurrying down to the valley. Only the Indian, the hunter or the trapper ventured into the forest or along the stream. Wild beasts roamed the mountain-sides, fish and game of all kinds were abundant, venomous snakes lived among the rocks, and eagles soared overhead, while Hendrick Hudson's men in summer time played nine pins and the sound echoed from cliff to cliff.

After the Revolution settlers came in from Connecticut and the Schoharie to Hunter, building grist mills and tanneries, and cutting a road to the valley over which they might draw their produce in rough ox-carts, exchanging it for the few necessities not produced on the farms.

The Indian trail developed into a Turnpike in 1823, which a broad highway now in part follows. The development of the village came with the establishment of the tanneries, the owners of which began about 1817 to purchase large tracts of hemlock timber land, and to erect tanneries. I am indebted to Mr. C. M. Britt of Catskill, formerly of Britt's Corners (where his grandfather Nicholas Arthur Britt, a soldier of 1812 settled), for the following: Palenville before the advent of Jonathan Palen was called "Lower Clove Village" and "Yankeetown." Palen lived on the right hand side of the road as one approaches the bridge at the foot of the Clove from Palenville, where there is now a high sustaining wall. The original house was burned some years ago.

The Palens were relatives of the Britt family, and frequent visits passed between them. They were well educated and had the first piano in that vicinity and the first Mr. Britt had ever heard.

The first toll-gate in the Clove was owned and kept by Martin V. Bonestell, another relative of Mr. Britt, and this gate was much farther up the Clove road than the last one, which is still remembered by many. The foundation of the first gate can still be seen on the side of the road, and its back door must have been perilously near the edge of the ravine. Across the road where there is a level space, now grown up with tall trees, was their garden. The toll-gate was afterward moved up to Fawn's Leap and kept by the Brocketts, and still later (the last one) was put up near the foot of the Clove. The artist Mason purchased the Bonestell property from the heirs, hoping to preserve the beauty of the surroundings, but he too passed on.

Formerly Palenville had several mills: those of McKinley on the south side of the creek, a powder-keg factory furnishing kegs for the powder mill at High Falls, a chair factory, and Griffin's stone-rubbing machinery, which did a big business, with a quarry in connection with it. Barton had saw mill and cider mill, later the turning mill, and Chauncy Goodwin a flour mill.

Below Britt's Corners is a stone house which was originally that of Wendell Saile, who was born in Germany and buried in the cemetery near by. The next house was that of G. N. Abeel, of whom two sons, Augustus and Eugene, and a daughter Nelly are remembered. They had colored help and built a school house for a private school which the Abeels, Wynkoops, Kings and Roots attended. The farm had the appearance of a Southern plantation. Between the two houses runs the present Ulster and Greene County line.

Mr. Britt was the personal friend of the Rev. Charles Rockwell who wrote the "Catskill Mountains." Mrs. Rockwell taught French and grammar at the old Dutch parsonage at Kiskatom, which was some distance south of the present one (now Hazard Morey's) with hair-flower, burr and seed-flower making, and music as accomplishments.

As you approach Palenville on the new highway the mountains rise higher and more impressive, an impassable barrier stretching for miles along the horizon. Gradually On-ti-ora, who was condemned by Manitou to lie forever upon his back for his pranks with the sun, moon and stars, his hatred of the Red Men, and the evil he did in the long, long ago, loses his individuality and merges from prostrate monster into the green fringe of treetops or the mists of heaven as the weather man decrees, and the cleft or clove between South Mountain and High Peak gradually opens before you.

The Palenville of to-day is a beautiful little village separated into two parts by the Kaaterskill Creek, which, having reached middle life, flows at will through the green pastures of the valley, twice trespassing upon Ulster County but yet returns to its native heath, encountering some rough passages on its journey, at last scarcely moving as if reluctant to mingle its waters with those of the Catskill.

CAUTERSKILL
1690-1800

Cauterskill proper is a collection of scattered homes, a mill and a chapel, west of Catskill village on one of the branches of the "Old King's Road." One can visualize the beauty of the scene in the time of the Indian. Here the Kaaterskill (or Cauterskill), after zig-zagging through the valley from the mountain top, finally rushes over its last obstruction with satisfied rumblings and roarings on the way to the Catskill. No doubt its banks were overhung with forest trees, and ducks and geese in their season swam on its waters, while the trail of the Indian followed it on the way to Schoharie.

KLEIN'S FALLS FROM CAUTERSKILL.

Later it became a part of the vast estates of the Salisburys and Van Bergens. Their first thought was to utilize the power of its falls, and there in 1690 Van Bergen had a saw mill opposite the present mill, and the stream was crossed by fording. Another ford was between what is now the Barringer and Brandow farms.

In 1733 Salisbury and Van Bergen had both grist and saw

mills. On the other side of the stream near the bend of the road in 1751 a house was built for Solomon DuBois, and tradition has it that it was a trading post where the Indians brought their furs.‡

In 1794 began the building of a bridge; the contractors, Martin G. Schuneman and John Cook. Those who had the matter in charge were William Van Bergen, William Brandow and Jacob Bogardus.† The last named had a plaster mill there. It is not known whether this bridge was at the Falls or farther up stream, but in 1815 a bridge was built across the stream, "on or near the falls of Joseph Klein," who had a mill at that place.

PIONEERS AND THEIR HOMES
DAVID ABEEL*

Christopher Janse Abeel, who was born in Amsterdam, Holland, in 1621, was left an orphan at twelve years of age. His mother just before her death left what money she had with a neighbor, to be kept for him when he should become of age. This neighbor put him in charge of the master of an orphanage, where he was taught the trade of carpenter, and when he became of age she gave him the money entrusted to her care.

HOUSE OF DAVID ABEEL.

Christopher Jans chose America in which to start in business for himself, and with a stock of hardware, about 1647, left Holland for Beaverwyck or Albany. In 1665 he had become a master builder, and erected the First Reformed Church which took the place of the log one at Albany. Two years later he was a deacon and treasurer

---

‡ See Pioneers and Their Homes.
† Catskill Recorder.
* From Abeel Genealogy.

GARRET ABEEL HOUSE, BUILT 1785.
(Courtesy of Mr. Geo. W. Holdridge of Catskill.)

of the poor fund of this church, and in 1665 it is recorded of him that he sailed for Holland to secure a legacy left him by a great uncle. His passport was made out in the name of the Hon. Stoffel Jans Abeel. He was a magistrate in Albany and filled other important positions, dying in 1684.

Christopher Jans had married in 1660 (Nov. 22) Neiltje Jans Croom (or Kroom), a native of Holland. Of their children, Johannes the eldest became a prosperous merchant and mayor of Albany; in 1701 Assemblyman, and again mayor in 1709. He married Catharine, daughter of David Schuyler.

Johannes Abeel, a grandson of Christopher Jans, was a fur-trader among the Indians and is recorded as an "alleged lunatic" because he married an Indian Princess, Aliquipiso, of the Turtle Clan of the Seneca Tribe. Their son was known as "Cornplanter" (correct spelling "Corn Plant"). In 1759 Johannes married Mary Knout, and during the War of the Revolution he was taken prisoner by the Indians and saved from death by Corn-Plant, who addressed him as "father," which secured him safety. "He was given his liberty either to accompany the Indians under the protection of his son, or to return to his white family. He chose the latter." After the close of the war Corn-Plant visited him at his home, and he was received with "much hospitality."

Christopher Jans Abeel who came to America about 1647 was the ancestor of David Abeel Jr., son of David, son of Johannes and Catharine Schuyler, who settled near Katskill. Above the bank of the Kaaterskill not far from what is now known as "Webber's Bridge," just off the mountain highway between Catskill Village and Palenville,* is still standing the stone house which David Abeel built, and where he lived until his death in 1813. The family burial place is between the house and the highway.

The exact date of the building of the house is not known, but as the land was a part of the Salisbury-Van Bergen Patent, and Van Bergen is not known to have built a house on this portion of his estate, it is presumed that Abeel built it about the time of his marriage with Neiltje a daughter of Van Bergen, which was in 1752. David was probably born in Albany, but at the time of his marriage was living in Catskill.‡

The house is of limestone with a wing on the east end, its interior much the same as the others at Old Katskill, excepting a cellar-kitchen beneath the house, where Lon and the other slaves

---

* Now the farm of Mrs. Charles Overbaugh.

‡ A patent dated Nov. 27, 1771, was granted by Governor Clarke to David Abeel Jr., John Dederick, Jacobus Abeel and James Abeel which gives possession to David Abeel Jr. in virtue of the will of Garret Van Bergen a part of the land composed of the first division of Catskill Patent called "Backover." The residences of the petitioners having been in their possession over fifty years, this may apply to the wing of the house.

of the Abeel family spent their days. There is the same hallway running north and south with door at either end, an enclosed stairway (which may not have been enclosed when the house was built) leading to the garret. On either side of the hall were rooms with fireplaces, and on the southern side of the house a Dutch stoep which has been removed.

David Abeel did not receive a patent for his thousand acres of land until 1771, "on the west side of, and adjoining the brook called the Caterskill, at a place called the Bak-Oven." The Van Bergens already owned this land but consented to the issuing of this patent.

Here David and his wife Neiltje lived and raised their little family, which consisted of Anthony, Garret, Catharine (or Caatje), Anna (or Annatje), in peace and comfort, receiving religious instruction at the church at Old Katskill, following the rough road through the forest on horseback or in rude sleighs,† drawn by oxen in the earliest days and later by horses.

The Revolution made an end to peaceful days, for David and his sons were strong Whigs. The few Tories of that neighborhood were their enemies, and it was necessary to be constantly alert and watchful. Of the Tories, Jacobus Rowe was the most feared, for he was not only Abeel's enemy but was friendly with the Indians who occasionally raided the valley. It was on a Sunday evening in 1780 that the family were returning from services at old Katskill when the blow fell (see "Indians and Tories"). David and Anthony were taken captive to Canada.

Garret Abeel, the second son of David, seems to have lived in the brick house, now best known as the Webber house, just below the bridge, at that time a part of the estate of David Abeel. He moved to Catskill about 1785. "Garret became judge of the Court of Common Pleas, which office he held for many years." He had never studied law, but had a vast amount of common sense, and a deep sense of justice.*

The mountain road in those day passed the Abeel house, crossed the Kaaterskill by ford below the farm buildings and continued through the Dederick farm, crossing the King's Highway and present state or Saugerties road south of the Young home.

Garret Abeel built a stone house in 1785 which stood on the site of the present Armory and was torn down forty years ago to make room for the present building by Contractor George W. Holdridge. The house faced the creek and was afterward the property of Captain Caleb S. Spencer.

---

† The deep boxed sleigh which was once the property of Dominie Schuneman was for a long time in the possession of the late William Newkirk of Leeds, and some time after his death was purchased by Miss Anna Abeel, great-great-granddaughter of the dominie.

* See Attorneys.

Town of Coxsackie

Coxsackie has been written Kocks Hackie, Kuxakee, and Coxsackie. The French defined it "owl hoot," Spafford the "hooting of owls," Schoolcraft "cut banks," and O'Callagan suggests a "corruption of kaaks-aki, country of the wild goose."

The town of Coxsackie has a more or less high ridge along its river front, while on top of this ridge the country stretches out into the Coxsackie Flats. This eastern section of the town has been called "the garden of Greene county," and the extensive flat land is backed by the Kaleberg, beyond which the country is more or less hilly and uneven, with other but smaller flat lands to the west.

The oldest highway in the town is the King's Road of 1710. A road leading from the King's Road to the river was laid out in 1790 and ran "between the line of Peter Bronk, Richard Bronk and Anthony Van Bergen" and so on * * -- * "to the dock of Ephrahim Bogardus on the North River, to the high water mark." The road at the head of the landing in 1793 is described as "leading from the dwelling house of Eliakim Reed to Coxsackie Landing." Johnny Cake Street belongs to later history, that of 1828, and the Coxsackie Turnpike was built in 1806.

John Bronk was the first supervisor, 1800-01, and the first known school teacher after the dominies (who were the first instructors) in the town of Coxsackie was Anthony Rogers, who taught in Coxsackie village in 1795. At Jacksonville at this date was John Bower. Rev. Henry Ostrander is known to have kept school in the old stone school house on the north side of the turnpike from 1801 to 1810, and here it is said "the sons of the wealthy Van Bergens and Bronks studied Latin."

Coxsackie according to her size has a large number of patriots of the Revolution to her credit. Some participated in the conflict, and others did good service at home. October 20, 1775, John L. Bronk was commissioned Major of the 11th Regiment, of which Anthony Van Bergen was Colonel. Bronk had been commissioned a captain of a company as early as 1740, with Sybrant Van Schaack as colonel.

Leonard Bronk was ordered by Governor Clinton in 1780 to "impress ten tons of flour or an equivalent in wheat, 20,000 weight of beef or fat cattle or equivalent thereto, for the use and service of the Army." Like most other settlements, they had Tories in their midst and Committees of Safety were necessary to see that the roads were patroled, and proper measures taken for the safety of the people and their property. Coxsackie also came to the front with a Declaration of Independence made before the accepted Declaration, on the "Seventeenth Day of the Year of our Lord One thousand

---

*Owing to the illness of Judge Hallenbeck during the winter and spring, he has been unable to put his valuable material in shape, and the County Historian has done the best possible within a limited time.

seven hundred and seventy five." This Declaration had two hundred and twenty-five signatures, and the original can be seen at Albany.

COXSACKIE VILLAGE

West Coxsackie and Catskill had much in common in the early days. Then they were known as Kocks Hackie and Katskill. Both were born on vast farm estates; had in part the same ancestors (Bronk and Van Bergen); and each was a twin, or rather triplet, for it consisted of two landing places and a country home. The landings were at first feeble infants, and some years later the upper one at Coxsackie gave up the struggle for existence as a landing, while the lower grew in length and breadth, and the sister on the hill was content to lead a farmer's life with less family to her credit but with more widespread possessions.

Old Katskill and Kocks Hackie shared the same pastor of the Dutch Reformed faith until 1797, but with separate churches; and every other Sunday the common pastor or dominie, whose home was at Katskill, traveled through the forest on horseback to preach two long sermons on "Lord's Days and feast days, catechising the children and youth and those of the German brethren residing among us, in their language."

Around this first Dutch church at Coxsackie* grew what is now West Coxsackie, then the most important part of the settlement. It is not known whether Peter Bronk, the first patentee, lived there or not. He died before 1687 and the land came to his son Jan. Marte Gerritse Van Bergen purchased the north part of the Loonenburg Patent adjoining Bronk's called the "Fountain Flats." The land purchased of the Indians by Peter Bronk Jan. 13, 1662, and confirmed by Governor Richard Nicolls June 11, 1667,‡ consisting of 252 acres, went "Westward of the woods to Katskill Path, and running along the said Path southward, it comes to the Stone Kill, from thence it runs Eastward over against the said Nutten Hooke, and so Northward along the river to the Forest Kill." This and the Fountain Flats, also the Corlears Kill Patent, all owned by Bronk & Van Bergen, composed the three patents for which they petitioned Governor Dougan to issue another patent covering all three parcels of land, which was granted May 23, 1687. This is called the "Coxsackie Patent."

Vol. 2 of Patents, Sec. of State office, Albany, Discrepancies in land areas is accounted for by the fact that the Dutch definition of land is that which was cleared or fit for cultivation. Rocks did not count with them.

Jan Hendrickse Bruyn's share came into the possession of Cor-

---

* See Churches.

‡ The north line of the "Fountain Flats" was the south line of Peter Bronk's line, and the south line (original line) ran about ten rods north of the house on the Ely farm.

nelius Machielis (Oct. 30, 1685) and was sold to Jacob, Casperen, and Jan Casperen Hallenbeck, Dirck Van Vechten and Jochem Collier. Machielis sold to Jacob Phoenix "the half of a farm called "Klinkenberg," with the barn and house, in 1685. This is the first mention of a house, although in a Staats and Proovost deed of 1670 a barn is mentioned. Klinkenberg or Echo Hill is north of Four Mile Point. In 1694 an old and a new orchard are mentioned as on this farm. This new orchard was used as a burial place by the Hallenbeck family, and was on the top of a hill west of the Houghtaling house. On the west side of the road near Four Mile Point was the dwelling place of Jan Van Loon's father (Jan).

At the headwaters of the Coxsackie Creek, under the high cliffs of the Kale Berg, was the home of the Van Schaacks, which was given by Jan Van Loon in 1719 to his son-in-law Arent Van Schaack, who married his daughter Maria. The annual rent to be paid for this land was "one scheppel (about three pecks) of wheat, and two fowls."

Martin and Garret Van Bergen of Old Katskill, after the death of their father and in settlement of the estate, conveyed their rights in the Coxsackie Patent to their brother Peter, who in turn relinquished his rights in the Katskill and Corlears Kill. In 1726 Jan Bronk made his home at what is now Leeds, and died there, but when Peter Van Bergen settled permanently at Coxsackie is not known. His brothers Gerret and Martin did not come down from Albany with their families to settle on their father's estate until after their houses had been built in 1729, at Old Katskill. Previous to this date the estate there had been leased.*

As Peter, Pieter, or Petrus, was married November 7, 1724, to Christina, daughter of Anthony Coster and Elizabeth Ten Broeck, it is likely he did not live at Coxsackie for any length of time before that date. The house of Peter was "on or near the site of the stone house which in 1884 was owned by William Farmer," on the north side of the street in the upper village.

Garret Van Bergen deeded a piece of land to Jan Caspersen Hallenbeck April 14, 1683, called "Kaniskeek," which was at that time in the possession of Jan Caspersen, and in which a house and barn is mentioned. This was the Hallenbeck homestead and long remained in the family.

Jan Bronk deeded to Philip Leenderse Conyn in 1710 land of which Conyn had been "in peaceable possession for several years." The house was on the opposite corner, west from the double house of Peter Van Bergen, and the farm on the south side of the street, and east from the King's Road.

In the second division of the Coxsackie Patent in 1730, Jan Bronk conveyed to his son Leonard, of Coxsackie, a piece of land next and opposite to the homestead of said Leonard, and also a piece called "ronde vlackie or round flat." 160 acres was sold in 1789

---

* See Old Katskill.

by Peter Van Bergen to Silas Rushmore. This tract was bounded on the west by the Catskill Path, and north and east by Murderer's and Coxsackie Creeks. Rushmore sold twelve acres of this at the junction of the two creeks to Martin Hallenbeck, the remainder to John L. Bronk. It is still called the Rushmore lot. The part next to Murderer's Kill was sold to Hendrick Vandenburg. The remaining acres were divided into 64 lots, and equally divided between the families of Bronk and Van Bergen. The whole of Lot No. 48 is now the business portion of Coxsackie Landing, Lot No. 50 is what in days gone by was the Upper Landing, while Nos. 46 and 47 are the Lower Landing. At the junction of the King's Road and the road to Greenville near the New Baltimore line, on the northwest corner, stood during the Revolution and for years after the noted tavern kept by Peter Bronk, a grandson of the first settler.

UPPER LANDING

At first the Upper Landing surpassed its sisters in growth and strength. One Ephrahim Bogardus established a ferry here just after the Revolution, and "one of the first acts of the County Court, in 1800, was to give him a license" for that purpose.

Before the war William Wells came from New England and built a stone house at the Upper Landing. It stood on the northeast corner of Lot 52, in the Coxsackie Patent, and south of the road from the upper village. In 1818 the house and land near by was sold to Leonard Bronck. This sale included Well's Island, which was opposite the house and contained eight acres. The oldest known name for this island when sold to Marte Gerritse Van Bergen, is "Nutten Flat," one north of it "Blinder Flat," and another still farther north, "Dover Flat." The island at the mouth of Coxsackie Creek is shown on old maps as "Marte Gerritse Island." Others who had homes here were William Rea and Peter Cuyler, but as time went on business moved down stream.

LOWER LANDING

Peter and Richard Bronk sold to "Israel Gibbs, merchant of the town of Catskill," March 7, 1794, Lots 46 and 47 of the Coxsackie Patent. One contained 14 acres, the other 35 acres. Of this tract small lots were sold to Joseph Chaplin, "on which (1794) the potash works now stands;" another to John Gibbs who had a house there, reserving "14 feet square where Miss Nancy Gibbs and Pauline Gibbs are buried." Mary Wells also had a house near the Knickerbocker ice-house. This was Lot 47, and known as "Molly Well's Point." Squatters settled farther south, and at this point was the wharf of Israel Gibbs, known as Gibbs Landing.

At the top of the hill, at what is now known as Coxsackie Landing, before 1744 stood a stone house built by Claude Ducalon, a French doctor, who had a daughter Catharine, baptised in the Lutheran church of Athens at that date. He was still living there in 1784 (on site of Collier house). What is now the landing was then a rocky point separated from the mainland by a marsh, at high tide covered with water. Eliakim Reed built a wharf on this rocky point and it became Reed's Landing. The hillside was then a forest, the streets and roads but paths cut through the forest, in some instances only blazed trails.

In the New York Magazine of December, 1797, is the following: "On Saturday last Peter W. Yates, Esq. by virtue of a dispensation from the Grand Lodge (previously referred to as "ancient Masonic fraternity") constituted a new lodge at Coxsackie, and installed its officers. He delivered to the officers and members, and the visiting members from adjacent lodges, an oration suitable to the occasion. Afterward they partook of a supper in an elegant lodge room, lately constructed by the members of the new lodge; and the next day the Rev. Mr. Knap preached a sermon for them in the new Presbyterian church."

JACKSONVILLE

Jacksonville is a small village in the western part of the town whose first inhabitant was Gerret Roosa, who owned a share of the Roseboom Patent. He lived on the south side of the road east of Jacksonville, and his memory is perpetuated by two rude stones, one bearing the inscription "G. R. 1776," and the other "Here lies the body of the wife of G. R., 1787, Apr. 28."

The first tavern here was that of Joseph Bullis, built 1799. He also had a distillery opposite it. The name of the village is said to have been given it by "James Farlee Burroughs who came from Greenville and established a store there." The story is that his goods arrived at Coxsackie Landing addressed to Jacksonville, Coxsackie, and for some time it was a mystery where the place could be, for previous to this, presumably because of the distillery, it had been called "Swill Street." Jacksonville was doubtless named for "Old Hickory," for it was in his time that Burroughs settled there.

In 1796 Shadrach Hubbell bought the farm on the south side of the road by the school house (Dist 8). The principal business in the early days of Jacksonville was sawing. Robert Vandenburg and Pazzi Lampman had saw mills there.

HOUGHTALING PATENT

The Houghtaling Patent was beyond the Kale Berg, from the Stony Kill on the south to the Diep Kill in the town of New Baltimore. This patent was granted to Mathias Houghtaling July 8, 1697, by Governor Benjamin Fletcher, who represented the English crown.* The Diep Kill crosses the county line and the Catskill Path at almost the same spot. Conrad Houghtaling, eldest son of Mathias, conveyed to his brother Hendrick a small tract along the Catskill Path, which was afterward the home of Conrad's son Thomas. His house stood a few feet east of the house which was afterward Truman Mackey's. Hendrick in 1770 conveyed the rest of the patent

---

* See Book 7 of Patents, page 127, Sec. of State's office, Albany.

(excepting that of his brother, and the land conveyed to Casper Collier) to Hendrick and Robert Vandenberg, reserving "one-half of all mines which may be hereafter found on the above lands."

There is an old tradition that when Coxsackie was young, Indians had gone out to the hills early one morning and had returned before breakfast with a quantity of lead. Tradition further states that an Indian chief offered to sell one of the pioneer Houghtalings the secret of the place where lead could be found, and upon his refusing to give the desired price the Indian "declared in a rage" that the mine should never be found while it remained in the hands of any who bore the name of Houghtaling. "This tract is commonly known as the Vandenberg Patent, but that is not the original grant. It was afterward divided into seventeen lots of fifty acres each, one of which for some reason contained sixty acres and was the cause of a suit in Chancery. Thereafter it was known as the Chancery Lot."

The Vandenbergs‡ were living at Coxsackie in 1729, for Richard Vandenberg purchased on April 18th of that year, land of Thomas Williams formerly owned by Jan Bronk, which began at the Spruyt or Slink (marshy piece of ground), bordering on the lands of Philip Conyn and the orchard of Peter Van Bergen. Vandenberg had evidently been living on the land previous to the purchase. The family seem to have been friends of the Van Bergens and it was through them that they settled here. The Vandenbergs also leased other land of the Van Bergens, paying annually five scheppels of good wheat until 1820, when a satisfactory arrangement was made between the heirs of both. With this land and the purchase of other tracts they became large land-owners west of the upper village.

About thirty rods east of the Kaleberg, on Murderer's Kill, was the early home of the Vandenbergs. The first house was built before 1725, the second of stone about 1764. West of the house on the ridge above was the Catskill Path, and the old Indian trail on a line with the back garden fence.

ROSEBOOM PATENT

This patent was south of the Houghtaling and Coeymans Patents, extending into the town of Athens, and was granted April 12, 1751, to Jacob, John Jacob, and John G. Roseboom. The last named had obtained his share for a friend, John Henry Lydias of Albany, and it was transferred to him in 1751. The tract seems to have been divided and transferred from one to another, denoting speculation, until in 1771 it had thirteen owners who employed an Albany lawyer, Robert Yates, to divide it into lots. These were set apart to their different owners by a kind of lottery, each drawing a number in turn from a box. Nos. 4 and 5 were drawn by Martin Lydias, who with his wife Genevieve sold them to Dirck Van Vechten, reserving "his mill and stream of water where his mill stands." This

‡ The name is spelled Vandenberg in early deeds but is known as Van Den Berg.

was called the "New Patent." It is a rocky tract and the north end of High Hill† is within its boundaries.

The Stighkoke Patent is in the western part of the town and in the form of a square. The village of Jacksonville is within its eastern limit. Five Indians—Herman Backer,§ Tanighsanow, Koughan, Aquahannit, and Tansaghoes—sold this tract of land to Casperus Bronk for thirteen pounds and ten shillings, June 6, 1743. The Patent was issued June 30th to Bronk, Martin and Garret Van Bergen and Hendrick Remsen.

The Coeymans Confirmation line runs through Stighkoke Patent from the east to near the west corner, and divides the patent into disputed and undisputed lands, for the Coeymans line at this point has been the cause of much ligitation. The Salisbury Patent lies south of the Stighkoke and contained 700 acres. A patent was granted to Casperus Bronk, William and Abraham Salisbury, of which Bronk sold his share to Teunis Van Vechten for 50 pounds, and he in turn sold it to the Salisburys, reserving one-third of the saw mill, and one-third of the utensils and implements belonging to the mill, with "liberty to ride or lay down saw logs and planks in a convenient place near the mill." Abraham Salisbury left his part by will (1756) to his son Wessel. Teunis Van Vechten left his share in the saw mill to his sons Teunis and Abraham. Wessel Salisbury and his brothers sold to the Brandows, and the land was divided and sub-divided until at last the mill, lot and streams passed into the possession of Henry Cornwell, a native of Duchess county who did an extensive business at what was widely known as Cornwell's Mills. He married Sarah, a daughter of Nicholas Van Hoesen. The mills were sold by his sons Henry and Richard to Reuben Jump. Robert Vandenberg had a saw mill on a branch of the Potick within this patent.

MORIN PATENT

This tract of land, for which a patent was secured in 1770 by John Morin Scott and seventy others, occupies only a small portion of the town of Coxsackie, the town line running through it only a little way east of the Stighkoke Patent.

CASPARUS BRONK'S ONE HUNDRED ACRES

This one hundred acres bordered on the Stony Kill and was on the "west side of the Catskill foot path where the Path crosses the Stony Kill." All this land came to Annetje Bronk, only child of Casparus, who afterward married John A. Whitbeck, and the upper half was sold to John L. Bronk in 1764, the lower half to the same person in 1773, together with her share in that part of the Fountain Flats which lay between the Catskill Path and the creek.

---

† Coxsackie High Hill.
§ Vol. XIII, Land Papers, page 134. The Patent in Book XII page 198.

COEYMANS PATENT

The first patent, the principal part of which is in Albany county, had its south boundary near West Coxsackie. This was granted in 1673 by General Lovelace to Barent Pietersen. The second patent was granted in 1714 at the request of Andries Coeymans, son and heir of the first patentee. A patent granted to Kilian Van Rensselaer in 1685 enroached upon the Coeymans Patent, but the contest over these disputed lands was settled by a deed from Van Rensselaer.

PIONEERS AND THEIR HOMES
LEONARD BRONK

The following has been taken from a paper prepared by Rev. Lewis Lampman and read before the Greene County Bar Association in 1911:

Leonard Bronk, fifth in descent from Jonas Bronck, was born in Bronk House (still standing and occupied) on Bronk Patent, about two and a half miles west of Coxsackie village, May 11th, 1751 or 1752. His first ancestor in this country was Jonas Bronck of Westchester County, after whom Bronck's Manor, Bronck's River and Bronck's Borough were named, the "ck's" being changed into "x" on account of euphony.

In 1639 Jonas Bronck, liberally educated and rich, with his friend Jochiem Pietersen Kuyter, a Danish officer, sailed in his own private armed vessel, named the Fire of Troy, from Hoorn, Holland, taking their families, farmers, female servants and stock, for New Amsterdam, reaching that place in July, 1639. The arrival of the ship was hailed by the colony "as a great public good." Where Jonas Bronck came from originally is yet a matter of dispute. I am inclined to the opinion that he was a Dane. His last European residence was in Amsterdam, and there he married Antonia, daughter of Juriaen Slagboom (probably his second wife). Riker's History says of him: "Signior Bronck was a family long distinguished in Sweden, though probably himself from Copenhagen, where some of his kindred lived." What adds emphasis to my suggestion that he was probably a Dane, is the fact of his intimate association with Kuyter, a Danish officer; and the Danish library which is mentioned in the inventory of his possessions after his death.

The probabilities are that the place of his location had been settled by him, and the necessary steps to secure the land had been taken, before he left Holland. Hudde spent the preceding winter in Holland, and met both Kuyter and Bronck. And we find that the Directors of the Colony sent explicit directions to the governors of the Colony of New Amsterdam to further the wishes of both Bronck and Kuyter. He secured a "Grond Brief," a tract of land of 500 acres north of the Harlem River, and became the first white settler in that section. It is interesting to note this characteristic of Jonas Bronck, for it crops out in his descendants, viz: he was not content with the deed from the authorities of New Amsterdam, but in addition made an honest purchase from the Indian Sachem, Tackamack, and his associates. The tract of land purchased by him was called by the Indians "Ranachqua." It lay between the Harlem River and the river Abquahung, now known as the Bronx. Here Bronck made his improvements and began his life.

Jonas Bronck died in 1643. Kuyter and Dominie Bogardus were his executors. From the inventory of the estate we learn of a fine Latin and Danish library, as also a large collection of works on law and history and divinity. Jonas Bronck left a widow and one son, Pieter Jonassen Bronck. The widow married Arendt van Corlear, Sheriff of Rensselaerwick, and removed with him to Albany.

It was this Peter Bronck, the only son of Jonas, who in 1662 purchased from the Indians a tract of land and secured for it from the Dutch authorities what is known as Bronck's Patent. On the overthrow of the Dutch by the English the purchase and the original grant to Peter Bronck were confirmed by a patent granted by Gov. Richard Nicolls, June 11th, 1667. The grant was bounded on the north by the Coeymans Patent; on the south by the Fountain Flats

BRONK HOUSE.

and Loonenburgh Patent; on the west by the ridge of hills running north and south that makes the west bounds of the valley; on the east by the Hudson River, taking in the whole fertile valley and the river's bank from an east and west line about a mile south of Coxsackie landing to an east and west line on the north bounds running from the mouth of the Coxsackie Creek to the ridge of hills to the west of the Coxsackie valley.

On this patent, by the terms of the grant, a house was built in 1663. I think the stone house at the southeast corner of what is known now as Bronk House was built at that time. My father-in-law, Leonard Bronk, youngest son of Judge Leonard Bronk, said many years before he died that that part of the house was a good deal more than two hundred years old. He died in 1872. The brick house was built in 1738. The date is cut in the foundation on the north side of the house. The kitchen extension was rebuilt in 1792.

The house, the mills and the land descended to his son Jan Bronck, and from the date of the original purchase the homestead and many acres of the original grant have never been out of the hands of the lineal descendants.

The immediate ancestor of Judge Leonard Bronk was John L. Bronk, who married Elsie van Buren. He inherited the old home and the traditions, and he was worthy of both. He was the most influential man in his section in his time. In 1770 he was commissioned Captain of Militia by Lieut. Gov. Cadwallader Colden. On Oct. 20th, 1775, he was commissioned Major of the 11th Regt. N. Y. by the Provincial Congress. In 1778 he was commissioned 2nd Major by Gov. Clinton. These commissions are in my possession. He was Justice of the Peace in 1782. The History of Greene County closes with this tribute to him: "John L. Bronk was in his day one of the prominent citizens of Albany County. Throughout his life he was a prominent man, and by his death Albany lost one of its most valuable citizens."

Leonard Bronk was an only child, and he inherited a large fortune in mills and lands. But that was not his only inheritance. He inherited the traditions of his father's house—kindliness to neighbors, uprightness in business and loyalty to his country. He saw his father living in friendly relations with all his neighbors, an officer fitting his men to fight for liberty, and a justice striving to resolve disputes and establish equity. And all of this entered into his life and became a part of it. When and where he got his education I do not know. The first documentary information I have of him is in 1773. It is a book of old patents, laboriously copied from the originals by Mr. Bronk. I have the book in my possession. He was evidently equipping himself as a surveyor. He seems at that time to have been in New York city. He was then twenty-one years of age and may have been finishing his studies in that place. In 1776 he is evidently an attorney at law.

But here comes in the documentary story a very sudden and abrupt transition. In 1777 he is appointed 1st Lieut. "in convention of the Representatives of the State of New York." The commission is signed by Pierre Van Cortlandt, Pres't; Robt. Benson, Sec'y. In the same year Adjutant in Colonel Anthony Van Burgen's regiment, and 1778 1st Lieut. by Governor Clinton.

In 1779 he married Catherine Van Den Berg, daughter of Robert Van Den Berg. She is said to have been a very beautiful woman. At any rate, for the evidence is abundant, she made her husband a very happy man and added to his influence.

In 1781 he begins that long civil career that ends only with his death, but in his multiplied activities he neither abates his interest nor his efforts for the success of the Revolution. He is selected a representative in the Assembly this year, and is at the head of the poll. He is also chosen Supervisor of Albany County. And John Wigram of Columbia County, writing to him a congratulatory letter, says that he is the youngest Supervisor yet chosen in Albany County. The list of honors conferred upon him by county and state is long and noted under another heading.

During all his life he was a slave-holder, and for the last twenty years of his life quite a large owner of slaves. When any of these slaves ran away Judge Bronk refused to go after them. When his friends remonstrated with him he would answer, "If they are not satisfied with my treatment of them I will not force them to live with me." And his children and his grandchildren not only honored him—they adored him.

His grave is just beyond the house to the south and west on a little knoll at the bend of the creek. In the little inclosure is a plain slab with this inscription: "In memory of Leonard Bronk, who died April 22d, 1828, aged 76 years. I am the Resurrection and the Life." And beyond the inclosure, crowding all the rest of the knoll, are the graves of the faithful servants who trusted him while he was alive and wanted to be buried near him when they were dead. On the whole I am proud that I am even remotely connected with him. He died as he had lived—trusted, honored and loved by all who knew him.

Town of Durham

The town of Durham previous to March 8, 1790, was a part of Albany County and belonged to the district of Coxsackie which was organized in 1772. In 1778 Coxsackie became a town. In 1790 this town was divided and the western portion became Freehold (Durham).*

The name Freehold originated either from the fact that there were no other claimants for the land, or as the late J. G. Borthwick believed, from the village of Freehold, which received its name because it was situated "in a section of land between two patents and was therefore a freehold."

The town of Freehold included the present town of Durham and portions of Greenville and Cairo,‡ and a large part of Conesville,

---

* The late J. G. Borthwick, uncle of William S. Borthwick, Supervisor of the town of Durham, from whose writings most of this sketch has been taken, states that in his opinion Freehold included at this time the present towns of Windham, Ashland and Prattsville, and the original Act of Legislature seems to confirm his opinion.

‡ Ephrahim Darby, Ebenezer Barker and Peter Curtis were the first Commissioners.

HISTORY OF GREENE COUNTY

Schoharie County. It may also have intruded on Delaware County, as the boundaries are indefinite and embraced 150,000 acres, a vast forest wilderness where fish and game were plentiful.

Ebenezer Barker was the first Commissioner of Highways, and Ephrahim Darby the second. Upon the formation of Greene County, Freehold became one of her townships. In 1803, Cairo and Greenville took away a piece of Freehold, and two years later (March 28, 1805) the name was changed to Durham. As many of the early settlers had come from Durham, Conn., the name New Durham had been used for the settlement from the first, and was finally decided upon for the town.

The section of the town north and west of the mountains was annexed to Schoharie County March 3, 1836, and the town portion thus annexed became Conesville in honor of Rev. Jonathan Cone, who was the pastor of the Presbyterian Church in Durham.

DURHAM BRIDGE.

The town of Durham contains 31,033 acres, is an agricultural town with varied scenery. Mt. Pisgah is in the angle of the western boundary, its northern slope in Conesville, its southern and western in Windham. This peak is 2,900 feet high. On its eastern side is its famous "Cold Spring," while the view from its summit includes portions of five states. This peak is one of several which may be said to be the northern frontier of the Catskills. To the south you may see Mitchell Hollow intersecting the Windham valley; beyond these valleys, tier upon tier of mountains. The peak stands alone, bleak and bare, no trees obstructing the view on any side, and one involuntarily quotes the old hymn, "When from Mount Pisgah's lofty heights."

Walter Doolittle in 1880-81 built up it a winding road, and the first vehicle made the ascent July 4, 1881. On the summit

Doolittle built a house and observatory equipped with a telescope. During the year 1883, 1,500 persons registered there, and probably another thousand, who did not register, visited the spot. The number of carriages was 600. To-day there remains only the wreck of house and observatory, and the road is but a trail which still lures the nature lover.

Mt. Hayden is near, and southeast of Mt. Pisgah, its height 2,775 feet and well wooded to the top. Between these two the road from Durham to Windham crosses through Blakesley's Notch. Jennie Notch divides Mt. Zoar and Ginseng Mountains, while southeast of Mt. Zoar, Windham High Peak raises its lofty head 3,500 feet. The town line as surveyed by David Baldwin in 1806 passes directly over the top of this mountain.

The Catskill Creek flows through the eastern part of the town of Durham, with Saybrook Creek its largest branch from the east. The latter received its name from settlers who came from Saybrook, Conn., and it is also called "Ten Mile Creek." From the west come Bowery, Thorpe, and Sawmill creeks.

Thorpe Creek received its name from Captain Aaron Thorpe, who in 1790 had a sawmill on its banks. It is a turbulent stream of rifts and falls and receives the waters of Cornwallville and Post Creeks. The gorge on this stream at East Durham is 50 feet deep, and here the wife of Joel Jewell lost her life while trying to save a weak-minded son. A few years later this son wandered away and was not found for several months, when a hollow pine "stub" was cut down. In the interior of this stub or trunk his remains were found. It was a favorite place for chimney swallows, and it is supposed he climbed to the top to secure the birds and falling in was unable to extricate himself. A man by the name of Vosdick rode off the rocks on the side of the gorge in the night, and was found lying partly under his horse, both dead.

Roswell, or Rozwell Post, built one of the first grist mills in the town on Post Creek. This stream has also been called Heifer Creek. The two branches of Post Creek unite forces at what is known as Johnson's Flats. This flat is supposed in early days to have been covered by the water of a huge beaver dam. Just below these flats the stream descends very rapidly over the rocks and enters a ravine called "Shady Glen."

Sawmill Creek, later called "Prink Creek," is now known as "Durham Creek," one of the sources of which is Cold Spring on Mt. Pisgah. Another source is near West Durham, and still another on Mt. Hayden. On Durham Creek are Sawmill Falls, a famous sheep-washing place; Bidwell's Falls, named after Benjamin Bidwell, and a spot called "Mrs. Bidwell's Tea Cup."

The town of Durham has very little Indian history. Their trail followed the Catskill, and there is a spot on what is known as the old Cleveland farm called an Indian burying ground. Hendrick Plank was carried captive to Canada by Indians during the Revolution, and died there. After the war a few still remained— a lazy, thievish set.

HISTORY OF GREENE COUNTY

Eliab Youmans, a surveyor of patents in 1767, and his assistants is supposed to be the first white man who spent the night in this section. He surveyed the Maitland, Stewart, and other patents. The first settlement in the town, probably about 1770 or 1772, was made at Oak Hill by Lucas DeWitt, John Plank, Hendrick Plank and possibly a Mr. Egbertsen, although the last may not have come until ten years later. Lucas DeWitt Jr. was a son of Lucas of Hurley, Ulster County. They came from Holland but were originally from France. Some of the family were civil engineers employed by the government of Holland in the construction of dykes. Their services were considered so great that a monument was erected by that government to their memory.

Lucas DeWitt's first house was of logs and he carried his grain to Madison (Leeds) or Katskill to be ground until he obtained a large portable mill, described as something like a coffee mill, with which he ground his grain by hand. As time passed he built a dam near the upper bridge in Oak Hill, attacned his portable mill to water power, and it became the first grist mill in the town. When the war of the Revolution broke out DeWitt hid his mill in a hollow log, and on his return found it intact and ready for business. It was used until some years later, when a modern one was set up on the bank of the Catskill.

The town of Durham was the home of Revolutionary patriots and soldiers who had come after the war, probably 1782-83, to settle there, or had returned to deserted farms from which they had taken their families to a safer place while they served their country. At any rate, shortly after the war settlements within its borders began to grow rapidly.

OAK HILL

Oak Hill was the earliest settlement in the town. It belonged to the patent granted by King George III of England to Colonel Richard Maitland, a Scotch officer in the British army. This patent was granted June 23, 1767. The settlers were obliged to take leases of Maitland's executors, he having died. These leases were dated May 3, 1774. Lucas DeWitt's lease stipulated he was to pay "one ear of corn, and a proportion of the King's rent per year, for five years," and at the expiration of five years the rent was to be 5 pounds 12s per year. As the war was on two years later, it is likely the King did not for long receive his rent. In the lease it is stated that Lucas DeWitt Jr., a yeoman from the Blue Mountains, was in possession of the land, and also that the place was known as DeWittsburg. After the massacre of the Stropes or Strops at Round Top the settlers took their families to Ulster County.

The first church organization in the town was at Oak Hill and of the Dutch Reformed faith. The church building was about a mile from Oak Hill, on the road to Preston Hollow, and the site donated by Stephen Van Rensselaer. It was probably organized about 1787. (Vosburg says, "the earliest date appears to be July 7, 1794. Before 1800 probably a part of Albany Classis").

Jan. 2, 1796, "At a meeting of the citizens of a place called Oak Hill in the town of Freehold, they being desirous of changing the name of said village, it was unanimously voted to call it by the name of DeWittsburgh" (Catskill Packet).

VILLAGE OF DURHAM

Durham or New Durham is second in time of settlement in the town. The Revolutionary War had left the country burdened with debt and now followed hard times for many a yeoman and his family. Land was cheap in the wilderness, and emigration to the newer parts of the country was one of the ways of solving the living problem.

Meeting-house Hill is one of the highest of the foothills in this section at the base of the Catskill Mountains, 1,100 feet above tide water, and this spot was chosen by seven young men from Durham, Conn., in 1784, as a suitable place for their homes. These young men came by boat to Catskill Landing, then with knapsacks, muskets and axes, continued their journey on foot. The names of only four are known, those of Jonathan and Abiel Baldwin, Phineas Canfield and David Merwin. Selah Strong came later in the same year. The next year five families came.

This choice of a settlement commands a fine view in all directions, but though there had been two meeting houses, a school house, blacksmith shop, and store, besides a number of dwellings, on this hill, there is now nothing but a forsaken "city of the dead" upon the hill-top. It became too small for all, and only Jonathan Baldwin and Selah Strong remained. The last purchased the farm which belonged to the late Horace Strong in 1798, and died there in 1837. His second son Elijah is said to have been the first child born at New Durham. These settlers endured many privations, for Mr. Strong's diary tells of "provisions being very scarce," but the influence of these God-fearing, thrifty men and women can never be measured. Many of them belonged to the Congregational Church of Connecticut, and among the first things they did was to build a log meeting house and provide regular services on the Sabbath. Deacon Christopher Lord of Saybrook, Conn., father-in-law of Jonathan Baldwin, came in 1787 and filled the place of pastor for ten years.

The first settler in what is now Durham village was Adijah Dewey. He was called Major Dewey and built a log house which is said to have been the first hotel there. He moved to Madison (Leeds) about 1820.* Dr. William Cook was the first physician. He was a soldier of the Revolution, and the following anecdote of General Washington has been handed down as related by him: The army wintered in Morristown, N. J., during the winter of 1777 and 1778, and so little did they have to eat that, at one time, their rations were limited to a single gill of wheat per day. Said Dr. Cook:

---

* His daughter Anna married Jarius Chittenden Jr. Polly, another daughter, married Peter Elting. Major Dewey also lived in Cairo.

"Washington used to come around and look into our tents, and he looked so kind, and said tenderly, 'Men, can you bear it?' 'Yes, General; yes we can,' was the reply, 'and if you wish us to act, give us the word and we are ready'." While they were at Morristown Washington had a dangerous attack of quinsy. The officers feared that he would die, and they asked him to indicate the man best fitted to succeed him, and without hesitation he pointed to General Nathaniel Greene.

It is said of a man by the name of Ford that he had the first cabinetmaker's shop, built the first bier and was the first to be borne to the grave upon it. Polly Chittenden taught school during 1787 and 1788, and Elizabeth Dudley in 1789. A Mr. Carter was the first lawyer, while Jacob Carter built the first bridge over the Katskill, and another at Brown's mills, soon after the completion of which he was drowned near it.

In the year 1788 Deacon Obed Hervey and others‡ settled in Hervey Street. They belonged to the North East Baptist church of Dutchess County. The Deacon was a godly man, and although well along in life was ordained a preacher, holding meetings at Hervey Street in houses and barns. He died in 1808, aged eighty-six. His son Obed was also a deacon, contributing much toward the welfare of the church. Elder Hermon, son of Deacon Obed Hervey Jr., was pastor for thirty years during which the church was built. He resigned in 1839. The Presbyterian church was organized Nov. 8, 1792, and with that of West Durham makes interesting history.

CORNWALLVILLE.

Cornwallville is one of those "below the mountain villages," set among the hills and farm lands of "Durham Town," for the southwestern boundary of the town runs on the tops of high mountains, the sloping sides of which meet the villages half way, and the shadows of the "Blue Mountains" grow long as evening falls.

Looking from East Windham Mountain the land shows little of its hills and valleys, of the many streams by which it is watered, of the gorges, glens and cascades of these same streams, but rather stretches like a great map to the Hudson River and the country beyond. Yet these villages overlook valleys of their own, and in addition have hills a-plenty, all of which form attractive and diversified scenery.

It would seem that Daniel Cornwall was responsible for the name. He was born in Connecticut about 1753, married Rachel Hall, and settled on a farm owned by Benjamin Hubbard in 1788. His first house was of logs. The pair were two weeks coming from New Haven, Conn., to Catskill in a sailing vessel. A defective title to his land caused him to pay twice for it.

Mr. Cornwall was a soldier of the Revolution, and both were members of the Congregational Church of Connecticut. They brought

---

‡ Among them were Captain Ashael Jones, Mr. Bumhourd, John Butler, Elder Arnold and Henry Bartell.

their faith with them, and in 1793 united with the church at Durham. In his old age he was often Moderator at the annual town meetings. Both he and his wife lived to extreme old age. They had six children, and his son David married Mary, a sister of the late Edward Johnson. One of his daughters married the Hon. Lyman Tremain of Durham, and another Robert E. Austin of Catskill (Jefferson).

John and Paul Percival were among the first settlers of Cornwallville. "Quaker Orchard," about two miles southeast of that place, was the last resting place of Capt. Thomas Smith and Charity his wife, and was named because of the springing up of self-sown apple trees, the seed scattered by people attending camp-meeting there. Deacon George Wright was one of the first settlers in Wright Street, and he came from Saybrook, Conn., very early in the history of the town, living on the farm afterward his grandson's. He was a soldier of the Revolution and musician for his company. The country about this settlement belonged to the Cockburn Patent.

METHODIST EPISCOPAL CHURCH, CORNWALLVILLE.

This church observed its one hundredth birthday October 16, 1921. Quoting from a "Historical Sketch" by William S. Borthwick, delivered on that day: "Many of the settlers of New Durham, which was the first English settlement in the town and was located on the hill north of where Platt Hill now lives, belonged to the Congregational Church of Connecticut, and among the first things they did was to build a log meeting house and to provide for regular meetings on the Sabbath.

"Quite a number of the settlers about New Durham were Meth-

odists, and they bought the church frame of the East Durham people and set it up on the hill near the Presbyterian Meeting House.
* * * This church is supposed to be the oldest of the denomination in the county. The church at Coeymans, Albany county, is the mother church, and the circuit included Coeymans, Catskill, Durham and part of Delaware county. * * * It was while the church was on the hill that it was incorporated September 21, 1819, and Harris Giddings was chosen President, Caleb Wetmore Secretary, and the corporation was known as the Methodist Episcopal Church of Durham, N. Y."

As the forests were cleared away, Meeting House Hill became very bleak and bare, and a majority of its members lived in Cornwallville, hence in 1821 they moved the church building there. Dr. Barrett was then preacher. In 1825 the Trustees were Caleb Wetmore, John, Jerome and Jabez Hubbard. (See Churches).

SOUTH DURHAM

South Durham is a tiny village at the foot of the Mohican Trail, and is composed of post office, store, hotel and a few dwellings. Its foothold seems precarious as you come from still lower levels, as if it might on an icy day slip and slide from its moorings. The shadows of Windham High Peak fall upon it early in the afternoon, and it is almost surrounded by the mysteries of deeply wooded mountain-sides.

EAST WINDHAM

A collection of summer hotels, a post office, a store and a widespread view of the Hudson valley to the Capital City and the Berkshires, constitutes East Windham. Its one-sided street is set close against the rock-terraced side of the mountain, at the front dropping precipitously down to the valley. It is the summit of the long and beautiful ascent up the mountain, now known as the Mohican Trail, which follows in part at least the blazed trail up which Jehiel Tuttle brought his family and household goods just after the Revolution, said household goods being fastened to two small trees which he cut at the foot and to which he fastened his ox-team.

Captain Peter Van Orden Sr. purchased 200 acres of land and built the first hotel in the town of Windham just outside this hamlet near where the toll-gate afterward stood, when all about him was a wilderness given over to the wild beasts of the forest. It was a log house and he entertained emigrants and chance travelers of all kinds. It is said of him that "he often rose on dark rainy nights, yoked his oxen, and taking hold of old Bright's bow in order to keep the track, drew emigrant wagons out of the mud." Peter Van Orden Jr. was born here in 1800, and the family burial place is near by.

In 1836 Ira Sherman had a hotel at East Windham. He was a son of Samuel Sherman, and a first cousin of Gen. William T. Sherman. Barney Butts, whose after life was closely connected with this vicinity, was born a mile from Hensonville.

PIONEERS AND THEIR HOMES
ADAMS

Joseph Adams lived at what is sometimes called Durham Center, on what was afterward known as the Lant place and then became the property of Henry S. Mace. The annual town meetings were often held there. Mr. Adams had four sons—Joseph, Gopher, and John by his first wife, and Platt by his second. John and Platt became eminent public men. Mr. Adams was born in 1738 and died May 16, 1832, aged ninety-four years; his son Joseph lived to be one hundred, and lived near South Durham at the time of his death.

John Adams became a teacher of district schools, studied law, and in 1810 was appointed Surrogate of Greene County by Daniel D. Tompkins. He was a Federalist, and, forming a co-partnership with Malbone Watson (afterward Judge Watson), removed to Catskill.

Platt Adams, a half-brother of John, was a man of great force of character, possessing great executive ability. He was a lawyer by profession although he never practiced much, preferring business and politics to law. He married Clarissa Dudley, daughter of the widow Dudley, who afterward married the Rev. Seth Williston, D. D. The name of Platt Adams is found frequently in the church records as clerk and trustee. He was Colonel of Militia, Town Clerk from 1821-25, when he was chosen Supervisor and filled that office for a number of terms. He was also Sheriff, and member of Senate and Assembly. He had two sons and two daughters. His son Grovener married Nancy Cone, daughter of the Rev. Jonathan Cone.

MOSES AUSTIN

The following was written by the late J. G. Borthwick over forty years ago: "Moses Austin was born in Wallingford, Conn., about 1768; came to Durham at about twenty years of age, and bought land where Asbury Strong now lives. The farm still goes by the name of the "Austin place;" the house long since disappeared, and the barn was destroyed by fire two or three years ago. His neighbors were Charles Johnson and a Mr. Ford who lived in the same house. Mr. Ford was taken violently ill, and Mr. Austin rode on horseback, and in the night, to the city of Hudson for medicine, but it was in vain. Mr. Ford died, and Mr. Austin was often heard to say that it was one of the most melancholy recollections of his life. In 1806 he bought the farm now owned by Charles Wetmore,† and built the large house now standing, occupying in the meantime the old block house which stood near by. He was a prosperous business man—owned a woolen factory in Cairo, was engaged in various business enterprises and became very wealthy. He was at

---

† He is said to have "built in 1806" the house where Edward J. Parks now lives.

one time Judge of the Court of Common Pleas, and in 1819-22 was one of the members of the New York State Senate. * * * *

"Mr. Austin was twice married. His first wife was Elizabeth Cooper of Chatham, Conn.; his second, Sallie Humphrey of Derby, Conn., a niece of the Hon. and Gen. David Humphreys, who was United States Minister to the Court of Spain and Portugal. He had a large family and one of his sons remained on the farm and became Supervisor of the town. Two daughters and one son lived in Cairo. His brother Aaron lived on the "old Austin place," and died in Cornwallville. Another brother lived in Durham, his descendants in Windham. Mr. Austin spent the evening of his life at Cairo, and died there on the 2d day of May, 1848, aged eighty years."

THE BALDWINS

The name Baldwin dates back to the year 864. The first Count of Flanders married Judith, the daughter of Charles the Bold of France. His first name seems to have been Baldwin, and his successors were called Baldwin down to Baldwin IX, who became the first Emperor of Constantinople. The first mention of it as a surname was in 1198.

Three brothers—Timothy, Nathaniel and Joseph—settled in Milford, Conn., in 1639. Joseph was the ancestor of the first Baldwins to come to Durham, N. Y. These were Jonathan and Abiel, sons of Abiel and Mehitable Baldwin of Durham, Conn., who came with five other young men in 1784 and settled on Meeting-House Hill. Abiel Sr., with his wife and younger children, did not come until 1804.

Jonathan is spoken of as a remarkable man and the means of bringing together the settlers for worship long before the church was organized. He was a blacksmith, and became treasurer and chorister of the first church; had charge of the building and received $3.25 per year for his care of it, which included sweeping it out at least once a month. He married Submit, youngest daughter of Deacon Christopher Lord, and in 1816 removed to Atwater, Ohio, where he died in 1843. One of his children, Elihue Whittlesey Baldwin, became a minister of the gospel and President of Wabash College, at Crawfordsville, Indiana.

Abiel was a soldier of the Revolution; married Eunice Coe, had nine children, one of whom became a minister; and Abiel is spoken of by the late J. G. Borthwick as "the most godly man I ever knew." Of the other brothers, Curtis, who came in 1785, married the school teacher Polly Chittenden. He had taken up land on Meeting-House Hill. David married Julia Chittenden. They had no children but assisted in the education of two nephews, who became ministers. David was a man of uncommon piety and had a wonderful memory. The Rev. Seth Williston called him "his concordance," and it has been said of him "his christianity was a living principle."

Seth Baldwin married Rhoda, daughter of Timothy Hull of

Durham, Conn. He lived on the old farm until 1804, and then removed to a place near Cornwallville. He had twelve children, one of whom, Dwight, was at one time principal of Kingston Academy, taught in Catskill and Durham, and finally, after his conversion, became a medical missionary to the Sandwich Islands. Aaron, another son of Abiel Sr., married Sarah Norton of Durham, Conn., and in 1816 removed to Ohio. Of the daughters of Abiel Sr., Eunice married Selah Strong, Mehitable married William Torrey, and Ruth, Leverett Chittenden.

The second family of Baldwins was that of Noah Sr., brother of the first Abiel, and eight years his junior. They seem to have been very firm friends, living and dying on the same farm. Their children were well educated, professors of religion, and became useful members of society. The three oldest children of Noah died in infancy, and Sally, the fourth child, on her mother's death (when Sally was sixteen) took the entire care of seven children younger than herself. She often said if it had not been for the assistance of her brothers she would have utterly failed in the undertaking. She married John Hull of Durham, Conn., and, removing to Durham, N. Y., settled on a farm one mile south of the village.

Noah Baldwin Jr., brother of Sally, married Phoebe Hull. James married Mabel, the daughter of Seth Jones, a Revolutionary soldier of Saybrook, Conn., who gave his life for his country. James and his brother Noah lived about thirty rods apart and each built a substantial hip-roofed house, with internal arrangements exactly alike, built the same year and raised the same day. One stood on the north side of the road and the other on the south. James was a very quiet man, much respected, and finally sold his farm to his nephew, Lemuel Baldwin.

Hezekiah and his wife Rachel did not come to Durham until 1816, when he bought the farm at that time owned by Deacon Jonathan, where he lived the remainder of his days. They had no children and his widow became the second wife of Captain Jehiel Cooley.

Adah Baldwin married Christopher Post, and died in 1854 without children. Hannah married Stephen Tibbals and settled on what was afterward the Van Wagener farm. Mehitable married Luther Hayes, born in Massachusetts. They came to Durham village, where he was a hardware merchant, and by honest industry gained a competence. He was Elder in the church, a faithful Christian man. His wife, Aunt Hetty, was a very cheerful, pleasant Christian woman. They had nine children.

Rhoda was the youngest and eleventh child of Noah Sr., and she married Constant Bushnell of Saybrook, and came to Durham about 1800; in 1815 removed their church membership to Madison county, N. Y., and at some later date to Marshall, Michigan. They had at least nine children. The name of Baldwin, originating in Durham, is scattered nearly all over this country, from New York to California, from Minnesota to Mississippi, and when this was written over forty years ago there were twenty-three in the Sandwich Islands.

Town of Greenville

This town was organized under the general act passed March 26, 1803. The name was changed from Greenfield to Freehold on April 6, 1808, and on Oct. 6th of the same year, at the house of Seymour Minor, inn-keeper, it was voted to change the name to Greenville, which was confirmed March 17, 1809.

The first town meeting was held at the home of Eli Knowles on April 5, 1803, and the first town officers were as follows:

Stoddard Smith............Supervisor
Charles Griggs............Town Clerk
Aaron Hall .... Overseer of Poor
Thomas George....Overseer of Poor
Eben Norton.............Commissioner
Daniel Miller ....Commissioner
Peter Brandow........Commissioner
Eli Knowles ....Pound Master
Joshua Baker ....Assessor
Henry Talmadge ....Assessor
Francis Hickock ....Assessor
Reuben Byington........Collector
Reuben Byington ....Constable
Robert Frazier ....Constable
Joseph Heath ....Constable
Nathaniel Fancher...Constable

"In 1804 it was voted that all hogs one year old and upward may run at large, being yoked with a yoke 20 inches long. All under one year with a yoke 12 inches long." If left unyoked there was a fine of 50 cents for each offense.

In 1813 fourteen school districts were organized. There were numerous grist and saw mills on the Basic, "Jan-de-bakker" and Potick creeks—the grist mill of Augustine Provost in 1800, the woolen mill of the Kings in 1802, and the saw mills of Reuben Rundle and David Baker, one built by Simon Losee in 1792, a short distance above where Losee creek empties into Potick; the mill of Henry and Peter Bogardus on "Jan-de-bakker" about 1820, and the Jennings grist mill on the Basic, built 1800. There was a tannery in Freehold in 1805, built by a Sanford; with several others at Greenville; also leather, stoves and shingle factories.

John L. Raymond was one of the first settlers on the Prevost Patent.

The town of Greenville is comparatively free from mountains and high hills, its land more rolling than that of any other town in Greene County, yet it has an elevation from 1,600 to 2,000 feet. Basic Creek is its largest stream. About the time of the town's organization there was a post route between Coxsackie and Westerlo, with a post at Greenville village, and shortly after one at Newry. The first post-rider was known as "Old Brownie." The mail of Aaron Hall and his near neighbors was left between two flat stones at the four corners near Hall's home. The post was weekly and soon became semi-weekly.

Godfrey Brandow, Stephen Lampman and Jacob Bogardus were the first settlers. Reuben Rundle came in 1786, with wife and two sons. He had been a lieutenant in the Revolutionary Army, and married Sally Holly of Stamford, Conn.; his home on what is known as the Dean farm. For a time he was a shoemaker, bringing leather from Catskill on his back and exchanging boots and shoes for grain. He was senior warden of the first Episcopal church. Joseph Waldron was an enterprising settler of 1790; Obadiah King of 1791. Reuben Stevens paid $2.50 an acre for land at "The Hemlocks," where he died in 1804. His eldest son was a soldier of the Revolution; his wife, Mary Williams.

GREENVILLE VILLAGE

Augustine Provost was responsible for the existence of Greenville Center village.* His patents covered 7,000 acres, and coming to the town of Greenville (1794) he immediately built a frame house a little west of the present village, near the center of his estate, and around it tenant-houses, grist and saw mills, a bark mill, and opened a real estate office where he disposed of small portions of his land on reasonable terms. He built roads and looked after the religious and educational interests of the people, by whom he was much beloved. A school house was built for his own children, and those of his neighbors were allowed to attend without

PREVOST HOUSE AT GREENVILLE, 1798.

charge. He improved his house and grounds until it looked like an old English estate. There was rich furniture of English manufacture, and valuable paintings. He was acquainted with the prominent men of his day and the notables of England. The portrait of the Duke of Kent, who was a personal friend of his own and his father's, hung on his wall. Three of his sons were in the English army and he a Royalist whose unspoken sympathies were doubtless with England, but he maintained a strict neutrality. It was written of him in 1799, "Major Prevost has a neat little house built on a tract of nine thousand acres, which belongs to him. He is a son of that General Prevost employed in the British service who dis-

---

* Once known as "The Hemlocks."

tinguished himself in the defense of Savannah, and disgraced his character by the burning of many American towns.

"Major Prevost, a native of Switzerland, has all the frankness of an honest Switzer, and of a genuine honest Englishman. He is beloved by his neighbors, seems just and impartial in his opinions, speaks well of the American government, and is a good-natured and agreeable man." Major Prevost was born in Geneva, Switzerland, August 29, 1774, was twice married, died in 1821, and lies in the Prevost cemetery with others of his family.

The Academy at Greenville was incorporated by Regents on Feb. 27, 1816. This act of incorporation was signed by Daniel D. Tompkins, chancellor of University of State of New York, and Gideon Hawley, secretary of state. The corporators were:

Jonathan Sherill	Stoddard Smith	Francis Hickok
Rev. Beriah Hotchkin	Levi Callendar	Daniel Miller
Dr. Amos Botsford	Abijah Reed	Joseph Bishop
Augustine Prevost	Truman Sanford	Daniel Hitchcock
Eliakim Reed	Alexander Calhoun	Josiah Rundle
Aaron Hall	Reuben Rundle Jr.	Obediah King
	Eli Knowles	

James Waldron came to Greenville in 1790 and purchased 100 acres of Levi Blaisdell, a part of which was in the Coeymans Patent. His father came over from Holland in 1757.

Dr. Amos Botsford married Elizabeth Clark (1801) and the young couple settled on the Eli Knowles place. The only physician in that vicinity for many years, he rode horseback on his innumerable calls throughout the town. He is said to have been very dignified, had a fine physique and commanded the respect of all. For fifty years he was the faithful and successful physician, a Supervisor for a number of years, and one of the incorporators of the Greenville Academy, to which pupils came from all parts of the county. His fourth child, Mary L., married Dr. Bradley S. McCabe, a later physician of Greenville.

On the road from Greenville to The Hemlocks was the house of the Townsends, afterward occupied by Russel Townsend, whose uncle, John Russel, was one of George Washington's life guards in the Revolution and had the honor of carrying him from the field when thrown from his horse. Abel Townsend kept a public house on the borders of Greenville and Coxsackie.

The first physician in the town is said to have been Dr. John Ely of Newry, whose fame spread throughout the county. Isaac Hallock kept a hotel in 1820. Among its merchants are Ransom Hinman (1803), Abijah Reed (1810), and Levi Callendar (1816). Buel Cheritree was the blacksmith and Eli Knowles another hotelkeeper.

FREEHOLD.

Freehold was once an Indian village. The Indian village disappeared in 1616, followed by squatters in 1700, for here was some of the best land in the Catskill valley. Then George III of England granted it, in all 1,000 acres of land, to Johannes Hallenbeck, and a part was sold to the Beckers in 1720. Near by came Christopher Kniskern, Morris Hazard and the Truesdell family. Of the three last their families have disappeared from this vicinity, leaving behind only a few brown stones whose dates are all before 1795. Stephen Platt was an early comer and lost his life in 1800, trying to save a bridge in time of flood. He was active in the business of the town. The King brothers came from Massachusetts. They were educated men, and Perkins King was justice of the peace in 1818 and for seven terms of three years; County Judge for twenty-four years, Member of the Assembly and Congressman. Andrew Dodge was a successful merchant. Formerly potash was manufactured, and there were two brickyards, one near the old cemetery.

GAYHEAD

The little village of Gayhead lies on the edge of the town, and partly in the town of Cairo. Peter Scriver (now usually called Scriber) came from Clinton Corners, in Dutchess County, in 1818, and settled on a farm which is now the village of Gayhead. He had seven daughters and one son. The son went to Ohio, and his descendants now live at Annapolis, Michigan. He was a soldier of the Revolution, and the great-grandfather of Counselor Ambrose Jones, and grandfather of the late Addison P. Jones of Jefferson.

PIONEERS AND THEIR HOMES
GODFREY BRANDOW

Godfrey Brandow, who married Catrina Overbagh, was the first settler (1750) in the town of Greenville. The Overbaghs of Sandy Plains were his nearest neighbors, and his daughter Catrina, whose baptism is found in the Old Katskill church records, was the first white child born there (1751), and the first marriage was that of another daughter, Maria, who married Stephen Lampman, their neighbor in 1752, coming from Coeymans by ox-team.

It is supposed that Godfrey Brandow was of Holland Dutch descent, but his birthplace is unknown, and previous to his coming to Greenville he lived near Saugerties. In the year 1750 he located land in the town of Greenville, and his log house stood on what is sometimes known as the Seabridge farm, his nearest neighbors for two years being the Overbaghs of Sandy Plains, who were his wife's relatives. Godfrey Brandow and his wife Catrina Overbagh, at the time he settled in the town, had two sons and two daughters.

His farm contained 800 acres, the southern part in the Livingston Patent, and the northern in the Coeymans Patent, afterward Lot No. 1 of the sixth allotment. He cleared a little spot on a ridge which was covered by thick forest trees of oak, hickory and maple. Ten years later it was a large clearing well stocked with cattle and sheep. He brought to this new home plenty of such farming tools as could be secured at that period, and are said to have been imported from Holland.

There are no records of Indian troubles or other exciting events in his life in the wilderness, only wolf-hunts and the killing of other wild beasts of the forest. His son John settled near him, and after the father's death, in 1795, the homestead came to his then only remaining son, Peter, who bequeathed it in 1830 to his sons, Jacob and Peter P.

Peter, son of Godfrey and Catharine Brandow, was born March 22, 1750, and married Hannah, daughter of Jacob and Maria Bogardus. Peter had courted the mother of his future wife without success, and thereafter had no use for any other woman. He also refused to be friends with Jacob and Maria, but when their first child proved to be a daughter they again became friends, and a bargain was made that in case he could win that child's consent when she became old enough, he should marry her. Her consent must have been obtained, for he married her in 1792, and they had eleven children.

JACOB BOGARDUS

Jacob, who came from Coxsackie, was the third settler, and in 1772 he commenced to clear land on the farm which in 1882 was occupied by his grandsons, Henry and David Bogardus. For two years he spent his summers clearing away the forest, and his winters in Coxsackie. Coming back with a family in 1774 to make a permanent home, he found it unsafe because of Indians, and returned to wait for more peaceful times.

He enlisted as a minute-man in the Revolutionary war, and it was not until 1783 that he returned to Greenville with his family. The log house stood only a few rods east of where the family residence stood later. He had 800 acres, half of which was afterward sold, 200 acres to his brother Manning, who settled there in 1784.

Jacob Bogardus was a direct descendant of Everardus Bogardus, who was the first minister sent over by the Dutch West India Company to New Amsterdam. Jacob had a strong character and was noted for honesty of purpose, retaining the customs and manners of the Holland Dutch until the day of his death.

Manning Bogardus, who settled on a part of Jacob's original estate, was born in Coxsackie; was a Revolutionary soldier, and had command of a company of rangers.

Town of Halcott

The town of Halcott is the smallest in the county and separated from its associates by high mountains, which have no gaps or cloves to render it easily accessible, excepting from the west and south, through Delaware county. The roads over these mountains are steep, difficult, and little used.

The town was named for George W. Halcott, a son of Thomas Halcott, who is buried in a field near Halcott Center. It is a part of the Hardenburgh Patent, and is divided into four valleys by the sources of the east branches of the Delaware. The first town meeting was held in the house of James D. Vandenburg, April 6, 1852, and the following officials were elected:

George Lawrence............Supervisor
James D. Vandenburg..........Clerk
Abel Lawrence................Assessor
Alfred Townsend..............Assessor
Reuben Lake..................Assessor
John Griffin.................Constable
Abel Griffin.................Constable
Martin Brazee................Constable
Lawrence Brooks..............Collector
Silas Lake...................School Supt.
John M. Todd.................Justice
Nathaniel F. Ellis...........Justice
James Peck...................Justice
Benj. L. Crosby..............Justice
Russell Peck.................H'w'y Overseer
E. Woolhiser.................H'w'y Overseer
Benj. Ballard................H'w'y Overseer
Martin Brooks................Overseer Poor
Buel Maben...................Overseer Poor

Indians were not common in this section, and there is no tradition of a trail having passed through it. The last Indian of whom anything is known was one named "Fromer," whose wigwam stood near a spring where the Halcott Center road crosses the county line.

Emigrants came from Connecticut before 1813, but they did not linger long. They were squatters and soon became discouraged. The earliest known settler (1809) was Helmus Chrysler. In 1813 John Van Valkenburgh with his mother and brother Peter moved into the house Chrysler had built. They cleared the farm which afterward belonged to Marchant Van Valkenburgh. Joseph B. Brooks built the first frame house and barn. John Banker drove the first wagon over the road the squatters had started as a path, when he moved Otis Miller's family. Wolves were so plentiful that many sheep were carried off in the daytime even when guarded by dogs, the dogs soon learning that when they ventured outside the clearing they would have the whole pack of wolves upon them. A school house was built in 1816, where Jacob Miller's daughter and Sally Kline were teachers. The school house was of logs and stood on the Miller farm. Another was built in 1834.

In 1814 Tenant Peck came to the farm which in 1880 was owned by Rev. Daniel Van Valkenburgh. Jacob Miller, Jesse Lockwood, Peter I. Vandenburgh, Cyrus Smallie, Aaron Garrison, John G. Van Valkenburgh, William Denton and Elijah Parker came in 1816-17. By this time the footpath of the squatters had reached the turnpike at Griffin's Corners and was made passable for carts and sleds.

The first birth occurred in Nehemiah Cowles' family in 1814, and the same year Peter Van Valkenburgh died. In 1880 the Rev. John P. Van Valkenburgh was the only survivor of the original settlers. He was born in Rensselaer county, Nov. 9, 1800, a son of Peter L. Van Valkenburgh, a captain in the Revolutionary War and grandson of John Van Valkenburgh, who came from Holland to Albany county before the Revolution.

The Rev. John P. came to Halcott with his widowed mother in 1813, and eight years later was married to Jemima, daughter of Daniel Griffin, who about 1805 settled in the northern part of the town of Middletown, Delaware county. In 1842 he was ordained by the Methodist Episcopal church, having preached under a license for nine years. He had six sons and three daughters.

In Munsell's History of Delaware county an early settler's wagon, such as came to Greene and other counties, is described as having wheels with spokes like small saplings and felloes like those in the wheels of a modern stone-truck. Poles were bent across bow-fashion from side to side of the stout box, and covered with stout canvas to keep out wind and storm and the sweltering sunshine. A span of jaded horses that had not seen a comfortable stable for weeks, and under the canvas a woman with two or three small children, completed the outfit, beside which walked the husband and father to ease the team, sometimes sinking knee-deep in mud or staggering over fallen log or a stone. He is a strong, well-built six-footer, with heart brave to every danger.   *   *   *
The wife knows some but not all of the hardships before her, and that she will never live to have many years' enjoyment of the fruits of their sacrifice and toil, but their children will—it is for these she has consented to risk the perils of pioneer life, for it is only after grave consideration the decision has been made to seek a new home in the wilderness.

At evening the tired horses are watered and tethered where they can get their fill of grass, a fire is lighted, a hasty meal prepared, and soon they are asleep, to be awakened later by prowling wolves. The gun speaks, the fire is rekindled and they return to their slumbers. When they reach the end of their journey a log cabin must be built, shelter for the horses, and furniture made by the man's own hands. The pioneer has brought with him a few tools, a frying pan, cast-iron bake-kettle, a few knives and forks, iron spoons, cups and saucers, and perhaps a few choice pieces of china. They will be miles distant from other homes, but with faith in God and themselves they begin their new life, full of difficulties and dangers.

HALCOTT CENTER

When Amasa Hill kept the post office it was named Halcott Center. Among business enterprises was the store of Ralph Coe south of the M. E. Church, and here also was the inn. Another inn or tavern was that of Nathan Applebee. There was a saw mill in 1824, an ashery about 1816, and the blacksmith shop of Richard Norris. Before the town as a town came into existence, a post office was kept at Conger Avery's, who was the postmaster. The post office was then West Lexington, and the mail came from Prattsville to Griffin's Corners once a week; later it became semi-weekly.

Although the town of Halcott is at the present time an isolated one, kept from much progress as to population by nature's barriers over 3,000 feet in height, between it and the town of Lexington, within its small area is much of scenic beauty, and should the proposed new road be built from Halcott Center to the foot of the ridge in the town of Lexington, a distance of about four miles, its residents, instead of traveling through parts of both Ulster and Delaware counties to reach the county seat, will be connected with the rest of Greene county, which will mean much for future growth in population.

Town of Hunter

The territory within the present boundaries of the town of Hunter was part of a large grant of land given by Queen Anne to Iohanus Hardenburgh and six others, April 23, 1708, which was called the "Great Patent." Hunter comprises portions of Great Lots 23, 24, 25, 26, and all of 43. These lots were purchased by Tomilson, Day, the Livingstons, and John Hunter for speculation.

Lot 25 belonged to John Hunter of New Rochelle and contained 12,500 acres. This land was deeded by John and his wife Elizabeth, to Henry Overing and wife Charlotte Debross. In 1829 Overing sold it back to Hunter. Seven thousand acres were purchased later by Isaac Showers at 62½c. an acre.

January 27, 1813, an act was passed erecting Windham into three towns, one of which was Greenland, the name Hunter first used in 1814. There were few settlers before 1800, but the names of Samuel Haines and Herman Mason appear in Windham records as pathmasters in 1798 and 1799.

At a town meeting held at the house of Daniel Bloomer April 6, 1813, it was "Resolved, to have three assessors, three constables, one pound near the house of Daniel Bloomer, and nine fence viewers." Twenty-five roadmasters were appointed and the following officials elected:

Daniel Bloomer	Supervisor	Benj. McGregor	Commissioner
Sumner Parmenter	Town Clerk	Samuel Haines	Poor Master
Samuel Haines	Assessor	John J. Artman	Poor Master
Nathan Miller	Assessor	Neven Wilson	Collector
Neven Wilson	Assessor	John Wilson Jr.	Constable
John Wilson	Commissioner	Benj. Jones Jr.	Constable
Matthew Winters	Commissioner	Caleb Carr	Constable

In 1814 it was voted to pay the town clerk $7 per year for his services, and school commissioner $6. They raised $175 for the poor, and voted to give the Clove road to the Turnpike Company. In 1824 it was voted to "relinquish the road between Perkins and the New York tannery to the Hunter Turnpike Company." In 1826 the bounty on wolves was $15, panthers $20, wild cats $2, and foxes 50c. Later wolves brought $40.

According to the New York Gazetteer, the people who first settled here were "Tory cow boys from Putnam County, and their property was confiscated by the Whigs;" but the names of many of the settlers are synonymous with those of the towns of Jewett and Lexington, making it difficult to be certain to which town they rightfully belong.

High Peak and Round Top are in this town, their names similar to those in the towns of Windham and Cairo. Round Top once had an Indian fort on its summit, and the peak and the surrounding mountain country and cascades have been made famous by many writers of early days, among them Bryant, Cooper, Dominie Murdock, Thomas Cole and others.

The scenic wealth of the Catskill Mountains lies within the borders of the town of Hunter. It has been more richly endowed in this respect than any other town in Greene County, and three cloves with their streams, ravines, cliffs and trails, smaller replicas of those found among the Rockies and the Klondike, here have a common meeting place. It is also from Hunter town that the door unexpectedly opens to that most impressive of all views, that of the Hudson Valley and portions of the Eastern states.

One hundred years ago the town of Hunter was assessed for $87,609 and to-day for something over two and one-half millions. A number of assessment books dating back to 1826, well preserved, with penmanship far superior to that of the present day student, are in the possession of Mr. Showers of Tannersville, who is a descendant of the first Isaac who came to this country and whose son settled on Showers Hill when Hunter was mostly a wilderness.

HUNTER VILLAGE

The location of Hunter village is very beautiful, situated at the foot of the highest peak of the Catskills in Greene county, and with a stream, which seems to be the accompaniment of every mountain village of any size, the beautiful Schoharie kill, adding to its attractiveness.

Hunter was first Edwardsville, named after Colonel William Edwards, who was the "man of the hour" for that village, which grew with great rapidity after his coming. His wife was Rebecca Tappan and they had eleven children.

Seth Green, the cobbler, squatted about 1790 west of the village. His wife was Ann Buckingham of Saybrook. John Haines was the first male child born in the town. Sumner Parmenter (or Palmatier) and wife (a Miss Schofield), a son of Jerry Parmenter, settled near the lakes on unclaimed land, and in 1810 this land was claimed by Anthony Loucet and Seth Green. $5 an acre was paid by the occupants for the land.

Hunter village was called an "ivy swamp," but with the coming of Edwards one of the largest tanneries in the state was built on the site of the Bronson saw mill. David Van Horn and Abram Harr were apprentices and afterward tanners at the West Kill. The leather from these tanneries was taken to Catskill or Bristol (New Malden) and from there by sloop to New York; sometimes in winter direct to New York by sleds. This became a tannery town and the output of leather was large until the supply of hemlocks was exhausted.

The first church was dedicated in Hunter in 1828 and was of the Presbyterian faith. Among its first members were Colonel William Edwards and wife, John Bray and Samuel Henson and wife. Before

ONTEORA PARK.

this services were held in the loft of Edwards' tannery, fitted up for that purpose and rudely furnished. There is considerable information as to the troubles and trials of this church to be found in the Catskill Recorder of that date, but this for lack of space must be reserved for the history of Greene County churches.

TANNERSVILLE

The name is a relic of tannery days, when tanneries were on almost every stream where hemlocks grew, and were the gold mines of the Catskills. It has been said her native place was in the Kaaterskill Clove, where if you follow the trail of the first turnpike you will see the ruins of a village, and a few gnarled and knotted apple trees. In this village at one time were two tanneries and two hundred people and a post office called Tannersville.

Mr. C. M. Britt of Catskill, a native of Britts Corners on the Catskill-Palenville road, says that when he was a boy the village in the Clove was known as "Upper Clove Village," and that then a big tannery was still standing and at least two houses were occupied. The village had two boarding houses and a blacksmith shop.

Near Fawn's Leap in his time the Brockett family, who had two sons George and Leonard, were the first to keep boarders in that vicinity and had a stand at the falls, charging admittance to them.

The great-grandfather of Supervisor Lackey was among the first settlers of Tannersville, and his father, Michael Lackey, Tannersville's most able and enterprising citizen, a lover of nature and of his native town (an associate of the late Jacob Fromer) with his twin sister was born in what is now the New Manhattan, best known as the "Cascade," a small portion of which is the original building, one of the oldest in the village. Mr. Lackey remembers when there were but three or four buildings in Tannersville, among them this house, for a long time a tavern or inn and at one time a store kept by Fromer. Another was the inn of Norman H. Gray at the four corners, first that of Harlow Perkins. Gray was accidentally killed in the Clove in 1865. His son succeeded him. The land upon which Tannersville now stands was once owned by the Egglestons.

Among several old houses still standing in the village are those of Newton Curtis on Spring street, of Allen on Main street, of Doyle on Lakeview Avenue, and the old Rogers house.

To-day Tannersville is probably the most enterprising of Greene county's mountain villages. The attractiveness of its situation, 2,300 feet above sea level and "Above the Clouds" as its slogan reads, has been commercialized at the expense of natural beauty as have all successful villages, making lakes where lakes were not, establishing recreation centers, tennis courts, golf links and theaters, but its surroundings have lost little of the beauty of the hills. Around it can still be found in great abundance the wonders of the forest and the widespread views for which the Catskills are noted, all of which is close at hand. Explore the mountain side and one comes upon unexpected glens, high cliffs and tumbling brooks, moss and fern-covered boulders, and in their season mountain laurel and azaleas in great abundance. Onteora, Twilight, Santa Cruz, Sunset and Elka Parks, summer colonies where those rich in this world's goods come to play and rest, have been so constructed as to become an asset to the landscape, but do not belong to the earliest history of the town.

HAINES FALLS

The first settler of this village was Aaron Haines, who came from Connecticut on horseback. Both village and falls retain the name and keep in memory the family which has been most numerous and active in building up this vicinity,* but have left little in the way of early records behind them.

Haines Falls is formed by the waters of the West Branch of the Kaaterskill falling over a precipice of 150 feet, and its waters continuing on their way leap from rock to rock and ledge to ledge, forming numerous other and smaller falls and cascades until they reach the "Village of Falling Waters" at the foot of the Clove.

The village of Haines Falls is the farthest eastern village outpost of "Hunter Town" and the first to greet the traveler at the top of the Clove. It sits on the edge of Nature's great cleft in the mountain's side, where the inhabitants can look down into the eerie depths and through the cleft or clove to the world beyond. Near it are Santa Cruz, Sunset and Twilight Parks. The last in winter seems to be in imminent danger of slipping and sliding into what seems a bottomless pit.

Back of Haines Falls is Clum Hill, where the father of Jason Clum (who now owns the farm) came from Columbia county over one hundred years ago to escape tuberculosis. The change must have effected a cure, for he was twice married and raised three sets of children. Some years ago the son Jason sold a portion of the farm to Welles Bosworth, a noted architect of New York city, who has built a house of Greek architecture upon the hill where the outlook in all directions is one of the finest to be found in the Catskills.

THE CLOVES

The greater parts of Stony, Plattekill and Kaaterskill Cloves are within the limits of the town of Hunter, and all three converge from widespread starting points toward a common meeting place on the mountain top. All are beautiful in their own way.

The Plattekill Clove is the "nearest to Nature's heart," still untroubled by improved highway which lures the motorist but often mars the beautiful. Through it a stream rushes from rock ledge to rock ledge from its first wild leap, down through the wooded gorge. At the top is Platte Clove village and the Devil's Kitchen, somewhat

---

*On an atlas of 1865 are shown the homes of fifteen different Haines families in the town.

commercialized but for that reason more easily accessible to the public. The view is an impressive one. It was up this Clove that the Snyders of Saugerties were taken captive to Canada during the Revolution, by Indians and Tories.

RIP VAN WINKLE TRAIL (KAATERSKILL CLOVE).

Stony Clove is widely different from the others. If it were not for the railroad, whose engines huff and puff up tnis narrow cleft in the mountain range from Ulster county into Greene, wayfarers might think themselves lost in the wilderness when they leave the valley of content in Hunter town, and are shut in at the foot of high peaks with only patches of sky far above and scant room at the side for the noiseless stream that glides softly and lazily by the way, and where in springtime acres of mountain laurel, its dainty calico flower, and other wild flowers bid once tarry for a while.

Edgewood is 1,787 feet above tide water, a little collection of houses and camps where Stony Clove opens out on the way to the valley; and four hundred feet lower is Lanesville of 1,355 feet elevation, and not far from the Ulster county line. It is rich in streams and mountain peaks, and grand old Westkill looks down upon it.

The Kaaterskill Clove is the product of the ages, and was the natural passageway of the Indians from the wilderness to the valley. It was also the runway of wild beasts, the bear, the panther, and the wolf, which came down to prey upon the cattle and sheep of the settlers. Down it the deer descended—warily on the lookout for enemies—to drink from its stream, or, when the snow was deep upon the mountain sides, to seek forage in the valley.

During the Revolution, Indians and Tories followed this cleft in the mountain range, looking for scalps or for reward from the

British for captives. The fort of the Indian was upon Round Top, and once a captive was secured and they had entered the wilderness fastness, pursuit was useless. The Abeels of the Bak-oven were taken over this steep and difficult trail to the Schoharie kill, on the way to Niagara. (See Indians.)

We know but little of the Kaaterskill Clove before the advent of the tanneries, which was a later epoch in its history, but a pioneer geologist writes of numerous copperheads and rattlesnakes, eagles soaring overhead, of trees interlacing over the stream where five-pound trout were caught; of perpendicular ledges crowned by enormous rocks, over which waved the pine with its funereal verdure, often projecting over the cliffs like nodding plumes.

Haines Falls and the Kaaterskill must have been much greater in volume than to-day. Giant hemlocks and great trees of all kinds covered the mountain sides, and when the glorious autumn coloring appeared and Indian summer was at hand with its soft overshadowing haze, the hush which pervaded the forest and the deep silence of the wilderness—like which there is none other—must have filled even the savage heart with awe as he stood upon some jutting rock or sped swiftly along the trail.

The whole region of country about the Clove is rich in legendary lore and South Mountain is the spot pictured by Irving as the place of Rip Van Winkle's long nap. To-day, in spite of modern road and gasoline monsters, you can still on occasion hear Hendrick Hudson's men playing nine pins, while the "Old Squaw of the Mountains" still empties her feather bed from some far-up pinnacle which she veils in mist.

Pine Orchard, where stands the Mountain House of to-day, was the favorite camping ground of the red men, and the legend still lingers of Lotowana, the daughter of the chief Shandaken, whom Norserreden, "a cruel and dissipated Egyptian," sought to win although she was betrothed to a young chief of the Mohawks. Norserreden, enraged at the failure of his suit and vowing revenge, caused the death of the beautiful Indian maiden by the gift of a casket which contained a poison dart. He was pursued and burned at the stake by the warriors of the old chief, and "his ashes left upon the rocks to be scattered by the winds of heaven."

The Catskill Mountain House is just over the line in the town of Catskill. In 1819 a party was taken there on horseback by Erastus Beach. They spent the night camping on the flat rocks with "all creation" below them. Soon a shack was built for the accommodation of travelers, and in 1823 "temporary buildings" were advertised as "taken by William Van Bergen, whose accommodations are good and the house well furnished." Erastus Beach ran a stage three times a week to meet the boat at Catskill. A company was formed and a road built from Colonel Lawrence's to the hotel the next year, and a grand Independence Day celebration was held at Pine Orchard, the small building enlarged to "140 feet length" with four stories, and the interior "fitted up in superior style."

HISTORY OF GREENE COUNTY

In the scant pages of this book justice cannot (if at all) be done to the varied beauty of the Catskills, which like most other ranges throughout the world have something personally appealing, something which distinguishes them from their kind. The beauty of Greene County Mountains is the hidden things; deep caves in the forests, mountain meadows on their terraced sides, an abundance of streams and cascades, crags and precipices, deep silent glens, little mountain-surrounded valleys, and above all a charm not well defined which brings one back again and again to their feet.

From the front of this famous white Mountain House you can watch the sun rise far across valley and river from behind the mountains of the Eastern states. The river is a golden ribbon, the clouds tinged with inimitable red, shadows chasing each other from village to village, and from waving grain to patches of woodland which grow dense and dark, turning suddenly to brightest green as misty clouds disappear and the sun rises higher, rousing the monster Ontiora from sleep and to another day of helpless reclining, to which he was perpetually doomed in the long ago, while his eyes, which are the twin lakes, glitter in the sunshine with a fierce longing to be free.

Below there is a glimpse of the old road over which day by day during the summer season toiled the faithful saddle-horse, or stage-horses with the creaking coach until supplanted by the Otis Railway, which in turn gave way to the smelly motor car. The old road is fast becoming but a trail, and the glen in which Rip Van Winkle slept is returning to its primitive state.

The Kaaterskill, first known as the Harding House, was a victim of fire in 1924. Its outlook was entirely different from that at Pine Orchard. To its surroundings belonged the grandeur and wildness of mountain and forest, the western wilderness of early days was about it, and the innovations of time hidden behind the green.

The Harding road up the north side of the Clove is reduced to a trail well worth following although passable only as a path. From it can be had grand vistas of the valley, glimpses of the new road, and a sweeping view of the forest-covered sides of High Peak. There are immense old hemlocks and beeches on every side, and precipices from which one draws back with a shudder. The mountains are more impressive from this road, chiefly because of its wildness and the forest stillness, and but for traces of man in bridges and telephone poles might well belong to past centuries.

The Kaaterskill Falls are near the head of the stream which flows into the Clove at Horseshoe Curve. Here at the falls is the Laurel House, inseparable from the memory of the hospitable Schutts and their captive bears. Its beginning was "a stand set up by Willard Cowen in 1824." The stream is the outlet of the two Lakes near the Mountain House, and after a short and placid journey through the forest leaps downward 180 feet and then pausing for breath drops 80 more. Behind the first fall, along the half circle, roofed by nearly 70 feet of rock shelf, is a narrow path by which one can safely walk to the opposite side of the stream. A little way down you come to Bastion Falls, and from there until it is joined by the West Branch and on to the valley, its life is a continual struggle against boulders and other obstructions, here and there pausing in deep pools and tarrying by moss-covered rocks, cool fernbeds and at the foot of towering cliffs.

Once there was a boulder of about fifty tons, measuring 175 feet, resting insecurely at the top of the Kaaterskill Falls. A party of men from Cairo and Catskill decided on a new way to celebrate Independence Day. On July 3, 1820, they made their way to the spot, camped for the night and next day succeeded in pushing the boulder over the falls. "The effect was awful and sublime, the crash tremendous, exceeding the loudest thunder—the tremulous motion of the earth and the long murmuring echo rolling from point to point through the ravine gave to the scene an indescribable degree of grandeur. The rock was shattered in a thousand pieces. Toasts were then drunk and vollies of musketry fired."

PIONEERS AND THEIR HOMES

The life history of only one of Hunter's pioneers is available at this time; that of Colonel William Edwards, "whose monument is the village of Hunter."

Colonel Edwards was born in Elizabethtown, N. J., November 11, 1770. He was a son of Timothy Edwards, and grandson of Rev. Jonathan Edwards, in 1775 president of Nassau Hall, Princeton. His mother was Rhoda Ogden, daughter of Governor Aaron Ogden.

When William was less than a year old his parents moved to Stockbridge, Massachusetts, where he is said to have been a merchant, but, as "the inhabitants consisted mostly of Indians," he very likely was a trader. He was a Whig and is said to have loaned $100,000 in gold coins to the Continental Congress, which was never returned to him.

In 1784 William was bound out to his uncles, Colonel Mathias Ogden and Colonel Oliver Spencer (both officers of the Revolution). He received his board, the privilege of tanning with his master's stock four sheep-skins a year. His clothing was not included in the bargain. Following this he worked as journeyman for one and one-half years while learning, for $30 per year.

When Colonel William Edwards came to Hunter from Massachusetts he is known to have been almost penniless, but with great foresight he realized the business possibilities of tanning and induced Gideon Lee, a shoemaker in whom he recognized talent, tact and integrity, to go to New York as his guest. Mr. Lee made an eminently successful agent, and after amendment to several state laws was made, relative to the manufacture of leather, the New York Tannery Company was formed in 1817 with a capital of $60,000, and William Edwards and sons as managers of the enterprise.

Under Edwards's supervision and according to his plans a tannery was built at Hunter, and 1,200 acres of land adjoining, in the heart of the hemlock region on the Schoharie kill. The tannery's output was 5,000 tanned hides a year, and it is said to have been the first covered tannery built in the United States. The first leather went to the market in 1818. Workmen on the building and in the manufacture of leather were imported from Massachusetts.

Reverses came to Mr. Edwards through no fault of his, and following them the tannery burned in 1830 and he lost all he had. Four years later he recovered from these losses and followed out a plan he had long had in mind. He sold his property to his sons, after first having it appraised by Foster Morss and Jonathan Palen, distributing his all (which amounted to $25,000) among his creditors, for debts from which he had been legally discharged sixteen years previous. From this time he retired from active business, supported by his children, and died December 29, 1851.

Mr. Edwards has been described as being "of commanding presence, six feet four inches in height, well proportioned, of great strength and self-control, prompt and decisive." He was an inventor of four patents—copper heater, hide-mill, application of hot liquor, and roller.

He had so large a head that children ran away at his appearance. It was caused while playing with an Indian boy at four years of age—while dodging around a chimney in his father's house their heads came together, rendering William unconscious, but with no bad results other than his deformity. A strict Christian, he was held in high regard by all. His sons grew up to be successful business men.

Town of Jewett

The town of Jewett as an organization is seventy-six years old, and is the namesake of Freeborn G. Jewett, a justice of the Supreme Court.

In 1813 it was called Lexington, in 1814 part of it was Hunter. Its boundary lines are mostly mountain heights which guard the valley, some rising to nearly 4,000 feet; and only at the west end of this long and beautiful valley is there an unobstructed opening of any width. The Schoharie creek finds a way through one corner of the town, while at the foot of the mountains flows the East Kill with its many tributaries.

Cole Mountain (named after Thomas Cole, the artist) rises 3,975 feet, Black Dome 4,004, Black Head 3,965, East Kill 3,190,* Parker (which is on the Hunter Divide, named in honor of Daniel Parker, who owned much of the land upon it), and Tower Mountain 2,980 feet (on its summit Pond and Hastings built a tower sixty feet high).

---

* Height of mountains according to Van Loan's map.

Jewett's first town meeting was held in 1850, and its first officials were as follows:

Fisk Beach	Supervisor	Luman Whitcomb	Justice
Henry R. Hosford	Town Clerk	Alanson Woodworth	Justice
David E. Woodworth	Assessor	Jesse Barker	Justice
John Egbertson	Assessor	John Peck	Commissioner
William Goslee	Assessor	David Williams	Commissioner
Norman C. Johnson	Collector	Ambrose Baldwin	Commissioner
Lucius Pond	Poor Master	William Ford	Commissioner
	D. M. Hosford	Superintendent of Schools	

William Gass had the honor of being the first settler in the town, in 1783, near the mouth of the East Kill. He was followed in 1788 by Zephania Chase. A year later Chester Hill came to what is now Jewett Heights. The following are among the known pioneers of the town: Laban, Ichabod, Abraham and Amherst Andrews, Benjah, John and Jared Rice, Theophilus and Samuel Peck, Zadoc Pratt, David and Stephen Johnson, Henry Goslee, Justice Squires, Daniel Miles, Adnah Beach, Isaac and Munson Buel, Gideon, Reuben and Joel Hosford, and Daniel and Samuel Merwin.

Munson Buel, known as Judge Buel, was one of the best penmen of his age, a man of push and enterprise. The land upon which these pioneers settled was owned by a Mr. Tomilson. They were not poor settlers, but had sufficient means for such comfort as could be had in a new country, and prosperity followed in their train.

Laban Andrews built the first grist mill, in 1795, and Elisha Thomson opened the first store. The first recorded birth was that of Henry Goslee Jr. The first mail-carrier was a man by the name of Cole who went to Catskill on horseback, bought the few available papers and brought out any letters which might be at the post office. On his way through the town he would blow a tin horn at the gate (if there were gates) of those lucky enough to receive news from the outside world. How much compensation he received for his long journey through the wilderness history saith not.

In those early days of settlement not the least of the dangers which were encountered was that of wolves, which were abundant and ferocious. Many stories of adventures and narrow escapes from death have been handed down to their descendants. It was not an unusual occurence to hear these wolves howling throughout the day as well as night. At one time a Mr. Peck, who lived in Big Hollow near the town line, discovered in his barnyard a big wolf which after a hard struggle was killed, but not until it had bitten Mr. Peck's son. Nine days afterwards the son was taken with hydrophobia and lived but a short time. It is said that, "as his remains were carried to the cemetery at Lexington Flats, and the procession moved along the side of Hog Mountain, the wolves set up a dismal howl."

Robert Turner of Ashland, returning from Buel's mills with a grist, found wolves following him too closely for comfort. As it was near night, he stopped at what is now Jewett Heights, tied his horse to a tree and managed by building a fire to keep them off until daylight, when they left.

JEWETT HEIGHTS

Jewett Heights, formerly known as Lexington Heights, is 2,000 feet above tide water. A high table land, it gives you a feeling of being "atop of the world," looking down to the foot of mountains rising 4,000 feet in height. Its surrounding scenery is of the finest.

The first church of the Presbyterian faith was built here about the year 1800, and before it was finished was sold for $50 at public auction to Elisha Thomson. He immediately gave it back to the society. In 1804 another one was built on the site of the present church, and this also remained unfinished for many years.*

In "Old Time Letters" by the Rev. H. H. Prout, we find the following: "About the year 1808, a certain class of the inhabitants thought it necessary to the securing of justice and order, to have stocks and a whipping post. [These were built near the Presbyterian church, Jewett Heights.] It was a local institution erected on mere neighborhood views, and administered only on local authority. It was imported from Connecticut, and probably a fragment out of the book of blue-laws. The stocks and whipping post were built mainly by the Congregational Society of Lexington, with the laudable design of punishing petty misdemeanors. * * *

"The stocks were used but once. A man known as Brom Pete swore terribly on regimental training day. The poor fellow was taken in hand, brought before Justice Ichabod Andrews, and condemned to the stocks for two hours. One night six or eight spirited young fellows demolished the stocks, and carried most of the timbers to Abel Holcomb's swamp.

"Wagons were scarce in those days. The father of Colonel Pratt had the first one-horse wagon brought into town. Seldom a clock was to be seen among the inhabitants at that time. Laben Andrews brought a brass clock and sun dial from Connecticut. From that the neighbors made noon marks in their windows."

At Mill Hollow the Buell Brothers built a grist and saw mill in 1810, buying the mill of Abner Hammond, which was fitted with two card machines, and they carded wool for most of the inhabitants in that region. The wool was brought on horseback by both men and women. The Buells also built "clothing works where they dressed cloth, had a blacksmith shop with a trip hammer that went by water power." Among the visions which proved failures was that of Parks and Wolcott, who thought to turn various sizes of barrels and kegs from logs, but the invention failed to be practical.

JEWETT CENTER

Jewett Center is the oldest settlement, two miles south of Jewett Heights. East Jewett includes the beautiful mountain valley

---

* See "Churches."

in the eastern part of the town. David Chase, the son of Zephaniah, was two years old when they came from Martha's Vineyard in 1788, and settled near the mouth of the East Kill. In 1808 he married Abagail, a sister of Hon. Zadoc Pratt. West Chase, youngest son of Zephaniah, married Julia M. Newton. He kept an inn and the post office at Jewett Center for over forty years.

SPEENBURG HOUSE AND OLD POSTOFFICE (BEECHES CORNERS).

Beach's Corners is on the main highway between Hensonville and Hunter. It was the home of Gilbert Beach, who owned most of the land, and was named for him. Here at one time was a post office and the town hall (still standing). The old burial place of the Beaches, Buttses, Lords and others is near the Corners, which today consists of dairy farms and private homes.

PIONEERS AND THEIR HOMES
ZEPHANIAH CHASE

The first of the name to come to America was Thomas Chase, who was a native of England, and settled in Hampton, New Hampshire, in 1636. Thomas married Elizabeth Philbrick, and Isaac, their third child, was born in Hampton in 1647. He married Mary Tilton and died in 1727.

Joseph was the second child of Isaac and Mary, and married Lydia Coffin. Their oldest child, Abel, was the father of Zephaniah, who was born at Edgarton, Martha's Vineyard, March 14, 1748. Zephaniah, whose wife was Abagail Skiff, had three sons, and although a joiner and cabinet-maker by trade he went with his brother Benjamin on several whaling voyages. Seeing no future for his boys except a seafaring life, he determined to find a farm which he could afford to buy. A relative owned land in Binghamton, N. Y., and offered to give him a farm if he would commence a settlement there.

HISTORY OF GREENE COUNTY

Zephaniah sold his property at Martha's Vineyard for $250, and with his second wife, Love, and their son David and his sons by his first wife (Benjamin, Joseph and Thomas), the oldest of them but thirteen years, started on the long journey to New York. They finally reached the valley of the Batavia Kill, and, resting at a cabin at what is now the village of Windham, he was told that, owing to a high wind storm which had felled many trees across the road, it would be impossible to get through with a wagon. While undetermined what to do, one Thomas Harriott offered to sell him a farm on the Schoharie Kill, ten miles distant, at what is now Prattsville. A bargain was made in which the oxen figured as part payment. Benjamin, the eldest son, was sent on with the oxen and goods while Zephaniah and his young family, the youngest but little over a year old, crossed the mountain range on foot by a path, or blazed trail, which shortened the distance by half. Both parties made their way safely and were reunited at the designated spot.

They found the house only two logs high covered with bark, but another was in course of building, and this the father and sons finished before cold weather. It was here shortly after that another son, West, was born. There was no saw mill within twenty miles and so logs for the house had to be hand-hewn, split, shaved and planed into boards, for furniture as well as for the house.

The deed from Thomas Harriott is dated August 19, 1787. They cleared away the forest in valley and on mountain side, and later a more pretentious house was built. This farm was in the town of Woodstock, Ulster County, and was subsequently included in the new town of Windham. It became successively a part of the towns of Lexington and Jewett, and is now a part of the town of Jewett.

Zephaniah was a Baptist, and a soldier of the Revolutionary Army. He is buried in the family plot in the cemetery north of the house which he built, and his wife Love lies beside him. Benjamin, the eldest son, spent his life at the homestead. He engaged in farming, lumbering and tanning, and lived to be eighty-eight years old. These were the ancestors of the late Judge Chase of Catskill.

Town of Lexington

Lexington was taken from "Old Windham," January 25, 1813. Previous to this it was known as New Goshen, after a town in Connecticut.

The town includes most of Great Lot No. 22 and part of Lot 21 of Robert Livingston's grant, and had been leased by him in smaller parcels before 1777. One of these sub-lots was leased to "John Darling and conveyed by him to the Kips." The conveyance was signed by John Maben and Richard Peck. In 1883 its boundary trees were still standing.

Lexington streams are the West Kill and Schoharie Kill; its principal peaks are Big West Kill, 3,900 feet high; St. Anns, 3,890;

LEXINGTON.

North Dome, 3,400; Eagle Mountain, Sleeping Lion and Blue Bell. Along the banks of the Schoharie Kill was the domain of the Indian,. mostly peaceful and inclined to be friendly in this vicinity although the trail during the Revolution led along the Schoharie to Fort

SWINGING BRIDGE AT LEXINGTON.

Niagara and was used for taking captives to Canada. A section of land north of Lexington was once called Barber Town. William Chamberlin is said to have built the first forge in the town.

Josiah Clawson came from Claverack in 1812 with his wife Peggy, and his old flint-lock musket, used in the Revolution and handed down to his son Jacob A., has killed many a panther, wolf and bear. Joel and Jonathan Ford, the Petit brothers and John Valentine came from Caanan, Columbia County. Near them lived David Foster, a soldier of the Revolution, and William Street, an Englishman. About a mile and a half above the village in 1792 Thaddeus Bronson had a grist mill.

The first town meeting was held at the house of Abel Holcomb,. and the first town board of Lexington consisted of Peter Smith, Jacob Van Valkenburgh, Abram Camp and Nelson Beach.

LEXINGTON VILLAGE

There is an atmosphere about this village and valley hard to define, different from others in the Catskills. There is dignity and also a suggestion of protection in these mighty mountain bulwarks. As you pass along the main highway you feel yourself to be the discoverer of a deep, secluded and peaceful valley where nothing can disturb or annoy. When the first white man came to hunt or trap, or look for a home, it must have been oppressively grand and beautiful with its age-old forest in all its wildness, reaching from the low lands to the summit of towering mountains full of dark shadows. tumbling brooks and cascades, wild animals roaming at will and making their dens among the cliffs or coming down to drink or feed along the stream.

The village of Lexington is divided in two parts, with at first a fording place between, and it was not until many years later that it was connected with a bridge. The first village was north of the present one where once stood the Bray tannery (1819). Here later were both grist and saw mills, a store and post office. The village no longer exists. It was not until 1823 that Bruce Smith built a dam, grist mill, and distillery just above the present bridge.

Derrick Schermerhorn established the first woolen mill, an ashery and forge. He was a man of considerable strength and weighed 300 pounds. Richard Peck kept an inn.

WEST KILL

West Kill lies in a scenic valley of great length and near the foot of Deep Notch,* which is a great gap in the mountain side seemingly provided by nature as a passage from one valley to another. On either side of the way the mountains rise abruptly above the traveller, and as he climbs the ascent toward Bushnellville he seems to be swallowed up in a pathless wilderness. In the narrowest part of the Notch it is said that ice can be found at any season of the year.

To this beautiful valley of the West Kill came Jerome Van Valkenburgh in 1780. He was one of three of that name but not related to each other. Three Butler brothers and a man by the name of Dryer followed, the last building a woolen factory. Darius Briggs, Hezekiah and Amos Petit and Ephrahim Dunham were among the pioneers. When they came to this spot there was little but Indian trails over which to travel, and their supplies were brought from Kingston. Fortunately game and fish were plentiful.

BUSHNELLVILLE

Captain Aaron Bushnell first settled here, and from him it was named. Captain Bushnell was the owner of a grist mill, and when grain was scarce he imported large quantities of it from England by way of Rondout.

BEACH RIDGE

Beers in his Greene County History says that "Beach Ridge is a portion of the town lying on the highlands between Lexington Flats and West Kill village, and to the westward. It is a high rolling tract, partly on the mountain range which divides the town from Halcott, and where it reaches an altitude of 3,800 feet at the summit, called by some Vly Mountain and by others Angle's Peak; named from Daniel Angle, one of the first settlers of this region. He was one of the Hessian soldiers who served in Burgoyne's army, and was captured with the army at Saratoga. He, however, soon enlisted in the American service, was honorably discharged at the cessation of

---

* Also called Bush Kill Clove and Echo Notch.

HISTORY OF GREENE COUNTY 109

hostilities, and afterwards granted a pension. The monument over his grave records his age as a hundred and seven years."

The Ridge was a great stamping ground for wolves, which often surrounded the cabins of the settlers and there were many narrow escapes. Panthers too were sometimes seen. A Mr. Peck looking for strayed cattle saw one ready to spring upon him from a limb above. Calling loudly for help, the sound delayed the animal for a few minutes, when Henry Cline, who was some distance away, with perfect aim dropped the animal dead at Mr. Peck's feet.

PIONEERS AND THEIR HOMES

JOHN MABEN

John Maben came to Lexington Flats in 1777, and died there in 1813. He had come to America in 1768, or perhaps a year or two later, as a traveller who expected to return to his home in Ireland when he had seen the new country, and his "baggage consisted of 24 linen shirts, a plenty of other linens, clothes and money. He was to live as a gentleman for three years." The country attracted him so much that he did not return at the end of the three years, but married Miss Sally Pierce of Connecticut.

It is written of John Maben that he was of strong and robust frame and at once threw himself into the patriotic movement, and was no slow participant in the skirmishes of the Connecticut colony. With the cessation of hostilities in Connecticut he came to what is now Lexington Flats as early as 1777, as at this date his name appears upon leases given by Robert Livingston for these lands.

The Mabens are descended from the hardy and thrifty Scotch-Irish, and the Scotch clan Gregories on the maternal side, and inherited honesty, frugality, energy, keen humor and wit. They were also God-fearing men and women. The church records of Norwalk, 1652 and later, show the Gregories to have been eminent freemen, and that John Gregory was the founder of the town.

JOHN NEWTON

John Newton, the son of Silas, was born Feb. 3, 1776, in Chesire town, Connecticut. Here he served as an apprentice at the wheelwright business, and in 1797 came to Lexington, settling at Westkill. A year later he married Captain Bushnell's daughter Eunice, whose mother was Eunice Pratt, and carried on his trade at this place.

The children of John and Eunice Bushnell Newton were Orlando and Julia. Orlando followed in the business footsteps of his father, received his education in the district school, became a highly respected citizen of the town, holding town offices for over thirty-two successive years. His first wife was Harriet P. Bump, and the second Mrs. Ruth Christina Van Valkenburgh of Lexington.

Town of New Baltimore

The town of New Baltimore was originally a part of the county of Albany and the district of Coxsackie. Scutters,* Little and Willow Islands were annexed from Kinderhook, April 23, 1823. A line of high slate bluffs rises from the Hudson from 100 to 200 feet where the village of New Baltimore now stands. The western part of the town is comparatively level; its principal streams—Hannekraai-kill (now Hannacroix), Deepe Clove kill, Cabin Run, and the east branch of Potick—nearly all flow in part through narrow and rocky ravines.

The Coeymans Patent nearly covered what is now the town of New Baltimore, and the patent of Thomas Houghtaling covered the rest. Andries Coeymans, son of the first patentee, had his patent confirmed by a new one August 26, 1714.

No record of the early organization of the town other than that of April 4, 1854, can be found. The officials at that time consisted of:

Nathaniel O. Palmer............Supervisor
Edgar Halstead............School Supt.   A. P. Smith ....Police Justice
Benjamin Hotaling............Assessor   Stephen Dean............Commissioner
Lee Wheeler............Collector   J. U. Gurney............Overseer Poor
Henry R. Miller............Town Clerk   Abraham Travis......Overseer Poor

The first marriage in the town is said to have been that of Garret Van Slyck and Annatje Turk, September 1, 1736. This couple had two sons, Peter and James; James was a soldier of 1812. Albertus Van Der Zee was the first settler, soon followed by Andreas Van Slyck. The latter lived near the river in a stone house built in 1713. A map of 1773 shows Hotaling Island as being three islands instead of one. The one farthest to the north was called "Vife Hook." What is now known as Bronk's Island was then designated as "Marte Gerretse's Island."

NEW BALTIMORE VILLAGE

The tract upon which the village of New Baltimore now stands, and some surrounding land, was sold by John Barclay and his wife, who was a daughter of Peter Coeymans, to Cornelius and Albert Storm Van Der Zee for 1,200 pounds. This also included the north part of Shuter's Island.

Hannacroix creek is the principal stream and called in early days Haanekraai-kill (Cock crowing creek). About 1787 Charles Titus built a saw mill on Titus creek, and in 1808 he had a store and ashery. He was an orthodox Quaker. Hallett Titus early built a grist mill, the first in that part of the town, on Honey Hollow creek. This mill was taken down in 1808, but his son Isaac settled a short distance west of Medway, where he built a steam saw and turning mill. He was a Hicksite Quaker preacher of great ability.‡

John Smith came into town about 1795 from Westchester County. Timothy Green, a son of William Green who emigrated from Wales, settled on a part of the Jonathan Miller Purchase about

---
* Sometimes called Shutters.
‡ Quaker meeting was discontinued years ago.

1790. Conrad C. Hotaling moved from Coxsackie to the town of New Baltimore a year later. Before this his father, Thomas Hotaling, had built a stone house for him. Thomas A. Hotaling had a son Peter H., who built a stone house on the east side of Bedell Hill bearing the date June 9, 1794.

Ebenezer Wicks came from Long Island to Rensselaerville in 1790, and to New Baltimore in 1802. He was a Baptist preacher of great force of character who often preached three sermons on a Sunday, following the trade of carpenter and farmer also. In 1805 he built a school house which served as both church and school, and it is said he was the means of building a church at Grapeville, doing most of the work without charge, and contributing liberally toward the material.

A grist mill on Coxsackie Creek in this town was built by Peter Van Bergen in the seventeen-hundreds, and another on Potick creek by the Powells at an early day. The first mill on the site of what is now known as "Dean's Mills" was known as Skinner's, built about 1780, and was deeded by Solomon Skinner and wife Catrina to Thomas Hotaling in 1794. Many other mills were built upon these streams, but they all have disappeared.

At first New Baltimore was a fishing village, and Paul Sherman, who settled there in 1795, began building schooners some time before 1815, carrying on a trade with the West Indies. The first settled physician in the place was Dr. Robert Fowler.

The village now commanded from the bluffs above an extended and beautiful view of the Hudson. It was also the home of the Indian, a few remaining until after the Revolution, who, like most Indians after contact with white men, were quarrelsome and had many drunken orgies but did not molest the settlers.

In a short history of the Reformed church of New Baltimore which will be given later, compiled by Miss Julia Carhart, Jennie Trego Wickes and Jennie Fuller Van Orden in 1902, in "loving remembrance of the many who have gone before, and for the interest and help of those who shall come after as followers of Christ and members of this church," it is stated that "the church building was not completed and prepared for regular service until the year 1834. Also a fact worthy of note is that the doorstones at each entrance over which five generations have walked, were originally in one piece, and was brought from the church at Coeymans Square (now Ravena) by James Hotaling, the old church having been erected in 1793. In 1834 the church was dedicated by Dr. Van Santvoord, with the assistance of Drs. Ludlow and Ferris of Albany." The cornerstone was laid July 4, 1833.

Rev. Staats Van Santvoord, the first pastor and under whom the church was organized with a handful of members, served these people for five years without "any other compensation than the gratitude and good will of a growing congregation."

The Medway Christian church is the first of its kind in county, town and state. Rev. Jasper Hazen of Vermont came westward on horseback, preaching wherever and whenever opportunity offered. In the course of his journey he came to the public house of Jonathan Miller. Young Hazen was regarded as something of a heretic, for he acknowledged no authority in the church but Christ the son of God. He found a friend in Jonathan Miller, and at this public house the first Christian Church in New Baltimore and the state was organized in 1807. The house and barns of Jonathan Miller served as a meeting place until 1832, when a church was built on the Miller farm. In 1861 the present Medway Christian Church was built.

PARSONS HOMESTEAD.

The Parsons house, said to be the oldest in the village and now owned by Clarence Bronk Parsons, was built by the present owner's great-grandfather, Stephen Parsons, whose sympathy in the project, and gift of $100, encouraged the Rev. S. Van Santvoord to commence the building of the Reformed church in New Baltimore village. The grandfather of Clarence B. was Melvin Parsons, also the grandfather of Melvin and Jasper K. Hotaling; his father Francis A. Parsons and his mother Berthena Bronk, a family closely connected with the early history of the town, one of the noted living descendants being Dr. Edmund Southwick, a scientist and naturalist of New York city, his "Garden of the Heart" in Central Park being internationally known. His wife was a daughter of Stephen Parsons and Rose Croswell. A brother of Miss Carhart married Elizabeth Croswell, sister of the latter.

PIONEERS AND THEIR HOMES
JONATHAN MILLER

Jonathan Miller is supposed to be of the family of Millers whose ancestor John Miller settled on Long Island as early as 1650. Jonathan came from Peekskill, and purchased 67¾ acres of land from Isaac D. Verplanck in 1791. The land is described as "situated in the west corner of Lot I, in the 10th allotment of the Coeymans Patent, bounded on the north by the north line of the lot, and on the south by the Diep Kill, or Houghtaling Patent."

His log house was built near the Diep Kill, and on the south side of the road at the east end of his purchase. A few years after his coming to the town, "a young man rode up to the house one day and asked permission to hold a religious meeting." This young man was Jasper Hazen, and the meeting which was held in Miller's barn was the beginning of the Christian church, to which the Miller family attached themselves, many of their descendants following in their footsteps.

Jonathan had married Lydia McCabe. Their oldest child Hannah married Ephraim Garret of New Baltimore. Jesse, another son, married Ann Kirk. Mrs. Miller had literary ability and was well known as a successful writer of children's books. Henry Powell Miller married Lydia, a daughter of Jesse Miller, and made his home on the old homestead.*

CORNELIUS ANTONISSEN VAN SLYK†

The New Baltimore branch of the Van Slyke family can boast of a strain of princely blood, for the Prince of Orange is on their family tree. According to tradition, the earliest member of the family came from Amsterdam to this country about 1635. His name was William Peterse Van Slyk, as the name was then spelled. He appears to have been associated with the enterprise of the Patroon Van Rensselaer of Fort Orange. His son Jacobus Van Slyk was appointed by Governor Stuyvesant, in 1658, as "Voorleser," or lay reader and instructor in religion, to the settlement of Esopus, now Kingston. Through his instrumentality a flourishing church was there founded.

It is believed that another son had settled in Bruckelen, (Brooklyn), whose name was Cornelius Antonissen Van Slyk. To this one, Aug. 22, 1646, Governor Keift executed a patent or deed for a large tract of land, lying west of Catskill, toward Kiskatom, and extending for several miles northward. It was intended that he should here plant a colony, after the manner of the Van Rensselaers of Fort Orange. It was, in fact, a transgression upon their claims, which were stretched much farther southward than Keift would allow. This gift to Van Slyk was a recompense for what Van Slyk had done for "this country, as well in making peace, as in the ransoming of prisoners."

Disregarding the patent which Governor Kieft had granted to Van Slyk, the Patroon Van Rensselaer with superior power dispos-

---

* Charles Lisk, Lydia and Antoinette Miller are descendants living at Coxsackie; also Miss Jessie Miller and Miss Abby Kirk Miller, living at Medway.

† From Beers History of Greene County.

sessed Van Slyk, who did not care to contend, and located on unappropriated land between Coxsackie and New Baltimore, where for two hundred years the Hudson River branch of the Van Slyke family, and the Bronks with whom they were closely allied, were "lords of the soil."

A short distance from the old stone house at the West Shore station stood the original home of the Van Slykes. The late Rev. J. G. Van Slyke, D. D., who preached in the Reformed church of Kingston with eloquence and power for many years, was a descendant of this family; also A. W. Van Slyke, M. D., of Coxsackie, who for many years has been the successful physician of that town, and Bronk Van Slyke his brother, who is a prosperous farmer living on the farm at Dean's Mills, formerly owned by their father, Ephrahim T. Van Slyke. Of the later generations are Marie Hotaling Van Slyke, daughter of the doctor, and Mrs. Bertha Brown, Mrs. Marion Halstead and Paul Van Slyke, children of Bronk, and his two granddaughters, Adelaide Halstead and Hilda Van Slyke.

The tract of land deeded to Andrew and Peter Van Slyke afterward became the property of Benjamin Gurney, then of his son Jacob B. Gurney, and was the birthplace of the mother of Miss Julia Carhart, her mother being the only child of Jacob B. and Mary Hoag Gurney.

The Vanderpoel family have always been identified with the town of New Baltimore, and among their descendants now living are Edwin C. Vanderpoel, a former Supervisor of Greene county and a trustee of the public school, Miss Abigail V. Whitbeck and others.

Town of Prattsville

Prattsville as a town did not exist until March 8, 1833, when it was named after Col. Zadoc Pratt. It was formed from the town of Windham.* A large number of Schoharie settlers before the Revolution had made camp on the flats at Prattsville, and during the war they were attacked by Indians and Tories under British leadership. The settlers won out and the Indian leader Captain Smith was mortally wounded. He was buried where he fell, opposite the battle ground, but high water washed out his bones, which a negro collected and buried in a safer place. This battle is said to have taken place north of the bridge.

Among the first settlers of Prattsville were John Laraway and four sons, Isaac Van Alstyne, Van Loan brothers, Henry Becker and

---

* So much of the town of Windham, in the county of Greene, lying westerly of a line drawn from the north line of the town of Lexington north to the mouth of Lewis Brook, thence up said brook to its head, thence to the north line of the town of Windham, shall be a separate town by the name of Prattsville * * * (act of Legislature May 8, 1833).

the Shoemaker family. The first inn was kept shortly after the close of the Revolution by Martinus Laraway, and with his brother John they built the first grist mill.

The first town meeting was held at the house of Colonel Henry Laraway, April 2, 1833, when the following officials were elected to office:

Hezekiah Dickerman	Supervisor
F. A. Fenn	Town Clerk
Nicholas L. Decker	Assessor
Isaac Haner	Assessor
Ariral Blinn	Assessor
John Brandow	Overseer Poor
Robert Moore	Overseer Poor
Mathew R. Bougton	Constable
Titus Atwater	Constable
Samuel Tompkins	Constable
Lawrence Brandow	Constable
Ezra Disbrow	Highway Com'r
John Brackney	Highway Com'r
H. W. Shoemaker	H'w'y Com'r
A. B. Austin	School Com'r
Leveritt Munson	School Com'r
John Frayer	School Com'r
C. K. Benham	School Inspector
W. M. Brackney	School Inspector
Willard Marsh	School Inspector
Nicholas Decker	Justice
David F. Moore	Justice
Elisha B. Minard	Justice

A little later Zadoc Pratt and John Laraway were elected at a special meeting in place of John Brandow and Robert Moore, who had neglected to take the oath of office. The first school was kept in a log school house a little east of Pratt's Rocks, and a Reformed (Dutch) church organized in 1802.

The history of the town and village of Prattsville is for the most part of a later date than that which would ordinarily be included in this volume, but of its very early history when a part of the town of Windham little is known.

VILLAGE OF PRATTSVILLE

In a narrow valley through which runs the Schoharie kill, is the village of Prattsville. It is principally composed of one long street through which passes the highway, although other short streets and highways intersect it. When undisturbed by the motor car it has that old-time Sabbath stillness peculiar to the mountains which rise on either side of the village, while the placid waters of the stream creep up to the back doors of some of the inhabitants. There are trees a-plenty along the streets, and in spite of seeming lowness it has an elevation of 1,200 feet.

The village was incorporated in 1883 with Dr. Thomas Fitch as president; Charles Myres, collector; A. P. Myres, treasurer; W. H. Paddock, A. Lutz, and Charles A. Layman, trustees.

Northwest of Prattsville, just over the line in Schoharie County was Devasego Falls, in 1765 called "Owlfleck." In 1800 there was a tannery built by Bell, and sold to Charles Smedberg, a native of Sweden. In 1823 it burned and the incendiary act laid to the door of Bell, who disappeared, leaving behind traditions of his having been a pirate, who was afterward hung at Philadelphia. Smedberg built another tannery which shared the fate of the first. He was also a miller, sawyer, storekeeper, and farmer.

VILLAGE OF PRATTSVILLE IN 1848.

It was not until 1825 that Colonel Pratt built his great tannery, 500 feet long and 43 feet wide, on the bank of the Schoharie. In 1839 a freshet carried the dam away, and in 1845 the tannery closed. Directly opposite the Reformed church he had a saw mill which was afterward Myer's cabinet shop, later used as a machine shop by Harlow Taylor. Benett Atwood and Alfred Doolittle had a distillery on Washington street in 1830. Fenn and Dickman kept

DEVASEGO FALLS (VICTIM OF NEW YORK WATER SUPPLY).

the first store, and Cornelius Decker was inn-keeper of what was afterward the Fowler House. Dr. Smith came to Prattsville in 1790, Dr. David Curtis in 1800, and Dr. C. K. Benham in 1825. (See Physicians of Greene County.)

Along the highway at the eastern end of the village one comes upon a park given to the town by Colonel Zadock Pratt, and fenced by a substantial stone wall above which are the rocks known by his name. The whole rises precipitously 500 feet above the Schoharie, the summit reached by a winding path along which there are many worthwhile vistas of valley and mountains.

Near the roadway is a large mound topped by a monument, erected to the memory of the horses and dogs of Colonel Pratt, and another more recent memorial to the boys of the World War. Upon the first is inscribed, "Of over 1,000 horses owned and worn out in the service of Zadock Pratt, the following were favorites: Bob, a sorrel, aged 24 years; Bogue, a bay, aged 18 years; Prince, a gray, aged 30 years." Below this inscription are the names and ages of his dogs.

The path a half-mile in length turns and twists through the trees and about the rocks, with here and there a resting place carved from solid rock. Various emblems, a scroll, a wreath with the names of his two children in the center, a mechanic's uplifted arm with hammer in hand, a horse and a hemlock tree, the Pratt coat of arms, and a striking bust of his son Colonel George W. Pratt, who was wounded at Manasses, Va. The path ends at a spring.

Colonel Zadock Pratt was born in Rensselaer County in 1790, removing to Greene County in 1802. He was five times married, and lived a life full of responsibility and important happenings, holding various county and state offices of importance as well as conducting a large tanning business—a life too eventful to be fully recorded in the limited space of this volume.

The Windham Journal says of him among other things at the time of his death, "He built up the village which bears his name, and disbursed thousands of dollars to make it attractive. The beautiful elm and maple trees which adorn the walks on either side, the whole length of the street, the sidewalks, and the hemlock shrubbery at the eastern extremity of the village, are enduring monu-

MORSS STORES AT RED FALLS.

ments to his public spirit and enterprise. The sculptured rocks and the walks with neat sofas cut from solid rock, were designed more to enhance the beauty of the place than for any gratification of vanity, as many suppose.

"The Colonel loved travel and adventure, was a close observer of men, and a splendid judge of human nature. * * * He was among the first who dared go the overland route to California. His funeral was attended by the largest concourse of people ever assembled at Prattsville. He was buried with Masonic honors and drawn to the grave by a span of noble gray horses." On his deathbed he requested that Peter I. Brandow be one of his pall-bearers, but Mr. Brandow was buried on the same day as his friend. The

HISTORY OF GREENE COUNTY

Colonel died in Bergen City, and left a daughter, the wife of Hon. Colon M. Ingersol, of New Haven, Conn.

RED FALLS

Red Falls or "Federal City" is a small village on the Batavia kill. It received its present name from the falls and the peculiar color of its waters which flow over red sandstone. Foster Morss and his son Burton G. did much toward building up this little village, flanked by mountains and running into what is indeed a "Pleasant Valley." It has been said that here Jay Gould made his first money in cotton mills.

PIONEERS AND THEIR HOMES
BURTON G. MORSS

Asa Morss, the grandfather of Burton G., was a resident of Massachusetts, where he had married Hannah Austin and soon removed to Lisbon, New Hampshire. They had fourteen children, and of these Foster was the father of Burton G. Morss, born in Windham April 15, 1810, his mother (second wife) dying when he was two weeks old. After attending the local school he received a year's education at Greenville, another at Lexington, finishing up at Ballston Spa, Saratoga. During one winter he taught school near Ashland. His brother Austin became a Presbyterian minister.

Burton G. acquired a knowledge of tanning when the vats were not under cover, the bark-mill was worked by horse power, and a stone wheel was used for milling hides. For twelve years after Foster Morss built his tannery on White Brook it was worked by Lyman Morss, who lost his life by being scalded in a vat at Carbondale, Pa. Foster built a second tannery in 1820, and this was conducted upon the new system of tanning, run by water power and furnishing employment for about fifty men. Loring Andrews of New York, working in this tannery, laid the foundation of his immense fortune.

The tannery of Foster Morss was burned in 1826 and was a total loss. Three years later he built one at Red Falls run by water power. When this was closed in 1849 it was conducted by Burton G. Morss, who had a foundry there and made machinery for a cotton mill at Gilboa, and soon after for one of his own at Red Falls, with a dam which cost $6,000, and several tenant-houses. The mill contained seventy looms and was in operation until 1880. He also had a grist mill.

Burton G. Morss became owner of 3,000 acres of land in New York State and thousands of acres in Pennsylvania, becoming devoted to stock and dairy interests. He served the town of Prattsville as Supervisor in 1869 and consecutively for nine years. In 1875 he was a member of the State Legislature. In the great freshet of 1869 the mills at Red Falls were all swept away.

Town of Windham
No Local Historian

Windham, at first a part of Woodstock, Ulster County, became a separate town March 27, 1798, two years previous to the establishment of Greene County. Its first settlers were Captain George Stimson and Stephen Simmons (who was Livingston's agent).

The town is guarded on three sides by mountains, and only the northwest line, which borders on the town of Ashland, is free from these wonderful obstructions of nature, along the summits of which run the boundaries between it and the towns of Durham, Cairo and Jewett. Between these mountain barriers, with one exception where Elm Ridge cuts across the town, is the beautiful Windham Valley rising abruptly in some sections, in others in more or less sloping pasture lands toward the forest-topped mountains, and through it winds the Batavia kill.

At a town meeting held at the house of Richard Peck in the town of Windham, Ulster County, April 12, 1798, with William Beach moderator and Reuben Hosford clerk, the following persons by a plurality of votes were appointed to office:

William Beach	Supervisor		
Samuel Gunn	Town Clerk	Richard Peck	School Com'r
Ephrahim B. Hubbard	Assessor	Zephaniah Chase	School Com'r
Martinus Laraway	Assessor	John Tuttle	School Com'r
Munson Buell	Assessor	Elisha Thomson	Constable
Enos Baldwin	H'w'y Com'r	Constant A. Andrews	Constable
Benjamin Johnson	H'w'y Com'r	Harmonis Garlick	Constable
Darius Briggs	H'w'y Com'r	Elijah Bushnell	Constable
Justice Squires	School Com'r	Richard Jersey	Constable
Alexander Boyd	School Com'r	Henry Becker	Collector

The settlers of the town of Windham were principally from Connecticut, a lesser number from Massachusetts, a few from the Schoharie valley. Churches and schools were the most important things in the minds of these people, then came roads and bridges. The North Settlement road was opened April 9, 1794. In 1800 it was "Resolved, that Stephen Simmons be appointed agent for. and in behalf of the inhabitants of the said town of Windham, to apply to the Honorable, the Legislature, for such part of the money to be raised by lottery for improving certain great roads within the state, as may be necessary for improving the public road through Batavia in said town."

A few years after this (1810) it was "Resolved, that the Commissioners of Highways erect a set of stocks near the Meeting House on the mountain, at the expense of the town." Also "Resolved, that if any person suffer his or her dog to go to meeting, he or she shall forfeit the sum of fifty cents for each and every offence."

WINDHAM VILLAGE

This village has been known as Osbornville (about 1830) and Windham Center (1844) and is 1,500 feet above tide water. The

HISTORY OF GREENE COUNTY

beginnings of the village can be traced back to the time when George Stimson, sixty years of age, and his son Henry, a lad of thirteen, came from Hopkonton, Mass., in 1783 or 4. He was a soldier of the Revolution and left behind him in Massachusetts, to be called for later, a wife and ten other children. Father and son lodged in the open air beside a high rock at the west end of what is now Windham village, and, pleased with the spot and the advantages of the surrounding country, built against this rock a log cabin with bark roof.

The history of Windham village from its beginning until about a century ago can be given only as it has been handed down through the families of its pioneers, and some scant remaining records. Col. George Robertson left behind a written record of the Presbyterian church and the Stimson family which has been freely quoted in this sketch.

Along the western border of the town Ebenezer Baldwin settled in 1798. Eleazer Miller (before 1805), William Clark and Elias Fancher (1811) were early settlers; Solomon Munson with wife and son Jarius in 1800. Solomon was killed at a house-raising in 1802, about two miles northwest of the village. His son Jarius married a daughter of Silas Lewis and moved to Windham.

When the tannery boom struck Greene county it opened up the way to settlements in the mountains, and around the tanneries villages came to life as if by magic. These were built along the streams, and when the mighty hemlocks of the forest were gone then manufactories took their places, while grist and saw mills were abundant.

Philetus Reynolds of Stockbridge, Mass., married Dremania Saxton in 1803, and he became a tavern-keeper in Windham. Tertius Graham and father Samuel, who first settled in Ashland, had a tannery about 1800. It is said to have had an "iron bark-mill and a rolling stone Falling-mill," which was used until 1832. Tertius became a shoemaker, his two sons following the same business. The second tannery was built by Joseph Edsall and was running in 1815. The Osborn tannery was near the lower end of the glen, built in 1823 by Bennett Osborn and Abijah Stone. In 1810 they had a grist mill. Another tannery was built the same year by Samuel Reynolds and Clark Twiss.

Esquire Jesse Holister kept the first inn and store, and manufactured potash. He closed his business in 1824 and the Osborn brothers continued it. The inn of Holister after seven years was kept by Bennett Osborn until he built the Osborn house in 1829. Osborn was the first postmaster, commissioned by Andrew Jackson.

There are no records of very early deer-hunts among the mountains, but in November, 1825, a long-talked-of deer-hunting expedition took place at Windham. Dogs had been trained, guns cleaned and polished, and it is said "Catskill poured all her hunters to the field and Durham sent her president to rule the sport," which continued three days. The muster was in the early morning amid the calling for horses, barking of dogs and the voices of the hunters. They succeeded in taking but two deer the first day, and seem not to have been particular whether they shot a doe or buck. Tray, Blanch and Sweetheart were the names of some of the numerous dogs, and the smallest one killed "as large a buck as ever scaled the mountains." When a deer was shot but escaped, then a large greyhound was loosened who soon brought it to the ground. A number of deer had been killed at the end of the last day's sport; a bear shot and pursued, but not taken.

The following was taken from the Windham Journal:

Messrs. Editors: January 9, 1877.

As the last days of the Centennial were passing away I recalled an incident in my father's (the late Curtis Prout) life which I think worthy of record. The day on which he first crossed the Catskill mountain and reached his home in the valley of the Bataviakill was the last day of the century, the last day of the year, the last day of the month, and the last day of the week. He emigrated from Middletown, Ct., with his father and at the time here mentioned was twenty years of age. As with an ox-team and cart he slowly neared his destination, a cheering spectacle met his gaze. The old meeting house was being raised, and then he halted and met his brother Harris Prout and brother-in-law, Russell Gladding, and Mr. Cook, father of the late Ichabod Cook, who had come on the year before and were at work on the building, being carpenters, and there also, for the first time, he saw his future neighbors, conspicuous among whom was the massive figure of Mr. Silas Lewis, Esq., standing on a corner of the frame. As my father lived about seventy years after that event, I presume the actors on that occasion all passed away before him. They were mainly men of stern integrity and nerve. Their descendants are widely scattered, and some have held high positions of trust and usefulness. It is easy to recall the names of many of the Stimpsons, Strongs, Fullers, Morsses, Steeles, Buells, Robinsons, Ormsbees, Hunts and others as men of marked ability and business capacity. D. B. PROUT.

HENSONVILLE

The mountain villages are built in the valleys, and as the motorist rolls through he sees little of their charm, for the state highway is a leveler of grades and not a seeker after views. It is only as you climb the mountainsides or follow rough roads, little better than the trails of a century ago, that you feel the "call of the wild," or appreciate the beauty of the hidden mountain meadow where fairies play in the moonlight; the rough boulder-strewn pasture lands with their "bar ways," where cows are not just cows but an asset to the landscape as they peacefully chew their cuds under a sugar maple; the picturesque old sap-houses whispering of sweets in the spring-time, when the snow is melting from the mountainside and brooks run full; the views of valley and mountain that open up on every side and the abundance of ferns and everlastings at your feet.

One mountain village, its wood-roads and cow-paths explored, will give you more richness of memory, more deep satisfaction than any motor trip with its constantly moving panorama can do. When old age, invalidism or poor pedal extremities forbid, then take the motor car and get what you can, but if you would get the best, tarry for a time where a few minutes' walk will bring you to the stillness of the forest or some high open spot where God's mountain country in all its beauty lies below and around you.

JOHN HENSON, PIONEER OF HENSONVILLE.

John Henson, known as the pioneer of Hensonville, was born in 1798 and died in 1881; his wife Almira died in 1854, and both are buried there. He helped clear the land and build the first log houses, afterward replaced by frame ones, and although he died forty-seven years ago is still remembered by some of the inhabitants. He was twice married, had two daughters by his first wife, and lived to see several grandchildren and six great-grandchildren, one of whom, Mrs. Edward Haney, is living in Hensonville and remembers his stories of early days when the wolves howled around the house at night. He is remembered as a kindly, peaceable neighbor, fond of children, who always called him "Uncle John." He was of strong physique and at one time walked to Catskill, twenty-four miles, and back again between sunrise and sunset.

Hensonville, like many other villages among the Catskill Mountains, is clean, healthful and homelike, with water from the mountaintop of incomparable purity. It was once the farm of John Henson, who is said to have owned a mile in all directions and to have lived in the third house below the fountain. He had a saw mill on the little stream, a part of which is still standing. He was a Revolutionary soldier and rests in the cemetery back of his dwelling. The graves of his father and mother are marked by two brown headstones. The portrait of Mr. Henson shows him to have been a man of considerable character. Only one direct descendant, Mrs. Edward Haney, now lives in the village.

The cemetery at Hensonville was given for public use by William Henson over ninety years ago. Beers says that the "first to be buried there was a squaw by the name of Proctor, and a woman by the name of O'Brien. The latter was drowned while attempting to cross the brook near the village during a freshet."

Hensonville was the birthplace of the late Judge Emory A. Chase,* and the homestead (now Supervisor Delmot L. Chase's) is on the outskirts of the village as you descend the hill from Brooksburg. It is a beautiful spot where one goes to see the sun set behind far distant mountains, the intervening landscape and nature's coloring making a picture no artist could ever hope to imitate worthily. It would seem that the judge must have acquired his high character, ideals and broad-mindedness in some measure from his surroundings, as well as from home and ancestral influences. The history of most of the present residents comes more properly under that of a later date.

MAPLECREST

Big Hollow for reasons unknown has become Maplecrest, although its baptismal name seems more fitting and to the point. It is situated at the extreme end of the town and is reached from Hensonville where Elm Ridge, like a monster beast resting after the hunt, stretches full length, leaving only space for highway, stream, and a small margin of lowland for an entrance. The "Hollow," the great bowl of which shelters a beautiful little mountain village, with three churches, store, post office, and various minor industries with steep mountain sides rising from the back doors, narrows to a valley below High Peak and Cole Mountain.

Here at the upper end of the bowl is the beginning of the old "Ridge Road" (now almost impassable), which climbs steeply over Elm Ridge and ends at the Sherman farm and foot of High Peak, where there are two roads, one leading to Silver Lake and the other to East Windham. Lieutenant Lemuel Hitchcock came to the Hollow in the spring of 1795, transported hither by ox-team and sled. He and his son the year before "had located a square mile of land on both sides of the head waters of the stream" which runs through the hollow. The land seems to have been mostly on the north side, and his log cabin and orchard were near where in 1883 lived John Barnum. His children numbered ten, one of whom, Lemuel, settled

---

* See Attorneys of Greene County.

on a part of his father's farm, dying in 1861. At one time Winthrop Bagley, who is said to have been at the head of a band of counterfeiters, tried to buy out Deacon Hitchcock so there might be no interference with the gang on High Peak, for they had cut a road from their camp to within a hundred rods of the Elm Ridge road.

Eli Robinson, father of Lucius Robinson, former governor of New York state, lived in a log house and attended school in the log school house at Big Hollow. When the call came for men to serve in the War of 1812, Captain Eli P. Robinson called his company of militia together and asked for men, signifying his own willingness to go. Almost to a man they volunteered, and on the eve of their departure gathered at the church at Windham where Rev. Henry Stimson addressed them. Next day they marched away while the whole countryside looked on.

After 1800 the Hollow grew rapidly. Isaac Payne, who built the first saw mill, came from Connecticut, living there until his death at the age of ninety years. Samuel Atwater, the grandfather of Erastus Peck, came from Hamden county; Samuel Law early settled on Hough Hill, named after Theron Hough. Other settlers were Samuel Chapman, Harry Avery, Mr. Saxton, grandfather of Sandford Hunt, the father of Governor Hunt. Ambrose Chapman built a chair-factory, one of the first in the Hollow, on the south side of the creek, and also made hay-rakes. Other settlers came later.

MITCHELL HOLLOW

A man by the name of Mitchell came to this place in 1800 and lived on the flats in a house of logs. Little is known of this man, but he was buried under an apple tree on the Brockett farm. This farm was afterward that of a Mr. Brown, who built the house of the teacher Sylvester Andrews.

Deacon Elam Finch also came to this place and was one of the organizers of the West Durham Presbyterian church. These two men built the first frame houses in Mitchell Hollow. In 1805 Peck, Fordham, Smith, Robb and Williams settled here and built log houses. Near the brook lived Mr. Fenton and Ephraim Stimson, Henry Casper lived near Mr. Robb.

Ebenezer and Polly (Westlake) Blakeslee came from Connecticut (1819) with seven children, and near them were the Nelsons. David Lake and family came in 1816. Others were the Platts, Addis, Wolcott, Roper, Waterman, Smalling, Atwood, Burhans and Carr. The son of Carr became a noted teacher. Jared Clark in 1817 built the first dam in Mitchell Hollow. Roswell Bump of Dutchess county came to Catskill, then to Mitchell Hollow (1810).

The road to Mt. Pisgah via Mitchell Hollow passes the Hayden house, built partly of stone; this stone part was built by Jonathan Bell,* who came from England about 1800, shortly after this build-

---

* Mrs. C. S. Van Vechten of Leeds is a great-granddaughter of Jonathan Bell.

ing the stone house, which has been added to and enlarged. He made tackling for ships in the lower part of the house, overseeing the work on the farm but doing no farm work himself. His daughter Ann was seven years of age when they came to this country, and married Jacob Saxton in 1816. A daughter of Jacob Saxton and Ann Bell (Mary Ann Saxton) married John F. Casper and lived for many years on the Casper farm at Cairo Junction, later sold to the late Adam Shultis.

BROOKLINE

Brookline or Brook Lynne is a collection of fine summer hotels with modern equipment, between Hensonville and Windham on the Batavia creek. Early in the nineteenth century Herman and Jared Mathews came from Southington, Conn., and commenced making

VIEW FROM EAST WINDHAM, ON THE MOHICAN TRAIL.

shaving boxes. Later Soper had a shaving box factory, and somewhere nearby Bennett Osborn and Abijah Stone had a distillery. William Tuttle and Hiram Clearwater were merchants at the "Old Fiddle" settlement in 1830, and had a tannery.‡

UNION SOCIETY

Union Society, now known as Brooksburg and Newcomston Park, is composed of a few private homes and several summer hotels. It is on the Mohican Trail between Windham and East Windham, and its approach is bordered by the maples set out by Col. Robertson where he had a hotel and mills. He was born in a house the foundation of which can still be seen under the shadow of High Peak.

---

‡ I have not been able to locate the "Old Fiddle" settlement.

A post office was established at Union Society in 1815 or 1816, kept by Major Cornelius Fuller. In 1826, when the new turnpike was built, Col. Robertson was postmaster. Mail was not carried by stage before the building of the branch road from East Windham to Windham, but on horseback, and afterward until 1826 by a one-horse wagon. Erastus Buck was the first to establish a mail-stage drawn by four horses.

PIONEERS AND THEIR HOMES
GEORGE STIMSON

As has been stated, George Stimson came to Windham in 1784 with his son Henry, and built a log cabin at the west end of the village, then a wilderness. The rock against which he built formed one side of the cabin and also a part of the chimney and fireplace. Eleven miles distant toward the setting sun lived their nearest neighbors, the Laraways and Van Loans, while sixteen miles east was Shingle Kill (Cairo).

Tradition says that during the first winter the father went to Hudson, thirty-eight miles away, to get provisions, leaving Henry alone at the cabin. The boy must have had plenty of pluck and courage, for all about him was the solitude of the forest where bears, wolves, wildcats and panthers were plentiful. He proved himself equal to the occasion, and even when several weeks had passed and his father had not returned he still remained faithful to his trust, refusing to leave with a chance traveler who remained over night with him. The stranger was persistent and determined to force him to go with him, fearing starvation for the lad, but Henry ran away and hid in the woods. When six weeks had passed the father returned, having been kept at Hudson by an extended thaw which made the river impassable.

Many years later when Henry had become a minister and was attending Presbytery he met the stranger and made himself known as the boy he had tried to rescue. In 1785 or 1787 the rest of the family came from Massachusetts. The elder Stimson became a herder of cattle on the mountains, and Henry a founder of churches in that vicinity.[†]

Increase Claflin and his brother John settled on a soldier's claim. They came from Farmington, Mass., about 1786 on an ox-sled. These men had married daughters of George Stimson, and it is very likely his wife and other children came with them.

Nathaniel Stimson bought of the grandfather of Col. George Robertson, about 1807, the land upon which the village of Windham now stands. Mr. Stimson lived for a time in the house which later was that of Truman Johnson. Abijah Stone and Dr. Camp soon after built houses there.

---

† See Churches.

COLONEL GEORGE ROBERTSON

Col. George Robertson was born in Windham March 15, 1805. His grandfather came from Scotland in 1774, and a year later joined the Revolutionary army. He settled and married at Troy, owned a large part of what is now that city, after the death of his wife coming to Windham, where he married Esther Judson. His eldest son James came with him and married Elizabeth, daughter of Elihu Rogers, a descendant of John Rogers, the Christian martyr, who was born in Bradford, Conn., but then lived in Windham. James Robertson was an elder and liberal supporter of the Presbyterian church, owned two farms and kept a hotel. In politics he was a Whig. He had eight children of his own and in addition brought up and educated a number of others, starting them out in life with a Bible, a new suit of clothes and $100. George was the only one of the four sons who continued to make his home in Windham.

Three and a half miles east of Windham village he built a hotel (1828) on the farm then his father's, and this hotel is known as the first temperance house in the county. He has been known to have kept as many as 600 cattle and 13 drovers in a single night, and it was not an uncommon sight to count a hundred loads of butter passing in a single day. He became an enterprising farmer and business man, dealing in lumber and merchandise, and a partner of Colonel Zadoc Pratt in the tanning business, afterward buying him out. He is said to have been concerned in seven saw mills, owner of four, and interested in a large leather store in New York city. In time he became the owner of 600 acres of farm land. Upon this farm on either side of the highway he set out 900 maple trees, and these trees are still giving shade to the passing public. He was a member and deeply interested in the welfare of the Presbyterian church. He was a member of the Assembly in 1853, and his title of Colonel was received by election to the position in one of the State militia regiments.

Illustrating the push and enterprise of Robertson, the story is told that when his saw mill was burned the timber for the new mill was gotten out on Monday, framed on Tuesday, raised on Wednesday, and on Saturday night the machinery had been put in and was in operation. When the Windham tannery burned this record was beaten, for on Monday the timber for the frame was standing in the woods, and on the following Saturday night a building three and one-half stories high, 40x210 feet, with a lintel 21x120, was put up and in operation, thus saving a large amount of stock on hand. The Colonel married a second time Esther Dorcas, widow of George E. Merwin and daughter of Deacon Elijah and Mary (Robertson) Strong, the latter a native of Ashland.

CHRONOLOGY

ASHLAND

February 12, 1926, a Community Club was organized for prevention and protection from fires. One year later it had 79 paid members.

The buildings on the Hiram Jenkins farm were burned July 14th of the same year. Neighbors succeeded in saving the large farmhouse and cow-barn.

August 12th the big barn of William Bonesteel at Pleasant Valley was destroyed by fire. This was known as the Cole farm.

CORWIN B. BRONSON

Corwin B. Bronson passed away suddenly on Wednesday morning, November 3, 1926, at his home at Ashland. He was a native of North Settlement, a son of the late Mr. and Mrs. Benoni Bronson, and was held in great esteem throughout the town as well as among county officials and the county associations, in the activities of which he bore an important part.

He was but forty-five years of age at the time of his death, yet he had accomplished as much if not more than many an older man in the public affairs of his town. For four terms he had filled the office of Supervisor for the town of Ashland, and his far-sightedness, quick grasping of a difficult problem, made him a valuable asset to the Board.

Mr. Bronson was also a member of the Greene County Farm

Bureau, himself a practical farmer, taking much interest in its work. With his wife, in connection with their farm at Pleasant Valley, they conducted a large poultry business. He was also President of the Pleasant Valley Telephone Company. It has been written of him that "he was a man who improved the opportunities afforded him for developing types of business, religious, and social traits of human nature, and it was a pleasure for him to pass the benefits he acquired to his home people and others with whom he came in contact. He was a man among men."

ATHENS

April 10, 1927, the barn, fruit and hen-house and a shed of Daniel Vosburgh, on the Albany road, was destroyed by fire.

A slight fire in the barns of Seth W. Halstead and Louis Nabert May 26, 1927.

ELMORE MACKEY

Elmore Mackey died Nov. 27th, after an illness of over a year and a half, all this time a great sufferer, rarely free from pain. The funeral was held in Zion Lutheran Church on Nov. 29th, the Rev. E. Branson Richards officiating. Mr. Mackey was born in the town of Athens fifty-five years ago, the son of the late William and Jane Van Valkenburgh Mackey. He was a prosperous farmer for many years, but giving this up in middle life he moved to the village, where he played a prominent part in its affairs, serving as president of the Board of Trustees at one time, representing the town as

Supervisor, and also served as Sheriff for the county. He was the first President of the Athens National Bank and the first of the Athens Supply Corp., which office he held up to the beginning of his fatal illness; he was a member of the I. O. O. F. Lodge, the Knights of Pythias, and Morton Steamer Co., and an active member of Zion Lutheran Church, being one of its elders. Too much cannot be said of his integrity and honest dealings with his fellow-men, his morality and his kindness toward all. Athens loses in his going a Christian, public-spirited man and a respected citizen. Attending the service in a body were both Lodges to which he belonged, and representatives of the various institutions in which he was interested. Surviving him are his wife, one daughter (Mrs. Philip Carlson), one son (Floyd), all of Athens.

On May 20, 1925, Athens voted to appropriate $200,000 for the installation of a water and sewer system, the culmination of over forty years of agitation for a water supply. Until after 1919 estimates were based on water from the Hudson. Finally impetus was given a gravity system by Warren E. Howard, then a student at Massachusetts Institute of Technology, by a thesis on "A Water Supply for the Village of Athens," and data furnished by Robert H. Every of Yale, in regard to rainfall and watershed of Hollister Lake. In 1923 a committee of citizens, with Dr. Alton B. Daley as chairman and Charles W. Stranahan secretary, decided to back a gravity system, and a special village election resulted in a majority for it and placed the matter in the hands of the Village Board. The entire job was finished May 30, 1927, and a celebration held June 11th.

CAIRO
1926

John B. Earl took possession by purchase, the first of the year, of the R. A. Austin drug store.

January 12th the new High School building, which cost over $50,000, was so badly wrecked by fire as to necessitate holding school sessions in different rooms in the village. On the 22nd, Cairo ladies pledged $1,000 toward a chemical engine. The new LaFrance pumper and chemical engine cost $10,000.

Two fine modern residences were erected in 1926 next the National Bank—one owned by R. A. Austin, Cairo's druggist for over thirty-three years; the other by Julius Schad, owner of Walters Hotel.

The bakery owned for many years by Barney Freleigh was sold to Moses Deyo and Floyd Simpkins. This partnership was recently dissolved and Mr. Deyo is now sole owner.

The Board of Supervisors granted to the Cairo Chamber of Commerce the "privilege of making necessary surveys" and conveyed to "said corporation certain lands owned by the county for the formation of an artificial lake" in that town. Resolution introduced by Supervisor Bogardus.

1927

January 8th Gilbert Holdridge was found dead in his barn. His death was due to exposure.

January 20th Fred Van Dyke of the County Alms House committed suicide by drowning.

In the window of L. A. Miller at Cairo the first flag to be landed on Roanoke Island in 1862 has been on display. It shows signs of battle that include several bullet-holes. This flag was carried by Captain Erastus Dayton, father of Mrs. Miller, when as captain of marines during the Civil War he made forced landing at Roanoke, Va.

Allyn Emens of Dist. No. 1 was declared champion speller of Greene county.

April 6th a large barn on the Courtney Wood place near Freehold was burned, and a sawmill back of Acra on the 12th. This was owned by Miss Elinore Geary and was on what is known as the Frank Simpson place.

A building belonging to Lerner Bros. at Cairo and occupied by William Fisher was destroyed by fire April 28th.

The summer home of Charles E. Barbier, between Durham and Oak Hill, burned May 31st.

CATSKILL

1925

1925 was ushered in by a New Year reception given by the Rip Van Winkle Club, and a shoot by the Fish and Game Club. These were followed throughout the month by the usual annual meetings and banquets of hose companies and lodges; a dinner to county officials on the 6th. Hendrick Hudson Lodge, I. O. O. F., of Catskill celebrated its seventy-ninth birthday on Jan. 20th, when we had a big snow storm, of from eight to ten inches.

A new order of things was the burning of Christmas trees on the Holdridge dock by Dwight Brandow, which called out a crowd of people. January 24th is marked by the total eclipse of the sun, when the thermometer registered from ten to twelve below zero. In this intense cold, darkness crept slowly over the snow-covered landscape, giving it an unusual and wierd touch, which affected both bird and beast as well as humans. February 11th the Catskill Creek broke up with two feet of ice.

A distinct earthquake shock was felt on Saturday, March 5th. On April 20th the mountains were covered with snow, and on the 26th at the County Seat clocks were set ahead one hour. During this month the Howitzer Co. received from the arsenal at Raritan, N. J., a German seventy-five millimeter howitzer, weighing with carriage 490 pounds. It has been placed on the Armory lawn.

May 4th was opening day for the Post and Riley Creamery. 3,334 pounds of milk from twenty-six patrons was the first day's record, and on the 17th it was increased to 9,361 pounds from forty-six patrons. Cream cheese as a by-product, and chocolate milk, have been added to their output. During May the ferry boat A. F. Beach was equipped with modern, collapsible iron guard-gates.

DEAN WARDELL JENNINGS, M. D.

During January, 1925, death claimed eight persons in the town, among them, January 25th, Dean Wardell Jennings, M. D. Not since the passing of Dr. Wilbur F. Lamont, in 1912, had the village and surrounding towns been so shaken and bowed with grief at the passing of a man to whom they owed so much of sympathy and help in times of illness and trouble.

Dr. Jennings was born June 3, 1883, to Daniel Webster and Suzette Wardell Jennings, in Cairo, Greene county, spending his boyhood there. After graduating from High School he entered Drexel Institute in Philadelphia, from there going to the Albany Medical College, where he received his degree. For some time he served in Rochester General Hospital, later, after practicing in his home town, taking a course in the Post Graduate Hospital in New York. About eight years ago he entered into partnership with his brother-in-law, Dr. Lyle B. Honeyford, in Catskill village. This was a partnership in every sense of the word, for they were comrades and friends as well as congenial professional associates and brothers.

Dr. Jennings volunteered his services during the World War and was in the base hospital at Camp Sevier, S. C. He was a member of County, State and American Medical Societies, and of various lodges and associations in his home town. As medical inspector for three years in Catskill village schools he was loved by the pupils, even the youngest trusting him without question. He is survived by his wife, who was Miss Margaret Ritchie of Orillia, Canada; a brother, the Rev. W. W. Jennings of San Francisco, Cal., and a sister, Mrs. Lyle B. Honeyford of Catskill.

Memorial Day of 1925 will long be remembered as a testimonial to the veterans of the Civil, Spanish-American, and World Wars. After a parade led by Capt. Percy W. Decker, the column halted in front of the Court House, where the monument to the World War Veterans had been erected.

County Judge Thorpe was master of ceremonies, the Rev. Andrew C. Hansen offered prayer, and John McMenamy led in singing "America." Donald Heath gave forcibly and well, Lincoln's Gettysburg Address, "Tenting To-Night" was sung, after which Francis Van Loan recited "Flanders Field" in a manner not soon to be forgotten. The oratory of Hon. P. Barton Chaffee, who was the principal speaker, held his audience spellbound.

The Community Band played the "Star Spangled Banner," the national salute was fired by the Howitzer Company, and the new memorial unveiled. Taps were sounded at the end of the program. The names of 492 men who served in some branch of the service are on the bronze tablets, and 24 have stars.

From these imposing ceremonies the members of Watson Post, G. A. R., able to be present, with their wives, retired to their annual dinner in the rooms occupied by them for forty-one years, but which it seemed best should be abandoned because of decreasing numbers in their ranks. A permanent place has been prepared for their use in the Court House by the Board of Supervisors, and their valuable records and relics have been placed there.

Flag Day (June 14th) was observed by a display of the national emblem. July 4th was observed by the Howitzer Company, which assembled at the Armory and was inspected under the direction of Capt. William Heath. The village was bright with flags, and it was said that "never in the history of the automobile was traffic so heavy" as at day boat time on the afternoon of The Fourth. The F. N. Wilson Fire Company staged a field day at the Cairo Fair Grounds.

The Elks held a Field Day (August 12th) at the same place. The usual races and contests of a Field Day were varied by the rough riding of Troop G, New York State Police, which won much applause. During August the largest boat ever put over by the Benter yard was launched on Catskill Creek. It was "Whileaway II," built for Herbert Carpenter Sr. of Ossining, N. Y.

No special demonstration marked Labor Day, but it is estimated that between eight thousand and ten thousand cars passed through Catskill.

Sept. 28th the Society of Cosmo and Damien held their annual celebration, witnessed by crowds of people. At 9 a. m. a band concert at the Court House preceded the march in a body to high mass at St. Patrick's church. In the evening a wonderful display of fireworks on the Holdridge dock on the Westside. This display surpassed any of former years and was enjoyed by crowds of people on either side of the creek and on the bridge. An aerial bombardment from one side of the stream to the other was a special feature.

During October a campaign for a new post office was begun by Harry B. Morris and other prominent men. Senator Wadsworth promised aid, but intimated difficulties, chief of which was the securing of appropriations for the purpose at this time.

Great damage was done to shade trees and shrubs during the storm of October 10th. Two trees on lower William street, Catskill, toppled over, carrying light and telephone poles with them; others on Thomson and Broad streets, while branches and leaves covered the ground. In the country orchards suffered heavily and immense trees apparently as stable as the rocks were uprooted.

October 14th the cleaning of the village reservoir was completed, and on the 17th the Evening Line laid up its steamers, bringing to a close its fifty-fourth season of navigation. For two years past the "Catskill" has not missed a trip, neither did the steamers "Storm King" and "Reserve." The Hudson River Day Line made its last trip up the river October 18th, and down the river October 19th. The new and handsome boat "Alexander Hamilton" was put on this season, and improvements to Catskill Point made. The "Washington Irving" was the companion boat. The "Daily Mail" came out October 19th with enlarged edition. A new flat web press was installed and mechanical plant moved to Hill street.

On October 19th the entire village felt, in more or less degree, the blowing up of Zarin's market on upper Main street. The building was entirely demolished. There were no casualties, but many narrow escapes.

This month (October) established a record for unusual weather and boisterous conduct with severe wind storms and sudden changes of temperature. An unusual sight was that of October 30th, when snow fell throughout the day while the trees were still wearing their autumn dress of varied colors.

Nov. 1st Gus H. Dederick shot the first deer of the season. On Armistice Day in Catskill grocery stores and meat markets closed at noon, and holiday hours were kept at the post office. There was lavish display of flags, and the Court House was decorated with the national colors.

Catskill High School observed American Education Week, November 16th to 22d, by a program for each day of the week to which the public was invited. These programs were arranged by Miss Avis Pattrell, and were both entertaining and instructive.

The matter of a hospital for Catskill was brought up by Dr. E. C. Van Deusen of Athens in a public letter. He emphasized the need of such an institution, and answered objections by telling how it could be built and maintained. He drew attention to the fact that the Board of Supervisors expended yearly approximately $7,000 for hospital cases; that the Bonesteel endowment would add $2,000 for its maintenance; that the state aid was available, and drives for subscriptions would add materially to its equipment and maintenance.

In December the laying of a new main on Lower Main street was finished. This new main connects with that on Broad street. The Trustees of Catskill Public Library refused to endorse the County Library project put before them by Mr. Asa Wynkoop, head of the Public Library Section, University of the State of New York. The chief objections were: inadequate facilities of Catskill Public Library as a central distributing point, and the fact that Catskill would be obliged to raise $1,000 more yearly than at present for library purposes.

During the year (effective April 30, 1926) the village passed an ordinance regulating the sale of milk within the village limits. Citizens Hose Company deeded their new automobile fire apparatus to the village. A new street-sprinkler, snow-plow and tractor have been purchased. By an agreement between Corporation Counsel J. Lewis Malcolm and the New York Central Railroad Company a refund of practically $50,000 was saved to the town of Catskill.

Secretary Wallace of the State Board of Charities, as a result of his inspection of the County Alms House at Cairo, found the building badly in need of repairs, with poor drainage, inadequate laundry, unsuitable toilets, no fire escapes, no lighting in rooms, no hospital accommodations. Following this report the Board of Supervisors made an extraordinary appropriation of $1,500 for repairs. In December, as the result of two inspections by Commissioner Pyrke, he stated that "among other improvements are a new cow-barn with all modern improvements; cement floors in hog-house, with steel partitions; painting of most of the buildings; new and better herds and improvements in crops." He also declared himself satisfied with the efficiency of Superintendent Barker.

CHAMBER OF COMMERCE

The first meeting of 1925 called by President Thomas resulted in the consideration of a change in the location of the Rest Room from the Sage building to that of the Y. M. C. A. An appropriation of $1,500 was made for a secretary, and a drive for membership put under way.

The February meeting decided the lease of the store lately occupied by Frank Morelli in the Y. M. C. A. for a rest room. A Hudson River Bridge Committee was appointed, and a resolution passed requesting the Board of Trustees of the village to appoint a commission of eleven persons selected by the Chamber of Commerce to "study our present Village Charter and the General Village Act. * * * ". A committee was appointed to go before the Village Trustees asking that $2,000 be placed in their budget for the Memorial Monument; also $500 to be asked for the same purpose of the Town Board. It was also decided to make the Rest Room "headquarters for an employment bureau."

HISTORY OF GREENE COUNTY 137

In July the Winter Sports Committee launched a 12x16-foot float at The Point and had it towed to Table Rock, at the foot of William street, for the convenience of bathers. In December the matter of the condition of the West Shore freight-yard and approaches was taken up with the New York Central Railroad. The latter company agreed to spend $23,000 to pave yard and approaches to the station, in the meantime temporarily improving Railroad avenue by the use of cinders. Better train service was also secured.

A number of members of the Chamber of Commerce, following a dinner at the Saulpaugh tendered by Edwin J. Thomas (president), had an important conference with Mr. Fred D. Bagley of Buffalo, on State Park Commissions. As a result a Greene County Park Commission was appointed.

Mrs. Marie Butler, the efficient matron of the Rest Room, reported at the end of the year 8,945 visitors during 1925, while general information of all kinds had been given out by her. Since the Rest Room was started in 1923, Mrs. Butler has entertained 27,500 persons. It has proved a great boon to out of town people. The summer booklet was re-written by Kenneth Palmer, of which 10,000 were issued, and Robert B. Greenberger was engaged to solicit in its behalf throughout the county.

REAL ESTATE CHANGES

The Greene County Amusement Company, with three hundred stockholders throughout the county, built the Community Theater in 1920 on the site of the Nelida Theater which burned in 1917. On June 1st both the Community and Smalley's Theaters were taken over by the Farkas Theaters Inc. of Schenectady, controlled by W. W. Farley, stockholders to receive $15 for every $10 invested.

In February the Alsen cement plant was sold to Robert F. Johnson of Brooklyn, later becoming the property of the Lehigh Portland Cement Company.

E. C. Barlow purchased from Capt. W. A. Bear the dock and buildings which formerly composed the landing of the Catskill & Albany Steamboat Company.

The W. J. Hughes ice-house and other buildings on Water street (Catskill Coal and Ice Co.) was sold April 7th to Clyde DeWitt of Columbia county for $13,600.

The Catskill Foundry & Machine Works acquired title to the old gas works on Water street, between Union Mills and foundry building. The Middlesex Manufacturing Co. also removed to Trenton, N. J., and Mayonne Brick Co. took possession of Freeman property. Walter G. Ladd established a drug store in the Lohman building at West Catskill.

Greene County Lumber Co. sold its lumber-yard and real estate foot of Church street to Welsh & Grey of Albany, and the building at Main and Canal streets occupied by the Community Restaurant was purchased by Stephen Chorvas of Saugerties. Fred Clarke, who came to Catskill in 1912, sold his business in October to Joseph A. Hill.

1925 was the fortieth year of Willis A. Haines' blacksmith business on Church street. The Catskill Foundry & Machine Works finished eighty-six years of its existence in the same building although in different hands.

Five historical places have changed hands during the year. The farm and brick house in Jefferson built about 1792 by the Rev. Johannes Schuneman, the "Dutch Dominie of the Catskills," and where he died in 1794, was sold to Mario DiCaprio. This is best known as the Prindle farm.

The old Salisbury mansion of 1705, with the farm, near Leeds, passed by purchase from Mrs. Earl R. Potter to Howard S. Tiffany. The house was known for years as the Van Deusen house and is one of the oldest still standing in the county. The barn, the frame of which at least dated back to 1682, built by the Whitbeck's, was burned to the ground in February, 1926.

The old Van Vechten mill property (known also as Cook's, Rushmore's, and Pixley's) was sold to Ivan Shestacovsky, who owns a part of the Van Vechten Patent. The first mill was built there in 1715, and the second in 1765, and the present one in 1830.

Another Van Vechten place known as the "Toll-Gate Farm," there having once been a toll-gate on the state road near the bend, was sold by Charles Van Vechten to Otto Margraf. The exact date of this house is not known, but in 1848, when it was purchased by the late Luke K. Van Vechten, the house was called old and needed much repairing. The farm was purchased by Samuel, his grandfather, from Francis Salisbury in 1792.

The McLaughlin property in Jefferson, purchased by George Badeau of Leeds, is on or near the site of the Souser tavern of 1797, perhaps earlier, where many important political and military meetings were held, and where crowds assembled on race days, for the race track was near.

The Salisbury House in Jefferson might also be included in the list. The first house was built soon after the Revolutionary War by Barent Staats Salisbury, a noted soldier, and was occupied by his descendants for many years. It was sold by Frank Lauria to Henry J. Fischer of New York. It is said that some portion of the old house is included in the present one.

The Jefferson Rural Cemetery Association added two hundred lots to their property during the year. The Town Board put up 5,000 feet of snow fence, and the committee upon snow removal reported "105 miles of state and county highways kept free for traffic." Eight snow-plows were purchased, and $1.50 each voted by Supervisors for bounty on gray foxes.

During 1925 no destructive fires occurred, although alarms were numerous, chiefly because of the soft coal situation and consequent overheated furnaces, which caused small fires promptly extinguished by the firemen. Out-of-town fires have naturally been more destructive, and to these the Catskill firemen have responded, although conditions were such that little aid could be given.

HISTORY OF GREENE COUNTY

In January the house of Mrs. Mary Young on the Saugerties road near the brick school house was destroyed by fire. In March the house of Mrs. Mary McMenamy on Thomson street was badly damaged by fire, and in June a slight fire in the Haines garage, in which Roy Couchman was severely burned. In July the Buckland bungalow between Leeds and Sandy Plains was burned to the ground.

A blast at Cementon destroyed a house occupied by Lester Mertz and family. They had taken the precaution to remove most of their household goods.

Automobile accidents in the town of Catskill were numerous during 1925, caused by all known and previously unknown circumstances and conditions of drivers, cars, and highways. Many indictments of intoxicated drivers were found, as well as many fines given for reckless and careless driving. The results were in some cases fatal, in others broken bones and injuries of various sorts.

On November 4th, Miss Anna Brooks was accidentally struck and fatally injured by William Myers of Tannersville, dying two days later. Arthur Gavigan was instantly killed near the Henry S. Van Orden farm on the Saugerties road. Charles Manning, a young man of Palenville, was fatally injured. Mrs. James J. Buhl of Jersey City died from injuries received in an accident in this town.

September 22d the car of Joseph Ernst of Woodhaven, L. I., which was parked on Cooke street, broke through the iron rail of the Finch house on upper Main street, and descended to the basement, breaking through the side of the house, wrecking the furniture and injuring the occupants, one of whom, Mrs. E. B. Engle of Cobleskill, received serious injuries.

Nicholas Ricci, a taxi-driver of Catskill, was held up by a passenger at the point of a gun near Rensselaer, and tied to a tree while the bandit and his accomplices made off with the car, which was afterward recovered.

Among tragic occurrences of the year was that of Warren Ostrander, instantly killed, and Ransom Gifford fatally injured by the falling of a telegraph pole (June 11th) near South Cairo. Joseph Holmes (Oct. 30th), son of Charles Holmes, was fatally injured at the Acme Cement plant. Sept. 26th Peter Martin Kraus met instant death at the same place. Edgar Brandow, six years old, was found dead at the foot of the cliff at Broome and West Bridge streets on November 25th. On November 14th Clinton H. Moon committed suicide by shooting himself. He had been for several years poormaster at Cementon.

Christmas was celebrated by a Community Tree in front of the Court House, in charge of Mrs. Edith Hubbard. Watch night services were held in the First Reformed Church, and the mill bell, according to its yearly custom, rang in the New Year. The ringing of the old Liberty Bell was plainly heard over the radio. On December 29th a star of great brilliancy shot across the sky, attracting the attention of many.

140 HISTORY OF GREENE COUNTY

1926

On Monday, January 4th, Earl C. Brougham assumed his duties as manager of the Greene County Farm Bureau.

January 12th the Town Board signed a contract with the Upper Hudson Electric & R. R. Company for lighting Spooky Hollow district, and also voted to purchase a gasoline roller. The following day Leeds taxpayers voted in favor of 23 electric lights, with power to increase to 80, to connect with Spooky Hollow. Lights were turned on at Leeds February 9th, making a continuous lighting district from Catskill to that village.

IRA BURR KERR

The Hon. Ira Burr Kerr passed away at his home on the Athens road (where he had lived since 1898) September 21, 1925, aged eighty-three years. He was born at South Kortright, Delaware Co., April 12, 1842, to Samuel and Hannah M. Burr Kerr.

Mr. Kerr obtained his education at the Delaware Literary Institute, Franklyn, N. Y., and graduated from the Albany Law School in 1865. For a number of years Delhi was his home, where he edited the Delaware Gazette, moving to Athens in 1880. Elected to the Assembly in 1894, three years later he entered into law partnership with the late Sidney Crowell of Catskill. For sixteen years he served as justice of the peace. He was a life member of Catskill Lodge, F. & A. M.; in 1908 appointed District Deputy Grand Master.

On Nov. 28, 1873, he married Mary Elizabeth Babcock of Stamford, who died in 1921, and he is survived by two sons (Frederick of Hudson and Robert of Catskill), and one brother, Henry Kerr of Davenport Center, Delaware county.

"This community and this town have lost in Ira B. Kerr a citizen of a rare type—intelligent, educated, thoughtful and upright; those who knew him well have lost a loyal friend, his sons mourn a kind father. In social gatherings he was known widely as a ready, humorous speaker, yet full of reverence, and one who could never express too often his love for the beautiful scenes about his home and in the mountains to which he lifted up his eyes in praise to their maker."

The Cauterskill Ice Company started to harvest ice 10½ inches in thickness on January 14th. During March the Hop-o'-Nose icehouse was filled with 16-inch ice.

February 2nd Bruin went back to his bed for another six weeks' sleep, and next day his action was justified. At 7:30 p. m. February 3d snow flakes began to fall; by morning ten inches covered the landscape, with high wind but comparatively mild temperature. The 5th saw twenty inches of snow, with blocked roads, and tractors and snow-plows busy throughout the county. All roads in the town were cleared in record time, and the village of Catskill spent $1,600, also making a record for quick snow removal. This month proved to be the coldest February known in years.

Catskill taxpayers without a dissenting vote appropriated $2,000 for a new fire alarm siren. The old one was repaired by the Gamewell Company without charge, but the result was unsatisfactory and a new siren was installed for a four months' trial, which was finally accepted in April, 1927, after readjusting boxes.

March 22nd crossing the river on the ice was discontinued, and on the 26th the river from below Catskill Point to Hudson Lighthouse was clear of ice. Three days later the first tow of the season passed north. At Easter time snow was still deep in the woods among the mountains, and the first week in April there was a background of white mountains on the landscape.

April 3d a thunder storm was followed by sleet and snow with a drop of 45 degrees within ten hours. On the 17th a snow squall swept the county, while on May 6th there was a storm of snow, rain and hail.

On May 15th the Washington Irving of the Day Line made her first trip up the river, and sixteen days later (June 1) she sank off the Jersey shore from collision in a fog.

On May 28th William Caniff, commander of Watson Post, G. A. R., died at his home in this village; and on Monday, the 31st, as he led the Pruyn Drum Corps, Drum Major Elmer Russel suddenly passed on.

Memorial Day was celebrated on Monday, and owing to rain the exercises were held in the Armory, where the old patriotic songs were sung, led by John McMenamy. Lincoln's Gettysburg Address, and the "Poppies of Flanders Field" were finely rendered by James MacAllister and Ralph Palmer. Rev. Francis A. Kelley of the

Sacred Heart Church of Cairo gave an eloquent and stirring address. Taps were sounded by Philip E. Elmendorf. The members of Watson Post, G. A. R., had luncheon at the restaurant.

Memorial Day of 1927 was celebrated by a parade, with Captain William Heath chairman of service at the village cemetery. William Freese of Cairo and David Chassy, winners of the Philip prize at Catskill High School, were the orators of the day. At a dinner at the New Saulpaugh, given by Mr. Geo. W. Holdridge, there were eleven veterans and their families, six widows, with Mr. and Mrs. Grant E. Robinson and Mr. and Mrs. Percy W. Decker as guests of honor.

July 3d 1,500 passengers landed from the Day Boat at Catskill, and from an extra boat that same night, 500 more. The traffic through the village over the week-end of The Fourth was unprecedented. No special demonstration was held at Catskill, but flags were in evidence everywhere. Hook & Ladder Co. No. 5 held a Field Day on the Cairo Fair Grounds on the 5th.

July 18th a severe hail storm damaged The Point property. The hail was general throughout most of the county, but did damage to crops and fruit only over a small area. At Catskill many of the hail-stones measured an inch and a half in circumference and covered the ground.

August 10th the New York City-Catskill auto-bus made its first trip up from New York. The Farm Bureau picnic on the 12th was attended by about 2,000 people. August 16th was opening day of the Cairo Fair. Former Mayor Hylan was the guest of Judge William E. Thorpe at a luncheon at the Saulpaugh given in honor of Mr. Hylan, who delivered an address at the Cairo Fair on Chamber of Commerce Day.

Labor Day was a great event in Catskill, planned for by the local firemen for months previous. The weather man was not kind, but this did not prevent throngs of people from being present, nor interfere with the firemen's parade in the afternoon. The carnival parade in the evening marched in a pouring rain. The Greene County Firemen's Convention (its 38th annual) held an enthusiastic session at which "practically every fire company in the county was represented." It is said to have been one of the best ever held. The streets were gaily decorated for the occasion, and everybody did what they could to make the day a success. The Boy Scouts were on hand with pails of water, first-aid kits, and cigarettes.

Catskill Public School opened September 8th, and on the 27th the societies of Sts. Cosmo and Damian held their annual celebration.

November 16th saw the heaviest rain storm of the year, which swept away many bridges in the mountain towns, where the most damage was done, changed the courses of streams, and for a time made roads impassable. The approaches to the concrete bridge on the Catskill-Palenville highway were badly damaged. A bridge at Palenville was swept away, and there were many washouts and slides on the Clove road.

December 2nd the mercury dropped to 10° above zero, with high wind. The mountains were covered with snow, and three days later snow fell all day. On the 7th the mercury fell to 5° below zero, and the A. F. Beach (ferry) was unable to make regular trips owing to heavy ice in the slips. At night the river froze over from shore to shore, but on the 8th the ferry boat resumed service. December 14th the ferry again stopped running.

The contract for new club house at Jefferson was given to Thomas Gordon for $8,200. Two Christmas trees were put up in front of Court House, and many bulbs of bright colors attached by the Upper Hudson Electric Co.

At 11:45 on Christmas Eve at St. Luke's Church there was a fifteen-minute carol service, and at midnight the bell tolled the hour. The music for the communion service which followed was written by Mrs. Edith E. Hubbard, organist for many years, in memory of the late Charles G. Coffin, who was for a long time choir director. Sunday evening about fifty members of the Catskill Lodge, F. & A. M., attended by invitation in a body, it being the eve of St. John's Day, a patron saint of the order.

On Sunday evening, instead of the usual Christmas community singing in front of the Court House, a union community meeting was held in the Reformed church. Sheriff Arbogast gave the prisoners a Christmas dinner, and the Elks are said to have distributed 103 baskets of food and 150 pairs of shoes to needy ones.

On Sunday, December 26th, eight inches of snow fell and mercury dropped to eight below on Monday morning. Town roads and village streets were cleared for traffic early Monday morning.

Among public village improvements of 1926 are the re-decoration of the interior of the Village Building; repairing walk on old railroad bridge; steel straps attached to lower town bridge to deaden sound; application of Kyrox to Main street, between Thomson and Mott streets; repairs made to Sheriff's house and jail, with widening of driveway; concreting of Division street and Railroad avenue, and the placing of signal lights at the foot of Jefferson Hill, Division street, Upper Main, and also at Main and Bridge. The Irving School has been equipped with fire-escapes and electricity, and two large boilers installed in Irving and High Schools. The interior of the Masonic Temple has been re-decorated and re-furnished.

Among the churches a new pipe organ has been placed in St. Patrick's, while the interior of church, rectory, convent and school have been renovated. St. Luke's is planning for a new rectory, and the interiors of the Reformed church and parsonage have been re-decorated. In the latter extensive repairs made.

The Rotary Club and the Chamber of Commerce leased ten acres of ground from Michael Poulos for the High School Athletic Association, with Ward Van Dusen in charge. A plan for the re-opening of the Y. M. C. A. building has been outlined and discussed, and the matter of a revision of the village charter placed in the hands of a revision committee.

The last of the rolling stock of the defunct Catskill Mountain

Railroad (two locomotives and four box-cars) was sold in June by Receiver Thomas E. Jones. A bus line between Catskill and Albany has been established, running regularly since early summer, and the bus line between Catskill and Leeds was extended in December to Cairo.

Harry B. Morris, retiring Secretary of the Catskill Chamber of Commerce, reported at the annual meeting 130 members. He had aided in organizing a Booster Club at Prattsville, and Boards of Trade in East Durham, Windham and Freehold, and had also organized a movement against the removal of the Leeds bridge, which was successful. The treasurer reported a balance of several hundred dollars. An Agricultural and Industrial Exhibition in the Armory was put on for a week, commencing October 25th, by the Chamber of Commerce, and, with the co-operation of farmers, Farm Bureau and business men, it was a marked success. The Rest Room continues to be of great and increasing benefit to the public, under the management of Mrs. Marie Butler.

STREETS

Fairview Avenue came into existence (1925) by acceptance of the village from Emma J. Robb, Almerin Van Loan, Mary E. Van Loan, and the Highland Security Company.

Bushnell Avenue was extended (1925) 350 feet, and Union Street from Long Dock to Dock Street.

Grace Court (1926) is a new street connecting Spring Street and Woodland Avenue.

West Main Street where it crosses Railroad Avenue was moved about 18 feet and widened to 25 feet.

1927

The concrete sidewalk under the West Shore bridge was finished in June, 2,000 feet having been laid, and West Main Street to Railroad Avenue, paved with concrete, was opened to the public the first week in July.

The Farm Bureau has lost two directors during the year by death: Supervisor Corwin B. Bronson of Ashland, and ex-Supervisor Osborn A. Cole of Windham. The organization has assisted in the formation of a Greene County Horticultural Society and a Dairy Improvement Association. A Farm Loan Association has been organized, and with the co-operation of the State Federation a vigilance service set up, to stop roadside thievery. The Bureau also co-operated with the exhibit at the Armory. These are only a few of its activities, and it started the new year with 639 paid members, the largest on its record. The annual picnic for 1927 was held on the grounds of the Osborn House, Windham, July 21st, and was a great success.

FIRES

During winter of 1926-7 small fires were frequent, due to use of soft coal. On Jan. 28th the Tiffany barns at Leeds burned; Feb.

19th the house of Mrs. Mildred L. Haner was destroyed by fire. The burning of Kingston Hospital (Feb. 20) was of local interest, and March 3d the Lerner residence on Main street was almost destroyed, while on March 6th the Richman building, store and apartments of Friedman and others was gutted. April 5th a tenant-house on the Buck farm at Cauterskill burned with all its contents. In May a small bungalow at Palenville owned by Sandy Kesler was destroyed.

June 17, 1926, the barns and cooperage of the Misses Frances M. and Helen L. Jones were burned to the ground, and two days later the house of Fred Cole in the village was badly wrecked by fire. During the storm on July 18th, the Haines house near Lawrenceville was struck by lightning and burned. At Cementon August 22nd the house and store of Michael Cotish, occupied by Samuel Liepshutz, burned. Oct. 10th the cold storage and ice plant of Harlan Duncan and Alexander Wiltse in Catskill village, also shed of Nicholas Leone, were completely destroyed by fire. On the 22nd the Country Club house fed the flames, and December 13th the Glenwood Hotel on the Catskill-Palenville road burned; it was the property of Stephen Mills. On Dec. 28th the house of Joseph Pesce at Cementon was destroyed and his children narrowly escaped with their lives.

OTHER FIRES IN THE COUNTY

Jan. 28th, 1926, Spruce Grove House was destroyed by fire. It was the largest boarding house in Greenville and owned by Fred Sarbacker.

Locust Shade House, East Durham, was destroyed by fire March 16th. It was formerly owned by George White.

Greene Valley House at Halcott was destroyed by fire Nov. 30th.

The house on the Branaugh farm at North Settlement, occupied by Henry Oliver, was burned March 19th, and Sept. 19th that of Shirley Cammer.

May 7th the barn of David Robinson was destroyed by fire.

Nov. 3d the barn of Alvin Hunt burned, with eight cows and three automobiles.

1927

Fire on Jan. 7th damaged the house of Otto Daucher at Leeds, Jan. 12th fire destroyed the house of F. B. Brown at Acra (Lone Pine Cottage). Two fires on Jan. 16th damaged the store of Frank Heinick and the house of Ebenezer Jeune on Bridge street, in which Mr. Jeune was badly burned. Feb. 5th fire was discovered in the engine house of Catskill Mountain R. R., and on the same night the ice-house of the Knickerbocker Ice Co., south of this village, was destroyed by fire; it had been used as a mushroom plant. Early Wednesday morning, March 16th, fire was discovered in the furniture store of Deane & Deane. Nearly everything in basement and first floor was destroyed. May 5th the interior of Henry Post's house on High street was badly damaged.

REAL ESTATE AND BUSINESS CHANGES

Among real estate changes was that of the Catskill Knitting Mills sold to Utica parties. Benjamin Wishengrad and Morris Silverman of Hudson took over the retail business of the Cauterskill Ice Company, the concern to be known as the Catskill Ice Company. DeWitt Coal Company disposed of business and stock to Morris Bloom of Hudson.

The farm of Katharine and Isabel Brooks was purchased by the Country Club, and also a part of John Heath's property.

The building known as the old Peyton house was torn down to make way for an addition to the New Saulpaugh. This house was once the home of Adonijah Sherman, a pioneer resident of Catskill. The Wilcox house on William street was torn down to make room for a new rectory, and the Medard Pierre building on Main street for a garage.

The Gonnermann farm of 160 acres on the Five-Mile Woods road was offered by the state for reforestation and game refuge. 10,000 spruce and 5,000 pine trees have been set out.

The Irving Theater property was sold by W. W. Farley to Lerner Brothers of Catskill and Samuel Lerner of Saugerties. This building occupies the site of the Boston Store, burned in 1913. The transfer took place Jan. 3, 1927.

The Community of the Sisters of St. Francis purchased a piece of property from the Hayden estate, including the residence on Prospect avenue.

Lawrenceville church was sold at public auction in June to William Bogardus for $500.

Gay's Commercial Hotel (now known as Marlborough Rooming House), formerly conducted by the late Philip Gay, and later by William and Ira Gay, has been purchased by Sam. Lerner of Saugerties and Max Levy of Catskill.

1927

The old Corcoran house on West Bridge street was removed early in the year. It is said to have been built one hundred and fifty years ago.

Lot No. 1 of the old Cantine Patent was sold to E. C. Barlow; and the old building and canal-boats on Rogers Island were burned to make way for a new enterprise.

Lerner Bros. store, owned by Hollenbeck estate, was sold to Benj. B. Bernstein. It was formerly known as the Egnor house, later Nelson Larabee's, who April 1, 1869, deeded it to Wm. H. Hollenbeck, and it was occupied for many years by Smith & Price as a dry goods store, later by Doty & Goldin. On the upper floor Frank Allen successfully photographed a large proportion of the townspeople.

The Andrew Overbagh farm was sold in January. It was once known as the Wynkoop farm, the first story of the stone house built in 1792. Otto Margraf sold his house at Leeds to Ira Jansen. This was formerly Odd Fellows' Hall, built by the late George Warner.

HISTORY OF GREENE COUNTY

Harring & Betts purchased the Ahreet & Cussler building, putting in a beautiful colonial front and taking possession June 20th.

Contractor James Holdridge started work in widening Bridge street at the Bank Corner April 27th.

Rogers Island was formally opened to the public on Memorial Day (Seymour M. Sweet, president).

AUTOMOBILE ACCIDENTS

Automobile accidents in 1926 of a most tragic character were those of Joseph Subel at Cementon, resulting in his death. Another at Cementon caused the death of Jeremiah Depuy of Adams, Mass., while George Walker of Gilboa (June 29th) and Lillian Oren of Catskill (July 13th) were fatally injured at the foot of Jefferson Hill. James P. Friar was killed on June 20th.

Casualties from other causes, some of them fatal, were those of John Cozes Jr. of Cementon, who was drowned in June at Claverack; William Harbin (colored), killed at cement plant Jan. 11th. His home was at Atlanta, Ga. Capt. W. A. Beare of the R. C. Reynolds ferryboat was drowned April 29th. Percy C. Bagley, son of Fred C. Bagley, was drowned at Buffalo in the Niagara River in July. George B. Wagner was killed by a bucket at Alsen, and Danda Sendik lost an eye while working on an automobile at Cementon. Donald Overbagh lost three fingers and a thumb while handling a dynamite cap, and Fred Haines lost the sight of both eyes in a premature explosion on Sept. 15th.

1927

May 21, 1927, four persons (Orrie V. Coons, Joseph Ten Eyck, Jean McLaughlin and Theodore Warner) were injured in an automobile accident between Catskill and Athens. Coons died six days later in the Albany Hospital.

June 1st Mrs. Delia C. Dodge fell from her piazza-roof and was instantly killed. On May 14th Jesse Peck Truesdell jumped from a window and died from his injuries. Dominick Pullili of Cementon was drowned in May, and Fred Jones (colored) at Palenville July 7th. In July James Hempstead of New York was fatally injured at Leeds while diving.

1927 was ushered in with fine sleighing along the main highways and throughout the county, and at the same time good automobiling.

Louis T. Beach of Catskill, assistant postmaster for twenty-three years, resigned Jan. 1st.

On the 16th a foot or more of snow fell, blocking the roads.

Three trial ornamental lights in the business section were burned for the first time on the 30th, and in July locations for thirty-seven new standards were laid out.

Bear day was fine and clear, with a few clouds at mid-day when Bruin is supposed to make his decision, and two days later a terrific wind did considerable damage.

The new Day Line steamer Peter Stuyvesant was launched Feb. 2nd at Wilmington, Del.

In February the Grandview School issued a monthly paper called "The Chatterbox," with Janice Piper editor in chief and Roy Moon assistant editor. Both were of the seventh grade.

On the 24th the ice in the river was reported as wasting rapidly. Cold weather came on and it was not until March 9th that the Athens ferry made the first trip of the season, the earliest in many years. On the 11th Catskill Creek was free of ice, and next day Catskill ferry made its first attempt to cross to Greendale.

In February the bronze railing was put in place on the steps of the Court House.

On April 22nd a heavy storm did considerable damage to roads, and on the 23d the Catskill Mountains were white with snow.

In May a new traffic overhead light was put in operation at Main and Bridge streets.

Day boats made first trip May 20th.

A Safety Campaign flag with an American flag above it was put up May 28th at the North American Cement Corporation, the flag to come down whenever a day's work is lost through injury to an employee. Nearly every employee has signed a pledge to do his utmost to keep the flag flying.

June 9th the new hall at Cementon was opened, and in June the new Catskill-Palenville road was opened to the public, and No. 181 Athabasca Council celebrated its eighteenth birthday by a banquet at the Saulpaugh.

The largest crowd ever known over the week-end was that of July 4th.

In July the Memorial Fountain of the late Frances Willard was removed, the Boughton spring having been condemned.

The Catskill Country Club opened June 17th, when Attorney Percy W. Decker raised a large American flag and the national anthem was sung. The golf links were formally opened by the president, M. Edward Silberstein, and the tennis court by Harry Joseph. A committee served punch and cakes. The orchestra led by Gerald Hallenbeck gave an excellent program. The vice-president is Dr. E. A. Bennett, with George Clewes professional instructor. Th Club is very popular, and many luncheons, dinners and card parties are held there.

COXSACKIE

1926

Jan. 24th, Robert Judson was suffocated by smoke from a small heater in his room.

Jan. 27th, the storehouse and contents of lumber-yard of John Frank, on the old Reed & Powell dock, was destroyed by fire.

Jan. 30th, Charles A. Waltman was fatally injured in an automobile accident.

March 31st, Richard George Stacey was burned to death and his store destroyed by fire.

April 17th, storehouse of Howard Carey burned.

Oct. 14th, fire destroyed Carey's cooperage, and damaged Brady's undertaking rooms.

1927

Rea ice-house was burned March 31st.

Coxsackie at her village meeting vetoed proposals of $14,000 for pumpers and $7,500 for sewer purposes in the park. Officers elected were Abram C. Fairchild, president; Arthur Spoor and Guernsey Wilson, trustees; W. W. Salisbury, treasurer. All are Republicans.

Rev. Jerold C. Potts assumed duties as rector for Christ's Episcopal Church on June 15th.

June 24th, Martha Owen was rescued from drowning by Zelda Smith and Mary McCarth.

HARRIE McKELVEY CURTIS

Harrie McK. Curtis, a popular and prominent lawyer of Greene county, died at his home in Coxsackie after a brief illness, April 11, 1925. He was born April 24, 1884, at Coxsackie, to Alfred W. and Mary Nelson Curtis. In 1911 he married Helen Winne, and to them two children were born, Harrie McK. Curtis Jr. and Robert H. Curtis, all of whom survive him.

Mr. Curtis graduated from the Coxsackie High School in 1900, from the Albany Law School in June, 1904, and was admitted to the

Bar in the month following his graduation. He immediately began the active practice of his profession in Coxsackie with Alberti Baker as partner, and 1906 with Leonard A. Warren. He held the office of Trustee in the Village of Coxsackie in 1910, and was elected to the office of District Attorney of Greene county in November, 1916, serving two terms. He was active in the Masonic fraternity and the Benevolent and Protective Order of Elks, and the Greene County and the New York Bar Association, and was a deacon in the Second Reformed church of Coxsackie. He was of pleasing personality, always courteous and smiling even when carrying heavy burdens of responsibility as a public official, and his friends were many, not only in his own county but throughout the state. From the Memoriam of the Greene County Bar Association we quote the following: "We are proud to have him as one of our associates and honored to have known such a noble character. To know Harrie McK. Curtis as only his intimate friends knew him, was to love him, and no man could work with him without being thoroughly impressed with his high ideals and the sincerity of his personality."

DURHAM
DR. GEORGE CONKLIN

On January 5, 1925, death removed from the town of Durham the familiar figure of the family doctor, aged eighty-five years, who "for over a half a century, day and night, summer and winter, through thick and thin, traveled over the hills and dales of Durham town, to relieve the sick and suffering." He was one of the oldest and most respected citizens, and as a physician was well known throughout the town and the community at large. He was a member of the Presbyterian church, having united with it soon after coming to Durham, supporting it liberally, and was for many years a Trustee. He was also a member of Cascade Lodge in Oak Hill.

Just four months later (May 7th) his aged widow followed him and was laid at rest beside him in the Greenville cemetery. She was of "a genial and kindly nature; and thus two old residents of Durham have joined the throng gone on before, leaving behind them loving thoughts and reminders of kindly deeds done in their lifetime," cared for to the last by those whom they had befriended in their youth—Charles Jenkins and John Whitbeck.

GREENVILLE
HENRY T. BOTSFORD

Henry T. Botsford, former Supervisor of the town of Greenville, died suddenly March 11, 1925, at the age of eighty-one years.

Mr. Botsford was born in Greenville to Dr. Gideon Botsford and Mariah Talmadge Botsford, spending his long life there. In his younger days he owned and managed several large farms, and was later closely identified with local insurance companies. He was a faithful member of the Presbyterian Church, serving it officially and as treasurer for nearly half a century, and was active in town and village affairs.

Mr. Botsford was twice married—his first wife Mary H. Robbins; his second Mrs. Lillie E. Story, who with a daughter, Mrs. Helena Vincent of Milbrook, survives him.

ORRIN C. STEVENS

Orrin C. Stevens died at his home in Greenville on July 28, 1925. He was born in Greenville Jan. 29, 1872, the son of the late James and Elizabeth Sherrill Stevens, and is survived by his mother, his wife (Arcia Cook Stevens) and four children (James, Alice, Walter and Charles).

"Perhaps no removal by death in the community in which he lived has drawn out such true feeling and heartfelt sympathy for the sorrowing family. * * * While the descendant of a line of insurance builders, he was logically qualified as a pioneer, having introduced many new and valuable features in the office system, which have proved a convenience to the force and a definite public benefit. The employees, second only to his family, are more properly conscious of the heavy loss they sustain than those of the outer circle of acquaintances. Mr. Stevens was intensely human in his love for clean, healthy sports, and had a governing influence in the promotion of baseball in the village. He was always a familiar figure at the home games, where in his unassuming manner he would suggest changes in tactics that often proved their worth and evidence of foresight. In civic pride he was foremost, a sturdy advocate of anything that added to the wellbeing of the village. By choice he was politically a Democrat; had enjoyed the highest honors his town could confer, and as a consistent exponent of the principles which he believed to be the best, he had held fast without undue fervor. In business relationship he ranked high, and was the soul of integrity and truth. He reasoned as a philosopher, but his interpretations were in the plain language of the day."†

He was an active member of the Presbyterian Church of Greenville, a director of the Catskill National Bank, and President of the Co-Operative Fire Underwriters' Association of New York State. He was also Secretary and Treasurer of the Pioneer Co-Operative Fire Insurance Co. and of the Greene County Fire Insurance Co.

TOWN OF HUNTER*

Jan. 8, 1926, fire at Haines Falls destroyed much property at the coal and lumber yard of W. I. Hallenbeck, and the drug store and residence of John W. Rusk.

The snow fall in Tannersville Feb. 3d and 4th was the heaviest of the winter, with high winds and drifts. The main roads were opened in record time, and by working throughout Thursday night all roads in the town were open by Saturday afternoon.

At Beaches Corners March 12th Richard Merwin suffered a broken leg when his oxen ran away in the woods.

In March the bungalow of Miss Miriam E. Lester, outside of Tannersville, was burned.

Hunter Creamery was destroyed by fire May 31st, with loss estimated $35,000. The owner was L. B. Samuels of New York city, and the creamery had been in operation for about twenty-five years.

Early on Wednesday morning, July 14th, fire broke out in Twilight Inn at Haines Falls, and proved the worst fire tragedy Greene County had ever had, resulting in the death of twenty-two persons. In the cemetery of that place, near the Methodist Episcopal church, rest the personally unidentified bodies of fourteen victims, over which a shaft will be erected and their names inscribed upon it. The burial was an impressive scene, witnessed by a large number of sorrowing relatives and citizens, and in which those of the Lutheran, Methodist, Episcopal, and Catholic clergy participated. Twenty members of Tannersville fire department, who had fought valiantly to save life and property, were pall-bearers.

In September the Police Commissioner of New York city, in company with four hundred members of the Police Department and their families, dedicated the new $500,000 Indian Head Hotel, the chief unit of the police recreation camp at Platte Clove.

On the occasion of the worst flood Greene County has ever known (Nov. 16th), "At the northwesterly end of the main street

---

† From Catskill Recorder.
* Information obtained from Catskill Mountain Reflector.

in Tannersville, the water rose to so great a height that automobiles were forced to travel through the west road to Elka Park, in order to gain a single block on Main street. The first floor of the Reflector Publishing Plant was completely inundated, and at 4 o'clock the entire staff of employees waded about ankle-deep and made their exit through a rear window; the greatest distance of any of the employees' residences is not more than two-thirds of a mile, and still they were compelled to travel from four to six miles to reach their homes." The first floors of other stores and residences were inundated and filled with debris, and required sweeping, scrubbing and even shoveling when the water subsided. Through Kaaterskill Clove the road was torn away in places and otherwise made impassable, necessitating the use of the Catskill and East Windham roads to Tannersville.

CHRISTOPHER A. MARTIN

Christopher A. Martin, former Supervisor of Hunter and proprietor of the Loxhurst at Haines Falls since 1899, died May 13, 1925, at the age of sixty-thee years.

Mr. Martin was a native of the town of Hunter and highly esteemed throughout that section. Always allied with the Democratic party, he was Supervisor for that town in 1922-23. He was an active member of Mt. Tabor Lodge, F. & A. M., and of various other lodges at Windham and Tannersville.

He is survived by his widow and one daughter, Mrs. Henry Myer of Haines Falls. He was laid at rest in the Haines family cemetery.

1927

Tannersville celebrated Independence Day by a parade of firemen, Girl Scouts, N. Y. City Board of Water Supply Police, and officers of the village, headed by the Community Band of Catskill. This was attended by a large crowd of people, and in the afternoon a ball game between Westkill team and Tannersville Juniors was played, the local team being defeated. At 1 o'clock a band concert was given in the village square. Then came another ball game between Southern Bells of Catskill and the big team of Tannersville, the latter again going down to defeat. In the evening there was a fine display of fireworks. The village was filled with tourists and traffic was very heavy.

CHARLES VOSS

* Mr. Charles Voss, one of the most widely known and highly respected residents of this village and Greene county, died at his home on Friday morning, Feb. 18, 1927, at the age of seventy-eight years.

For many years Mr. Voss was a prominent figure in business and political activities of the county. He took a great interest in public affairs and was always ready to give his aid to any project that was a betterment to this community or for this county. He was behind the movement to have the Clove Road converted into a state highway, a plan for which he worked unceasingly until it was consummated.

---

* From Catskill Mountain Reflector, Tannersville.

HISTORY OF GREENE COUNTY

The deceased was a lifelong Republican and for many years was closely identified with his party. He held several offices, among them being President of this village and Supervisor for the town of Hunter for two terms. In the year 1904 Mr. Voss was appointed postmaster, a position he held for eighteen consecutive years.

Mr. Voss was born in Holstein, Germany, February 14, 1849. His ancestors, however, were from Holland. When a young man he came to America, and forty-two years ago he settled in this village, where he has since resided.

The funeral took place on Monday afternoon at the Methodist Church, the Rev. John K. Benedict officiating. The burial was in the Fair Lawn Cemetery, Prattsville. The Mt. Tabor Lodge, F. & A. M., of Hunter attended the funeral in a body, and the Masons' burial services were held in the church. The pall-bearers were from the Kingston Lodge. The large crowd attending the funeral, and beautiful floral offerings were evidence of the esteem in which the deceased was held.

Rev. John K. Benedict in his few brief remarks used the words of Emerson, "What you are speaks so loudly I can not hear what you say." No more fitting words could be used in the life of the deceased.

The immediate survivors are his wife, who was formerly Miss Jane E. Haner of Prattsville; one son, Ralph Voss, and two daughters, Mrs. Oliver Perry and Mrs. Edward Smith, all of this village.

JEWETT
ROMAINE A. BUTTS

Romaine A. Butts, former Supervisor of the town of Jewett, died suddenly on Thursday morning, July 15, 1925, at his home in Hensonville. Mr. Butts was a native of the town of Jewett, having been born there October 29, 1845. His father, Justus Butts, was one of the original settlers of that part of the county. On October 30, 1867, he married Lizzie S. Barkley, who died in 1911.

Mr. Butts served the town of Jewett as Supervisor for two terms, and while a resident of Hensonville was Assessor for the town of Windham for twelve years, his term ending with the close of 1925. He was also a member of the Farm Bureau and of the Official Board of the Hensonville M. E. church.

It is said of Mr. Butts that "he was a natural trader and lover of horses, a trait well evidenced by his splendid team," and also that "his is a record of a life well spent, and further comment could not add thereto, but would rather detract."

TOWN OF LEXINGTON
1926

A reunion of the descendants of Peter H. Miller and his wife Hannah was held at Lexington Sept. 4th. One hundred and five descendants were present.

In December Norman Deyo of Westkill was fatally injured while riding down hill, by an automobile driven by Harry Dunham of Westkill. This sad accident was unavoidable on the part of Dunham.

During the freshet of Nov. 16th the Schoharie kill was the highest within the memory of the oldest inhabitant. Main street was covered with water and eight families were obliged to move out, while horses and cattle were removed to safer places. Chicken-houses and other farm buildings went down stream, while others were kept from following by being anchored to trees. In the general cash store in the village the water rose until it ran over the counters. Nearly every bridge between Westkill and Spruceton was swept away, and the roads beyond description.

1927

Later the Supervisors voted $10,000 for the improvement of Lexington town roads.

On July 16th more than 250 women attended the Women's Democratic Club picnic, held on Mrs. George Van Valkenburgh's lawn.

EDWIN L. FORD, M. D.

Dr. Edwin L. Ford, one of the oldest and best loved among the older generation of physicians in Greene County, died Saturday afternoon, March 19, 1927, at his home in Lexington. For fully half a century he ministered to the countryside, always greeting his patients with a smile and a pleasant word.

His daughter, Mrs. Frederick J. Zinck, wife of the pastor of the Methodist Episcopal Church at Lexington, and her three children are the only near relatives surviving Dr. Ford, but he is mourned by a host of friends throughout the mountains. Funeral services were held on Wednesday at the Baptist Church, Rev. George Rustin of Halcottville officiating, assisted by Rev. Ward Howlett, pastor of the church.

Dr. Ford was a son of David and Abigail Faulkner Ford and was born Oct. 13, 1842, on the farm where he always resided and which has been in the Ford family for over one hundred and twenty-five years.

When the Civil War broke out he enlisted as a private in Co. F., 120th Regiment New York Volunteers, and served in the principal battles of the war. He was wounded in the battle of Gettysburg and after recovering was taken prisoner at Mine Run, being held in Libby, Andersonville and other southern prisons. Nearly a year later he was returned to the northern forces in an exchange of prisoners. After receiving his honorable discharge he returned to his home. In the fall of 1866 he entered the Albany Medical College, from which he graduated Dec. 22d, 1868. In 1872 he married his first wife, Frances Cox, daughter of Rev. Leonard Cox, a Baptist minister and once a resident of Lexington; she died at the age of forty. In 1887 he married Annie L. Dunham, and of this union there were two children, Mrs. Zinck, who survives, and Edwin, who died in 1906.

NEW BALTIMORE
1926

Fire destroyed Edwin Vanderpoel's garage and bungalow on Jan. 5th.

Four prize awards on five exhibits of eggs were awarded Francis W. Wardle during Farmer's Week at Cornell.

New Baltimore was one of the towns which reached her quota of membership in the Farm Bureau.

At the State Firemen's home on April 2nd John Bortle of New Baltimore passed away. He was a member of Cornell Hook & Ladder Company of that village. He was seventy-eight years old.

Explosion of an oil heater in the laundry room of Miss Bertha Wade's residence May 22nd caused fire which did considerable damage, but house was saved by the quick work of the firemen.

In September ground was broken for Echo Grange Community Hall by County Clerk Floyd E. Jones turning the first spadeful of earth.

1927

Harry Omrisk and Thomas Williams were drowned in the river near New Baltimore June 15th.

June 22nd, W. D. Hull, principal of Dist. No. 10, committed suicide, owing to ill-health.

BYRON MANSFIELD

Byron Mansfield, son of Jehoikim and Maria Mansfield, a highly respected resident of New Baltimore who spent his entire life of seventy-five years in that village, passed on Jan. 24, 1925. He was an instructor in New Baltimore and also in Castleton, retiring several years ago. He was President of the Board of Education, Treasurer of the Baptist church, Trustee of Chestnut Lawn Cemetery, and for more than twenty years Secretary of Social Friendship Lodge. He had also filled the office of justice of the peace. He was the last of his immediate family, his parents and sisters dying several years since, and is survived only by three cousins (Miss Ryder, who kept house for him; George Ryder of Albany, and James Mansfield of New Baltimore). He will be missed in the church, the lodge room and all walks of life, his best eulogy being such utterances as that by the much younger man who exclaimed, "He was like a father to me."

He was buried with Masonic honors, with interment in Chestnut Lawn Cemetery. School was closed for two days and the pupils attended his funeral in a body. A bronze tablet to his memory has been placed in the school building by the Board of Education.

TOWN OF PRATTSVILLE
1926

Superintendent of Highways, Harvey S. Olmstead, in January asked that the bridge over the Schoharie kill be condemned. During the summer it was wrecked by an automobile, and later a temporary bridge was built while a permanent structure was in process of building. During the flood of November 16th the temporary bridge was carried away. At the present writing (July 15th) the new bridge is nearing completion. It is 150 feet in length and runs diagonally across the stream, with deeply imbedded concrete abutments. Its roadbed is 22 feet wide and made of eight-inch concrete, and its strength is such as to meet future as well as present-day demands upon it. Its cost was about $118,000. The bridge which it replaced cost $12,000 in 1870, and the iron was hauled from Catskill by horses. The earliest bridge now remembered was a wooden lattice bridge and carried away by high water in 1869. This bridge served the people well until the coming of the automobile weakened it by increasing heavy traffic, and a year ago one of these machines put it out of business and a temporary bridge was put up until another should take its place. This lasted only about two months when the flood of 1926 swept it away, and the old bridge, having been strengthened, again became an active factor in crossing of the stream. The plans for the new bridge were approved by recommendation of Supervisor Rosecrans.

The Prattsville-Ashland road has been re-surfaced by George

HISTORY OF GREENE COUNTY

E. Williams; a Booster club formed; the Methodist church wired for electric lights, the work under the supervision of Mrs. Elmer Hull, Claude V. White and Chester D. Conine.

Donald Osmar Rickard, aged one and one-half years, was accidentally drowned in a brook near his home on Clay Hill, July 9th.

During the storm of Nov. 16th "the tea room of Vernon Chatfield on upper Main street was threatened and only by prompt action on the part of those gathered there it would have been seriously damaged. Villagers carried the Frigidaire plant and practically everything else of value to a place of safety, and the building was chained to a large maple tree. All but one post was washed from under the building. Considerable damage was done to the barn on the Fred Hill farm on the Lexington road. He also lost a shed, stack of hay and a hog-house. Cellars were inundated. Carman's garage flooded to the depth of twelve inches, and Edward Lutz was forced to move shingles and lumber to higher elevation.

WINDHAM*
1926

Windham's fire district was enlarged in 1926 with only two dissenting votes; $115,000 of taxable property added. The Windham Hose Co. voted to purchase and present to Windham fire district an electric fire alarm system, and in May a new siren weighing 600 pounds was placed on top of the hose house by Foreman George McCoubrey and a force of men.

The Silver Lake property near East Windham was sold to T. M. St. John. It contains several hundred acres, and is being laid out in streets and sections by the purchasing company, of which Charles H. Belknap of Brooklyn is president.

Munson & Ferris of Windham purchased the store and stock of Patterson Brothers, one of the oldest concerns in Windham.

On Nov. 15th Edwin Probst, a World War veteran, was lost on South Mountain. On the 18th he was found dead by Roland E. Miles and brother of Hunter, having accidentally shot himself.

During the flood of Nov. 16th Windham residents became alarmed because of dangerously high water and storm accompanied by high wind. Cellars in stores and residences were flooded, putting out furnace fires and doing much damage. Charles Phelps lost several thousand feet of lumber. Clarence Marquoit was taken to safety by Harold Moore through waist-high water. The water was pumped from some of the cellars on Wednesday by the fire company pumper.

1927

May 20th the Butts Hotel at East Windham burned to the ground with heavy loss to the owner.

Descendants of Miles Merwin (1623), David S. Merwin (1816) and Jane Winchell Merwin held a reunion on Independence Day at Ashokan Dam.

---

* Taken from Windham Journal.

OSBORN A. COLE

Osborn A. Cole, former Supervisor of the town of Windham, died at his late home near the village of Windham on Monday morning, November 8, 1926, aged fifty-two years.

Mr. Cole was born at North Settlement, in the town of Windham, and was the son of Mr. and Mrs. John M. Cole. For many years he conducted a boarding house which was very popular and never lacked for guests. Three years ago he developed Cole's Glen Lake, making it a water sports resort, not only for his own guests but for the county—a far-sighted, successful business venture.

He was Supervisor nearly twenty-five years ago, and again during 1924-25. At one time and for six years he was a successful Commissioner of Highways. An active Democrat with hosts of friends. He was a member of the Methodist church of Windham, of Mountain Lodge, F. & A. M., Mountain Chapter, Windham, the Commandery and Shrine. He was also a member of the Executive Committee of Greene County Farm Bureau, and President of the Dairy Improvement Association.

Mr. Cole is survived by his wife, formerly Miss Tennie West of North Settlement, and one son Millard. His funeral was largely attended and conducted with Masonic rites.

DIRECTORY

GREENE COUNTY
OFFICIAL LIST, 1926-27.

Harcourt J. Pratt, Highland	Representative in Congress
Arthur H. Wicks, Kingston	State Senator
Ellis W. Bentley, Windham	Member of Assembly
William E. Thorpe, Catskill	County Judge and Surrogate
James H. Reilly, Catskill	Surrogate's Clerk
Harrison I. Gardner, Greenville	District Attorney
James Lewis Malcolm, Catskill	County Attorney
Wendell S. Sherman, Catskill	County Treasurer
Sada Haas, Catskill	Deputy County Treasurer
Charles H. Arbogast, Catskill	Sheriff
Andrew H. Speenburgh, Jewett	Under-Sheriff
Floyd F. Jones, Cairo	County Clerk
Irene Glennon, Catskill	Deputy County Clerk
Sadie Durwin, Catskill	Recording Clerk
Henry W. Barker, Greenville	Superintendent of Poor
Harvey S. Olmstead, Cairo	Superintendent of Highways
Horace G. Baldwin, Hunter	Coroner
Ichabod T. Sutton, Prattsville	Coroner
William E. Brady, Athens	Coroner
Mahlon H. Atkinson, Catskill	Coroner
Thomas J. O'Hara, Prattsville	Commissioner of Elections
Lincoln S. Hart, Catskill	Commissioner of Elections
Ruth Whitcomb, Catskill	Clerk Board of Elections
Thomas C. Perry, Catskill	School Supervisor, First Dist.
Robert M. MacNaught, Windham	School Supervisor, Second Dist.
Walter J. Decker, Hunter	School Supervisor, Third Dist.
Harrold R. Every, Athens	Chairman Board of Supervisors
Theron Lawrence, Jewett	Clerk Board of Supervisors
James Lewis Malcolm, Catskill	Referee in Bankruptcy
Pearl R. Simmons, Catskill	Court Stenographer
Archie D. Clow, Catskill	Sealer of Weights and Measures
Earl G. Brougham, Catskill	Farm Bureau Manager
J. J. Bogan, Catskill	County Veterinarian
Mary G. Rowan, Catskill	County Nurse
Madge A. Morris, Catskill	Child Welfare Agent
J. V. V. Vedder, Leeds	County Historian
Allene R. Davis, Catskill	County Librarian
Henry Van Dyke Smith, Catskill	Court House Janitor

Greene County is in the Third Judicial District, comprising the counties of Albany, Rensselaer, Columbia, Schoharie, Greene, Ulster and Sullivan.

It is in the Twenty-Ninth Senatorial District, which includes Greene, Ulster and Delaware Counties.

Is in the Twenty-Seventh Congressional District, made up of the counties of Greene, Ulster, Sullivan, Schoharie and Columbia.

Board of Supervisors.

Floyd L. Ives	Ashland	Fred Bouton	Halcott
Harrold R. Every	Athens	J. Frank Lackey	Hunter
Herbert Bogardus	Cairo	Frank H. Haner	Jewett
Clarence Travis	Catskill	Abram V. Roraback	Lexington
Edward A. Webb	Coxsackie	Levitt C. Powell	New Baltimore
William S. Borthwick	Durham	Frank Rosecrans	Prattsville
Robert Van Houten	Greenville	Demont L. Chase	Windham

Greene County Bar Association.
Incorporated Oct. 9, 1902

Emory A. Chase, President
Arthur M. Murphy, Vice-President
Frank H. Osborn
Albert C. Bloodgood, Treasurer
Jesse M. Olney, Secretary
Clarence E. Bloodgood
Edwin C. Hallenbeck

1927

William E. Thorpe, President   John C. Welsh, Secretary

Greene County Medical Society.
Organized in 1803; Dr. John Ely, President.

1927

Dr. Norman S. Cooper, President   Dr. William M. Rapp, Secretary

Agricultural Society.
Organized in 1819; John Bagley of Durham, President.

The first annual "Fair and Cattle Show" was held at Cairo Nov. 2, 1819. The animals were exhibited in a field of Daniel Sayre, and articles of domestic manufacture, vegetables and fruit were displayed in an unoccupied store. The Society assembled at Osborn's tavern for dinner, their hats adorned with heads of wheat and a green ribbon band. The dinner cost them 31c. each.

The first year's expense was $193.50; balance in the treasury in 1820, $126.12½.

1927

Dr. L. L. Parker, President   George W. Squires, Secretary
Herbert Bogardus, Superintendent

Farm Bureau.
Organized 1917 with

C. W. Gilbert, Manager   George M. White, President
Francis Wardle, Secretary   Oliver Palmer, Treasurer

1927

Charles Peck, President   Earl G. Brougham, Manager

Sheep Breeders' Association.
W. A. Finch, President   William S. Borthwick, Secretary

Guernsey Breeders' Association.
Floyd Miller, President   A. D. Morse, Secretary-Treasurer

HISTORY OF GREENE COUNTY

Jersey Breeders' Association.
Clarence H. Jennings, President   Henry R. Ingalls, Sec'y-Treas.

Fish and Game Club.
Dr. Walter Conkling, President   Michael Cimorelli, Secretary

Firemen's Association.
Charles Thorpe, President   Roy H. Freer, Secretary

Letter Carriers' Association.
Herbert Antus, President   Myron B. Van Schaack, Secretary

Committee for the Blind.
Wendell S. Sherman, Chairman   Miss Ruth Hall, Secretary

Red Cross Society.
J. Lewis Malcolm, President   Mrs. J. Lewis Malcolm, Secretary

Tuberculosis Committee.
J. Lewis Malcolm, President   Mrs. Champlin Clarke, Secretary

Humane Society.
George W. Irwin, President   Miss Georgina Jackson, Secretary
Loren J. Hubbard, Agent

Board of Child Welfare.
Harvey S. Scutt, Chairman   Percy W. Decker, Secretary

State Charities Aid Association.
Miss Madge Morris, County Agent

Democratic Women's Club.
Miss Ruth Hall, President   Mrs. Clifford B. Dykeman, Secretary

League of Women Voters.
Mrs. Norman Cooper, District Leader   Mrs. Lauren Crook, Secretary

Home for Aged Women.
Mrs. James P. Philip, Pesident   Mrs. C. Allen Hayden, Secretary

Greene County Horticultural Society.
Organized Jan. 21, 1926.
A. D. Gibson, President   Thos. J. Riley, Secretary-Treasurer

Directors for One Year
George H. Hallenbeck, Athens   Harvey Cole, Cairo

Directors at Large
Charles Post, Catskill   William Albright, New Baltimore
Hiram Palmer, Catskill   H. E. Utter, Durham
Otto Hille, Coxsackie   O. P. Carey, New Baltimore
P. W. Stevens, Greenville

Greene County Federal Farm Loan Association.
Organized June 25, 1926.
W. M. Van Hoesen, Athens, President   H. A. Steele, Windham, Sec.

Greene County Bible Society.
(111th year)

Rev. Andrew Hansen, President   Rev. Geo. W. Rockwell, Secretary
Miss Anna Gonnermann, Solicitor of Funds

Greene County Sunday School Association.
1926

Chas. F. Robson, President   Mrs. R. W. Plusch, Secretary
George Seward (Coxsackie), Treasurer

Greene County Ex-Supervisors Association.
Established 1921 with 122 members, 17 of whom have died.

1926-27

Edward A. Webb, President   W. S. Borthwick, Secretary-Treasurer

Dairy Improvement Association.
Organized at Windham, March 29, 1926.

Osborn A. Cole, President   Raymond Meddaugh, Vice-President

Greene County Pomona Grange.
George D. Hall, W. M.   Ralph Latta, Secretary

Catskill Mountain Electric League.
1927

Harold N. Warden, President   Lester A. Minkler, Secretary

Greene County Boy Scouts.

Athens, Troop 1 ....Edward Kisselberg, Scout Master
Cairo, Troop 1 ....Rev. Harl E. Hood, Scout Master
Catskill, Troop 1 ....C. Lauren Crook, Scout Master
             2 ....H. C. Cowen, Scout Master
             3 ....George F. Parks, Scout Master
             4 ....Joseph Della Morte, Scout Master
             5 ....John Cummings, Scout Master
Cementon, Troop 8 ....Horace Cross, Acting Scout Master
Coxsackie, Troop 1 ....Rev. Jerrold Potts, Scout Master
Greenville, Troop 1 ....Gerald Goff, Scout Master
Hunter, Troop 1 ....Lorenzo D. Edwards, Scout Master
Leeds, Troop 1 ....Otto Daucher, Scout Master
Prattsville, Troop 1 ....B. R. Blakeslee, Scout Master
Tannersville, Troop 1 ....George Woodworth, Scout Master
Windham, Troop 1 ....Rev. George F. Wells, Scout Master

The Columbia-Greene Council was chartered in 1924 with John MacLauren president. Greene County Council was chartered January 1, 1927, with J. Frank Lackey president. Scout Camp Half Moon is one and a half miles from Cairo on Freehold road.

Greene County American Legion.
Levitt Powell, New Baltimore, County Commander

HIGHWAYS.
Catskill-Palenville, No. 8231, calls for 8.25 miles, beginning at

HISTORY OF GREENE COUNTY

village line on West Bridge street and connecting with state road leading from Saugerties to Palenville. To be concrete highway; Garrison Contracting Corporation of New York. Figures of contract, $471,482.50. (See Supervisors' Report,* with map reference, pages 45 and 46.)

Cooksburg-Greenville (See Supervisors' Report, with map reference, page 55.)

Greenville-Dormansville, No. 3858 (page 53, with map ref.)
Tannersville-Haines Falls (page 41).
Coxsackie-Ravena (page 54).
Coxsackie-Ravena, part 2 (pages 15-16).
Palenville-Saugerties (pages 15-16).

Catskill-Cairo, to be built in 1927 (9.19 miles) by Troy Paving Company.

Westkill-Spruceton, to be built 1927 (5 miles).

TOWN OF ASHLAND.

Census 1920, population 560

Census 1925, population 596

TOWN OFFICERS

Floyd L. Ives	Supervisor	Charles Tompkins	Assessor
Arthur C. Lee	Town Clerk	Sanford Tompkins	Assessor
Claude Tompkins	Justice Peace	Hugh Lee	Overseer of Poor
Irving Tuttle	Justice Peace	Dwight Tuttle	School Director
Melvin Wier	Justice Peace	Floyd Ives	School Director
Frank Griffin	Justice Peace	Alvah Tuttle	Constable
Perry Wiers	Collector	Alden Ferris	Constable
William Griffin	Highway Supt.	Lewis Case	Constable
Ernest Patridge	Assessor	Claude Sutton	Constable

One election district in the town, with polling place in building used as Town Hall. No voting machines are used.

Post Office

Ashland (Fourth Class) .... Francis L. Dodge, Postmaster

No R. F. D. Routes.

Mail carried from Ashland to Hunter; William Winter, owner-carrier
Prattsville-Cairo stage stops at Ashland; Charles Alle, owner.

Corporations.

Ashland Co-Partner Dairy Corporation, Ashland, N. Y.
Organized for the manufacture of dairy products.

George A. Cobb, President   Hugh Lee, Secretary

James A. Campbell, Treasurer

---

* All references are to 1925 Supervisors' Report.

Ashland Community Club.
1927

Roy Cornell, President   Frank Munson, Secretary-Treasurer

This club was organized Feb. 9, 1926, and now has (Feb. 9, 1927) seventy-nine paid members. Its purpose is to secure fire protection for the town.

CHURCHES

First Presbyterian.

Church erected before 1799, and stood on present site of Ashland cemetery. Its first pastor (1802-1806) was Henry B. Stimson.

First Trustees:

Noah Pond	Philetus Reynolds	Nathan Osborn
Timothy Hubbard	Elijah Strong	Jarius Munson

Present church built 1842. Present pastor, Rev. John Entwistle.

Trinity Episcopal.

Organized by Rev. (afterward Bishop) Philander Chase, May 11, 1799. First rector, Rev. Joseph Perry (1803-1817). First church built 1814. Present church built 1879. Present Rector, Rev. Pierre McD. Bleecker.

Organizers:

Samuel Gunn	Norman Collins	Silas Lewis
Ebenezer Osborn	Eli Osborn	John Tuttle
Benjamin Johnson	Samuel Goodsell	Eliphalet Wheeler
Almond Munson	Amasa Tuttle	Orange Munson
Jehiel Tuttle	Jabez Barlow	Samuel Merwin
Constant Andrews	Justin Coe	Daniel Merwin
Enos Baldwin	Samuel Wolcott	Ebenezer Johnson
Elisha Stanley	Samuel Chatfield	William Tuttle

Methodist Episcopal.

Organized in 1841, church built in 1842, first pastor, Rev. S. Lakin. Present pastor, Rev. Ralph S. Thorne.

St. Joseph's Roman Catholic.
No regular service.

North Settlement.
Church built about 1826, now a Windham charge.

West Settlement.
No regular service.

Civil War Veterans.

George Tompkins   Pratt Brewer

World War Veterans not listed on Honor Roll at Catskill:

John Cleveland	Riley Waterman	John Zegel

Harry Titsworth and Raymond Rivenburg came to Ashland after war

TOWN OF ATHENS

Census 1920, population 2,361
Census 1925, population 2,505

TOWN OFFICERS

Harrold R. Every.........Supervisor
William J. Clark.........Town Clerk
W. F. Hitchcock.........Justice Peace
Peter Van Valkenburgh.........Justice Peace
J. K. Van Woert.....Justice Peace
Orin Q. Flint.........Justice Peace
Geo. M. Day.........Highway Supt.
Wicks B. Spoor.........Assessor
Willis Brandow.........Assessor
Sylvanus H. Cooper.........Assessor
Emory E. Allen.........Collector
Charles Starke.........Overseer Poor
Fred Bock.........Overseer Poor
Robert Hosford.........Constable
Charles Hitchcock.........Constable
George Scott.........Constable
Lawrence Ford.........Constable
Abram Post.........Auditor
Gardiner Clawson.........Auditor
David F. Whiting.........Auditor
Luella Bard.........School Director
Isabelle Rainey.........School Director

Places of General Election.

Dist No. 1—Village Building, rooms of Wm. H. Morton Engine Co.
Dist. No. 2—Methodist Society Hall, Lime Street.
Dist. No. 3—Village Building, rooms W. C. Brady Hook & Ladder Co.
Voting machines used since 1901.

Post Office.

Athens (Third Class).........Clare Masten, Postmaster

Rural Routes.

Terminal, Athens.........Russell Page, Carrier
Vosenkill Road, Spoonburgh Road, Kings Highway, Athens-Coxsackie Turnpike, Schoharie Road and Leeds Road.

Village Officers.

Abram Post.........President
Wm. H. Jamieson.........Trustee
Thomas Lampman Sr.........Trustee
Wm. T. Van Loan.........Trustee
Garret S. Dollar.........Trustee
Frank Nichols.........Treasurer
O. Gates Porter.........Police Justice
Edward Slattery.........Street Com'r
Charles Hitchcock.........Police Chief
William Boyles.........Constable
George Scott.........Constable
Robert Hosford.........Constable
Claud B. Whiting.........Clerk

One election district in the village. Election held in Village Building on third Tuesday in March.

Physicians.

Dr. Norman S. Cooper.........Franklin Street
Dr. Alton B. Daley.........Washington Street
Dr. Edmund C. Van Dusen.........Franklin Street

Attorneys.

Orin Q. Flint.........Washington Street
O. Gates Porter.........Franklin Street

Registered Nurses.

Clara P. V. Flint .... Washington Street
Myrtle Hotaling .... Warren Street
Harriet Rainey .... Warren Street
Sarah Smith .... Washington Street
Mary Van Valkenburgh .... Washington Street

Banks.

Athens National Bank, organized July 5, 1916.

First Officials.

Elmore Mackey, President   O. Gates Porter, Vice-President
P. A. Carlson, Cashier

Capital Stock $25,000. Surplus $5,000. Deposits first year $144,000.

Directors 1925.

Jacob H. Decker	Joseph Mayone	Samuel Applebaum
Richard Lenahan	William W. Rider	George H. Hallenbeck
John Nichols	Frank Nichols	William H. Miller
	Abram Post	

Officers 1925.

Jacob H. Decker .... President
Richard Lenahan .... Vice-President
John Nichols .... Vice-President
Samuel Applebaum .... Cashier
Louis Kortman .... Teller
Isabel Van Loan .... Clerk

The Bank's first home was located in the Tremaine Building on the South-east corner of Second and Washington streets. A new Bank building was erected in 1925 on the North-east corner of Second and Washington streets.

Athens High School.

John Severance, Principal

Libraries.

D. R. Evarts Memorial Library, erected 1907.
Presented to the village of Athens by Daniel R. and Elizabeth Evarts.
Librarian, Jennie H. Van Woert.
Number of volumes, 5,535. Circulation 1926, 17,432 volumes.

Athens Lodge, No. 129, Knights of Pythias.

Dec. 24, 1874.

George Brady	C. C.	Wm. E. Church	M. of A.
Edward Ashley	V. C.	William Dumary	I. G.
Gordon W. Brady	Prelate	Richard M. Watson	O. G.
George S. Seaman	K. R. S.	Albert Brown	Trustee
Wm. J. Coffin	M. of F.	Henry True	Trustee
Albert L. Whipple	M. of E.	George Clapper	Trustee

Charter Members.

George Brady, Gordon W. Brady, Edward Ashley, Judson N. Cooper, Henry H. Van Loan, Richard M. Watson, Chas. F. M. Greene,

Erastus Brady, Frank Edwards, Chas. W. Lyons, William Bogardus, Henry True, Geo. S. Seaman, Isaac H. Tice, Alvin G. Howland, Isaac Newton, Wm. C. Brady, Wm. E. Church, Rufus Watson, William Dumary, Wm. J. Coffin, Casper Brady, Albert L. Whipple.

Officers, 1926.
Gilbert Wells _____ C. C.   William Bergamini _____ K. F.
Percy Brandow _____ V. C.   Benjamin Whiting _____ M. F.
Norman Cooper Sr. _____ K. R. & S.

Custer Lodge, No. 508, I. O. O. F.

Instituted March 7, 1889, and the following named officers installed by District Deputy Grand Master F. A. Stahl and Staff from Hendrick Hudson Lodge of Catskill, N. Y.

Charles W. Roe _____ Noble Grand   Ezra Cooper _____ L. S. N. G.
John E. Palmatier _____ Vice Grand   Dr. A. H. Getty _____ Conductor
George E. Bates _____ Secretary Edmund Dickman _____ Warden
George E. Gordon _____ Treasurer M. Boyle _____ Inside Guard
Harvey Kennedy _____ R. S. N. G. Gustave Tertring __ Outside Guard
Ira Cooper _____ L. S. N. G. W. A. Brady _____ R. S. S.
Geo. E. Palmatier _____ R. S. V. G. Louis Minerly _____ L. S. S.

After the installation ceremonies, Past Grand George E. Mitchell of Hendrick Hudson Lodge was called to the N. G. chair, and instructed eight candidates in the Degree.

Officers 1926.
Lawrence Palmatier __ Noble Grand   Elmer Benn __ Financial Secretary
Harmon Borfitz _____ Vice Grand William C. Brooks _____ Treasurer
Chas. W. Hitchcock _____ Secretary

Frances E. Willard Rebekah Lodge, No. 343, I. O. O. F.

Instituted May, 1905.
Ida E. Mackey _____ Noble Grand   Katie Delamater _____ Secretary
Susie Peloubet _____ Vice Grand   Annie Fyfe _____ Treasurer

Elective Officers 1926.
Angeline Requa _____ Noble Grand   Lucy Lackie _____ Financial Sec'y
Leah Clawson _____ Vice Grand   Fannie Boughton _____ Treasurer
Florence Brown _____ Recording Secretary

Teator-Guilfuss-Miller Post, No. 187, American Legion.

Organized in 1919.
August Brady _____ Commander   James Dumary _____ Secretary
Floyd Mackey ____ Vice Commander   John Ford Jr. _____ Treasurer

Officers 1926.
Frank Nedtwick _____ Commander   Joseph Michael __ Vice Commander
W. Hallenbeck __ Vice Commander   Leslie Delamater _____ Secretary
C. Van Loan _____ Vice Commander   Floyd A. Mackey _____ Treasurer

Soldiers and Sailors.

Joseph Schill (Died Sept. 17, 1926)   George Mower
George W. Garrison (Died Jan. 28, 1926)   George Spoor

Spanish War Veterans:

James Westfall   Charles W. Stranahan   Louis Kortman

New Street.

From State Highway east to the Brick Row, Village of Athens, by petition of tax-payers and resolution of Board of Trustees and purchase from the American Briklath Company, price $500.00.

Deed—Date March 24, 1925. American Briklath Company.

TOWN OF CAIRO

Census 1920, population 1,487
Census 1925, population 1,816

TOWN OFFICERS.

Officer	Position	Officer	Position
Herbert Bogardus	Supervisor	Frank Dorpfeld	Assessor
James P. Post	Town Clerk	Barney Chichester	Overseer Poor
N. M. Howard	Justice Peace	Frank Every	Overseer Poor
F. C. Burnham	Justice Peace	Lysander Lennon	School Director
Henry Chadderdon	Justice Peace	Wm. K. Hobart	School Director
Ira D. Vail	Justice Peace	Peter Hood	Constable
Guy E. Meddaugh	Collector	Benjamin Bennett	Constable
Ross Ruland	Highway Supt.	E. W. Mangam	Constable
Vernon Titus	Assessor	Elmer Sherman	Constable
H. H. Bogardus	Assessor	Richard Baker	Constable

Election Districts.

No. 1, Schermerhorn's Hall   No. 2, Masonic Hall

Voting machines first used in 1919.

Post Offices.

Cairo, Third Class	L. P. Miller, Postmaster
Acra, Fourth Class	H. Chadderdon, Postmaster
Purling, Fourth Class	R. Palmatier, Postmaster
Round Top, Third Class	J. M. Fiero Jr., Postmaster
South Cairo, Fourth Class	J. Fiero, Postmaster

Carriers.

Charles Alle	Cairo to Prattsville, Windham Road
O. E. Kelsey	Potter Hollow to Cairo, Freehold Road
Elmer E. West	Cairo to Catskill, Susquehanna Turnpike
Charles Vincent	Cairo to Cornwallville, Durham Road
Vernon Arnold	Cairo to Round Top, Purling-Round Top Road

Schools.

Cairo High School, Charles D. Coutant, Principal.

1927 Graduates:

Ruth Isadore Baldwin	Peter Noval	Elmer C. Chadderdon
Elizabeth Canniff	Anita F. Sutter	Edsall J. Meddaugh
	Dorothy S. Story	

Professional Persons.

Ray Eugene Person, Physician   Otto Pfordte, Mining Engineer
Miles Chadderdon, Attorney

First National Bank of Cairo.

Organized October 16, 1924.
First Officials:

Ira T. Tolley, President   Elliott A. Jones, Vice-President
Harry C. Emens, Cashier

Directors:

Ira T. Tolley	Norman N. Howard	William H. Freese
Elliott A. Jones	John Cryer	Barney W. Freleigh
Herbert Bogardus	Roscoe C. Lacy	S. E. Cozine Jr.
Harvey S. Olmsted	Lysander Lennon	Charles H. Phelps
	Harry C. Emens	

Capital stock, $25,000; Surplus $5,000; Resources, $264,209.18.

Calvary Episcopal Church.

Established August 13, 1832.
Rev. Ephraim Punderson, Rector
Eli Brooks and George Wickes, Wardens

Vestrymen:

Ira T. Day	Horace Austin	Henry E. Hotchkiss
Amasa Mattoon	Hiram Hine	Harlow Hine
William C. Howell		John Lennon

In 1924 the Rev. Culver B. Alford was appointed as rector, remaining until June 1, 1926, and resigning to become chaplain of the Actor Guild, in the Church of the Transfiguration, better known as the "Little Church Around the Corner," located on 29th Street, New York city.

Present pastor, Rev. Harl E. Hood

Presbyterian Church.

Was first organized at Acra but moved to Cairo and established there May 1, 1799. The first business meeting was held in the "Meeting House" August 27, 1808. The early records and papers of the church were burned in the house of Daniel Sayre, Jan. 28, 1808. At this first meeting Abner Benedict was moderator and Daniel Sayre clerk. David Reed and Daniel Sayre were among the first deacons.

Present pastor, Rev. Andrew Imrie

Methodist Episcopal Church.

The Methodist Society began in 1815 in the house of Mrs. Sally Stevens. The first "Meeting House" was built on land donated by Benjamin Hine, the building still standing on Bross street. The first regularly appointed minister was Rev. J. Ham in 1851.

Present church property built in 1866.

Rev. M. S. Ryan, present pastor

HISTORY OF GREENE COUNTY

Sandy Plains Methodist Episcopal Church.

This society was organized very early in the settlement of the town. One of the first places where services were held was at the house of Henry Weeks (or Wickes) on Indian Ridge, the circuit rider coming around every four weeks. John Pine was the second class leader. The first church was built in 1837.

Official Board of Leeds and Sandy Plains, 1866:

Charles Gorse, pastor

Stewards:

Wm. G. Wolcott	Frederick Brink	William Fullager
David Dunham	Orlando Hopson	Frederick Salisbury

Leaders:

S. W. R. Showers   Platt Pine

James H. Hawkshurst, pastor 1866-68

The second and present church stands near the north end of South Cairo bridge, and is now a part of the Cairo charge. The present church was built in 1905.

Round Top Methodist Church.

This church was founded in 1838, by the following trustees: Peter Fiero, Samuel Jones, Harvey Stoddard, John Remsen (owner of the grove) and others.

Present pastor, Rev. Samuel A. McCormick

Sacred Heart Roman Catholic Church.

Pastor, Rev. Francis A. Kelly.

Chamber of Commerce.

Organized 1924.

Richard A. Austin, President	Harry Emens, Secretary
William Freese, Vice-President	Norman M. Howard, Treasurer

1927

Barney Freleigh, President   Elliott Jones, Secretary

166 Members.

St. John's Lodge, No. 196, F. & A. M.

Organized in 1801 or 1802. The officers were John C. Burhans, W. M.; Amos Cornwall, S. W.; Rufus Byington, J. W. Forfeited its charter during the Morgan excitement.

Kedemah Lodge, No. 693, F. & A. M.

Organized January 30, 1869. Its first officers:

Elias L. Dutcher, W. M.	J. Seymour Miller, S. D.
Egbert Youmans, S. W.	Benjamin H. Waldron, J. D.
Edward Adams, J. W.	Levi K. Byington, Tyler
Luke Roe, Secretary	Rev. Edward Pidsley, Chaplain
Seymour Adams, Treasurer	Zanoni Beckwith, M. of C.

Thomas L. Wood, M. of C.

Other Charter Members:

Henry Steele	George Weeks	Geo. W. Mead
Reuben W. Green	Francis G. Walters	Solomon Christian
Edwin E. Darby	Dennis M. Stewart	John A. Mower
J. S. Miller	Alvin B. Felt	Robert Bridgen
Martin Smith	A. L. Walters	Lucius K. Byington
A. Timmerman	D. S. Eckler	Edward M. Lennon

1925

John B. Earl, W M   James P. Post, Secretary

Angelus Rebekah Lodge, No. 604.
Instituted 1922.

Charters members: Mr. and Mrs. Ross J. Ruland, Mr. and Mrs. Garret Becker, Mr. and Mrs. Frank Hotchkiss, Mr. and Mrs. Frank Vaughn, Mr. and Mrs. C. P. Roe, Mr. and Mrs. F. Bonesteel.

Fraternity Lodge, I. O. O. F.

This lodge was instituted at Leeds, Jan. 22, 1875; moved to Cairo April 1, 1897, and house was destroyed by fire Nov. 17, 1913.

First Officers:

George H. Warner, Noble Grand	J. Martin Vedder, Vice-President
Charles C. Teich, Secretary	H. Fiero Vedder, Treasurer

I. O. O. F. Hall was deeded to the Odd Fellows by William H. Ford May 28, 1918, and possession was given at once. Mr. Ford died in Oklahoma Feb. 7, 1920, and was buried in Cairo Cemetery by Fraternity Lodge, Feb. 14, 1920.

Yonderbocker Lodge, No. 289, Knights of Pythias.

Established July 30, 1890, Pythian Period 27. First meeting held in Walters Hotel. Moved to lodge rooms in Masonic Hall about 1913.

First Officials:

Dr. N. H. Griffin, P. C.	Charles Person, Prelate
George H. Lyons, C. C.	Joshua Travis, Keeper of R. & S.
Francis G. Walters, M. of E.	Selden H. Hine, M. of F.
W. Burr Hall, Inner Guard	Johnson Smith, M. of A.
John C. Person, V. C.	Platt R. Weeks, Outer Guard

Other Charter Members:

Ira Jump	J. H. Palen	J. W. Mulberry
E. E. Guthrie	John Hahn	John E. Greene
H. F. Williams	J. C. Palmer	J. H. Lent
Hiram P. Lacy	G. B. Holcomb	H. R. Wells
Richard Cartan	H. S. Duncan	C. H. Riesdorph
W. S. Stanley	J. C. Lennon	J. L. Jacobs
J. H. Cammer	George M. Weed	F. H. Ford
	James H. Sheridan	

Mohican Post, No. 983, American Legion.
Organized January 16, 1925.

Louis P. Miller, Commander Joseph Francel, Adjutant
Percy Mower, Vice Commander Herbert Knapp, Finance Officer
James Bonesteel, Commander

Cairo Hose Company.
Organized Sept. 16, 1919.

William H. Freese, President Louis A. Miller, Treasurer
Barney Freleigh, Vice-President Moses Deyo, Foreman
S. Cozine, Second Vice-President Nathan Fiero, First Asst. Foreman
Howard P. Crum, Secretary W. Walters, Second Asst. Foreman

Directors:

Wm. H. Freese	Floyd Simpkins	Louis A. Miller
James A. Bonesteel	Augustus Hof	Barney W. Freleigh
Sidney Timmerman		Samuel A. Cozine Jr.

Other Charter Members:

Abram Bonesteel	George Simpkins	William Dyce
George Arnold	Courtney Weeks	James P. Post
Elliott Mangam	Louis Egnor	Julius Schad
George Holdridge	Andrew Freese	Seymour Haines
John Duncan Jr.	William Simpkins	Lucius Lennon
S. E. Elliott	Howard P. Crum	Oscar Horton
Frederick Barlow	George Van Buren	Walter P. Jones
Claude Story	Harry Rasmussen	John Turner
	Floyd Hempstead	

Joseph O'Connor, charter member, died 1924

1927

S. E. Cozine, President William Dyce, Secretary

John S. Betts Post, No. 348, G. A. R.

Meetings were held in the Lodge Rooms on the top floor of Walters Hotel in the early establishment of the Post.

First Officials:

Jonathan B. Webster, Commander W. H. Rice, Vice Commander
William Howard, Vice Commander Isaac Howard, Delegate
Albert Weaver, Alternate

Civil War Veterans.

James Akeley—Born Sept. 3, 1846, member of 4th Regiment, Heavy Artillery, N. Y. S. Vol. Enlisted at Poughkeepsie.

Aaron Betts—Entered service April 19, 1861, as Fife Major in 20th Regiment N. Y. S. Militia. Discharged Aug. 2, 1865; re-enlisted as private in Co. E, 91st N. Y. Vol. Inft.

William Brandow—Born Dec. 20, 1840, enlisted in 15th N. Y. Engineers N. Y. Volunteer Regiment.

Isaac S. Howard—Born Feb. 13, 1839; died Dec. 31, 1923. Enlisted Aug. 19, 1862; discharged June 29, 1865. Promoted Nov. 1, 1864; wounded March 25, 1865. Enlistment in 120th Regiment N. Y. S. Vol., recruited in Ulster and Greene Co.

Enoch Walters—Born Feb. 24, 1846. A member of 100th N. Y. S. Vol. Inft. Enlisted at Kingston Oct. 3, 1864; discharged Aug. 28, 1865, at Richmond Va. (Capt. Sam. Ely's Co.)

At the breaking out of the Rebellion, Alanson Walters with his four sons resided in Greene County. All five enlisted and the father was shot and killed in the battle of Winchester. One son died in Andersonville prison (Nelson), another was killed in the battle of the Wilderness, a third lost his leg above the knee at Gettysburg, and the fourth, Enoch, still living (1926) came out of the conflict uninjured. Moses who lost his leg was keeper of the Four-Mile Point Lighthouse, in the Hudson River.

Prominent in the life of the John S. Betts Post, No. 348, G. A. R., was their commander, Jonathan Brown Webster, familiarly known to Cairoites as Captain Webster. He was the descendant of a long line of military ancestors. His maternal grandfather, Jonathan Brown, after whom he was named, was a major in the war of 1812, and his great-grandfather was a Revolutionary soldier.

The paternal grandfather, a Connecticut man, was a Revolutionary soldier whose grandfather served on the three lists of the Colony in the Pequadsh war. On an old English coat of arms in the family, a five-pointed star on its shield shows military service of an oldest son, granted by the King, by whom he was knighted at Bosworth Field.

During the Civil War he was appointed captain in the 20th Regiment, Co. A, N. Y. S. M., April 31, 1861. The regiment was mustered into service at Kingston, N. Y., the place of general rendezvous. He had been captain in the 28th Regiment of the 12th Brigade, 3d Division of N. Y. S. M., which appointment took place November 11, 1852, and he resigned to take command of the 20th Regiment N. Y. S. M., Co. A.

He was born in New York city in 1824, the son of Samuel Webster, born at Freehold, N. Y., where his father, Samuel Sr., a Revolutionary soldier, located from Connecticut after the war. His mother, Eliza Brown, daughter of Jonathan Brown of Morris county, N. J., a major in the War of 1812. Captain Webster was recommended by Colonel George H. Sharpe for the position of Colonel or Lieutenant-Colonel in place of Colonel Pratt, who expected to resign, but later changed his mind. The recommendation is dated August 25, 1862. Mrs. S. A. Mangam of Cairo and New York city is his niece.

TOWN OF CATSKILL.

Census 1920, Population 7,670
Census 1925, Population 8,563

TOWN OFFICERS.

Clarence F. Travis.....Supervisor
Geo. W. Swartwout....Town Clerk
Mrs. Eva Swartwout.......Deputy
Melvin Waggoner....Justice Peace
Paul R. Morrison....Justice Peace
W. J. Saxe................Justice Peace
Louis F. Teich........Justice Peace
Walter Dederick ....Collector
Eugene L. Wolfe..Highway Supt.
Oliver Palmer ....Assessor
C. J. Hammer...................Assessor
George Badeau ....Assessor
Joseph Obert ....Overseer Poor
Frank Durwin.........Overseer Poor
Stewart Parks ....Auditor
John V. Bogart ....Auditor
F. C. Kniffen.......................Auditor
Patrick Ryan ....Constable
John Hines ....Constable
Bernard Cummings ......Constable
Van Dyke Smith............Constable
John Fitzsimmons ....Constable
W. S. C. Wiley..... School Director
John V. Bogart .. School Director

Post Offices.

Catskill Post Office (Second Class).....Wm. B. Donahue, Postmaster
R. F. D. Route No. 1..Elmer E. Palmer, Carrier
R. F. D. Route No. 2...........................Raymond E. Boomhower, Carrier

Route No. 1 goes up Spring street to Hamburg, crosses to Lime Street, circles Green Lake and follows Spooky Hollow road to four corners, from there goes through Leeds to Cairo Junction, returning on Five-Mile Woods road to stone school house, then to Cauterskill bridge and Catskill.

Route No. 2 goes up Spring street, delivers mail on part of Allen street (not in corporation), crosses the concrete bridge to Cauterskill and Kiskatom, going south through High Falls, and back to Catskill.

Between Catskill and Palenville mail is distributed by Irving Saxe.
Between Catskill and Cairo by Vernon Vaughn.

Palenville.

Palenville Post Office, Third Class ....C. J. Hinman, Postmaster

Leeds.

Leeds Post Office, Third Class.................Harry C. Teich, Postmaster
This office has a Star Route, Leeds-Gayhead; Oscar Swan, carrier.

CORPORATIONS.

Catskill Hardware & Lumber Co.

Catskill Supply Co. Inc. 1910, consolidated Jan. 1, 1926, into Catskill Hardware & Lumber Company, to furnish "everything used in construction of buildings from foundation to final cost of paint and varnish."

Welsh & Grey Lumber Corp.

To supply contractors and builders with lumber, masons' supplies etc. Office located on Water street, Catskill.

New Era Apple Products Co. Inc.

Incorporated April 30, 1926. Principal business office, Leeds, N. Y.

Directors:

Adolph L. Hausold, Hoboken   Adolph Schaefer, Leeds
Joseph Bartke, Leeds

Mayone Brick Co.

Incorporated 1916 at Glasco.

Took possession July 1, 1925, of Freeman property, West Bridge street (Powder Spring Farm), formerly owned by Frederick Cooke. This company operates yards at Athens and Glasco.

Catskill Creamery Co. Inc.

Edison Post, President   Thomas J. Riley, Vice President
Mamie D. Post, Secretary and Treasurer

Incorporated April 24, 1925, for the purpose of buying tested milk, which after being pasteurized is shipped to New York markets (also home consumption).

Edison Post Apple Products Corporation.

Incorporated Sept. 29, 1924, for the manufacture of sweet cider and vinegar, and shipping of apples to New York city markets.

Rip Van Winkle Golf and Country Club.

Martin Cantine, President   Mrs. J. R. MacAllister, Secretary

Catskill Country Club.

M. Edw. Silberstein, President   Percy W. Decker, Secretary
Dr. E. A. Bennett, Treasurer

Jefferson Heights Improvement Society.

Leroy Phinney, President   Mrs. Fannie I. Clay, Secretary

Exploration Club.

Clifford B. Dykeman, President   Miss Elizabeth Chadwick, Secretary

CATSKILL VILLAGE.

Officers.

Earl C. Sandt	President	Elias Reynolds	Assessor
George W. Irwin	Trustee	Irving Linzey	Assessor
Champlin Clark	Trustee	Harry Millspaugh	Assessor
H. C. Smith	Trustee	Patrick Ryan	Police Chief
G. E. D. Parker	Trustee	Paul Morrison	Police Justice
W. O. Edwards	Clerk	John Fitzsimmons	Constable
James McNee	Treasurer	John Hines	Constable
Mary A. Deady	Collector	Van Dyke Smith	Constable
J. L. Malcolm	Corp. Counsel	Bernard Cummings	Constable

Henry Shear.........Street Superintendent

Board of Water Commissioners.

Harvey S. Scutt
M. Edw. Silberstein
Frank H. Cooke
J. C. Beare, Superintendent
Mrs. Mark McGovern, Bookkeeper
William Shufelt, Engineer
Joseph Bennett, Fireman
William Saxe, Fireman

Attorneys and Counselors at Law.

Josiah C. Tallmadge
Orliff T. Heath
J. Lewis Patrie
Ambrose Jones
Osborn, Bloodgood, Wilbur & Fray
John C. Welsh
Lee F. Betts
Lester R. Smith
Charles G. Coffin
G. Howard Jones
John D. Whittaker
Clarence Howland
Decker & Malcolm

Physicians.

Lyle B. Honeyford
George L. Branch
George R. DeSilvia
Charles E. Willard
Mahlon H. Atkinson
F. W. Goodrich
William M. Rapp
James B. Rouse
S. A. Holcomb

Veterinary Surgeons.

Leon L. Parker*
J. J. Bogan (County Veterinarian)

Nurses.

Teresa H. O'Shea
Mary G. Rowan

Druggists.

William L. Dubois
Louis B. Decker
Champlin Clarke
Walter G. Ladd

Dentists.

E. A. Bennett
Geo. A. Englert Jr.
Louis Schecht
Walter A. Conkling
Samuel L. Newman

Optometrists.

P. W. Hallenbeck
E. C. Pratt
H. B. Wilcox
Edward H. Jones
Joseph A. Hill
Benn Hartmann

Civil Engineers.

Robert W. Jones
George H. Penfield

Surveyors.

Geo. W. Goetchius
George Stauning

Catskill National Bank.

The Catskill National Bank was incorporated March 26, 1813, under the name of "Catskill Bank," and re-incorporated July 20, 1865, under its present name. In 1813 its capital stock was limited to $400,000. Its first president was Thomas B. Cook.

Capital stock $150,000.00

James P. Philip, President P. Gardner Coffin, Cashier

---

* Dr. L. L. Parker, veterinarian, has been assigned the towns of Catskill, Cairo, Athens, Coxsackie and New Baltimore. Dr. G. Clark DeWitt of Oak Hill, for Durham and part of Greenville. Dr. Frank L. Haner of Jewett, all mountain towns excepting Halcott and a portion of Prattsville.

Tanners National Bank.

This bank was incorporated under the name of Tanners Bank (safety fund) March 14, 1831, and re-incorporated under present name in 1865. Its first president was Orrin Day; cashier, Frederick Hill; vice-president, S. Sherwood Day.

Directors, 1831.

James Powers	Charles L. Beach	John Breasted
Edgar B. Day	George H. Penfield	John T. Mann
S. Sherwood Day	Rufus H. King	Joshua Atwater jr.
Francis Sayre	Joshua Fiero jr.	Francis N. Wilson
	Isaac Rouse	

Its capital stock in 1831 was $100,000.

1926

Orrin Day, President William Palmatier, Cashier
Capital stock $150,000.00 Surplus $150,000.00,
Undivided profits $85,434.45.

In November, 1925, County Treasurer Wendell S. Sherman, who had been assistant cashier since 1912 and associated with the bank for nearly twenty-six years, was promoted to vice-president.

Catskill Savings Bank.

This bank was incorporated under its present name April 1, 1868. Its first president was John Breasted; Edgar Russell, secretary. It began business in the main room of the Tanners Bank, and there remained until January, 1909, when it moved to its own building.

Wm. W. Palmatier, President A. C. Bloodgood, Vice President
Addison P. Jones, Second Vice President and Secretary
C. Edsall Fiester, Assistant Secretary
Assets July 1, 1927, $6,484,804.29

Catskill Savings and Loan Association.

It has been stated that William S. Torrey and Charles A. Wardle fathered the Association, and its first officers were

Thos. E. Ferrier, President W. E. Torrey, Secretary
P. Gardner Coffin, Treasurer W. W. Bennett, Attorney
John L. Kennedy was first to secure a loan.

1927

Josiah C. Tallmadge, President Thos. E. Jones, Secretary
Assets $515,547.79 Loans $103,773.75

CHURCHES.

Christ's Presbyterian Church.

Incorporated 1803. Church built 1808.
Rev. Andrew Hansen, Pastor Rev. C. G. Hazard, Pastor Emeritus

First Reformed (Dutch) Church.

First church built 1828, present church 1853
Pastor, Rev. Jacob Van Ess.

St. Luke's Protestant Episcopal Church.
Rev. Walter E. Howe (1926)

St. Luke's parish was founded before 1800; First church dedicated 1809; Corner stone of present church, 1883. Incorporated on St. Bartholomew's Day, August 24, 1801.

Methodist Episcopal Church.
Pastor, Rev. Grant E. Robinson.
First church built 1824, present church 1864.

First Baptist Church.
Pastor, Rev. G. W. Rockwell.
Church organized 1803. Present church built 1873.

St. Patrick's Roman Catholic Church.
Established 1853. Present church built 1885.
Rev. John L. Smith, Rector.   Rev. William Martin, Assistant.

Second Baptist Church.
Pastor, Rev. Trussie Johnson.

The corner stone was laid July 26, 1925; its cost, $9,000. Rev. George W. Rockwell of the First Baptist Church preached the dedicatory sermon from these words, "Thou art Peter, and upon this rock will I build my church and the gates of hell shall not prevail against it." Dr. Hazard spoke in connection with the corner stone. A review of the church history was read by Mrs. Julia Gunnel, one of the founders. Mrs. Julia Cobb, organizer and president of the Silver Leaf Building Club, which inaugurated the drive for funds for the new church, also addressed the gathering.

Mt. Tabor A. M. E. Zion Church.
Pastor, Rev. J. H. Edwards.   Organized 1914.

Christian Science Church.

This church was started with a few members in 1917. The first meetings were held in the Sage building, and from there in 1918 they moved to Clark street. In 1923 a church was built and dedicated on the corner of Broad and Livingston streets, and, free from debt, its service was held in September of that year. This church has two readers and six trustees.

Temple of Israel, Catskill.
Rabbi Benjamin Schwartz.

Leeds Reformed (Dutch) Church.
Organized as Katskill and Kocksackie, 1732.
Present church built in 1818.   Rev. George D. Wood, Pastor.

Methodist Episcopal Church, Leeds.
Church built 1860. Rev. G. O. Wilsey, pastor.

St. Bridget's Roman Catholic Church, Leeds.
Established and church built in 1878.

Methodist Episcopal Church, Palenville.
Rev. Leslie G. Davis, pastor.

Gloria Dei Episcopal Church, Palenville.
Rev. Harl E. Hood, in charge.

St. Mary's Roman Catholic Church, Cementon.

Catskill High School.
George H. Chadwick, Principal.

1927 High School Graduates.

Ruth Baker	Francis Doorly	Ruth MacClain(H)
Beatrice Bartoo(H)	Katharine Eckler	Mildred Morehouse
Edith Bates(H)	Francis Fowks	George Parker
Mabel Beare	William Freese	Donald Rightmyer
David Chassy(H)	Doris Heath	George Rosengren
Harriet Cole	Georgiana Heath(H)	Irving Seeley
Orlando Craft	George Holdridge	Marian Silberstein
Carlton Coutant	Mamie Kiebart	Lena Smith
Naomi Decker	Hertha Latimer	Harry Townsend
Mary Vicevich		Virginia Winans(H)

Grandview School
Alice L. Babcock, Principal.

Mrs. Thomas C. Perry, instructor in the second grade, and wife of Superintendent Perry, died at her home in Catskill, March 17, 1926. She was devoted to her work and greatly loved as a teacher.

Miss Helen Finnigan, instructor in the third grade, died at the Albany Hospital Jan. 30, 1926. She was a successful teacher.

St. Patrick's Academy.
Opened 1890.
Graduates 1927.

Marie Van Loan   Julia Styga   Michael Hodor

Hebrew School, Catskill.
Rabbi Schwartz, Instructor.

Town of Catskill.

There are fifteen school districts having school buildings in the town. No. 1 (Catskill) is a Union Free School. No. 5 contracts with No. 1, and No. 14 contracts with Nos. 1 and 10.

Palenville (Rowena Memorial).
Alice E. Jones, Principal.

Leeds.
Arthur C. Lewis, Principal.

Cementon.
John W. McMenamy, Principal.

Catskill Public Library.

Endowed by Andrew Carnegie, 1901.
George W. Irwin, President. Mrs. Frank H. Osborn, Treasurer.
Miss Emily Becker, Librarian. Mrs. Mabel Sommerville, Assistant.

Emory A. Chase Memorial Law Library.
Trustees

Percy W. Decker   Benjamin I. Tallmadge   J. Lewis Malcolm
Miss Allene Davis, Librarian.

Catskill Lodge, No. 468, F. & A. M.

Organized 1859. John H. Bagley, W. M.

The Masonic Order is closely connected with the early history of Catskill village. It is first heard of during the years 1793-4 and was then known as "Harmony Lodge." Among those who instituted it were Thomas Thomson, Jacob Bogardus, Hezekiah Van Orden, George Taylor, Rufus Stanley and W. W. Wetmore.

In 1818 Catskill Lodge, No. 302, which numbered among its members many of those formerly of Harmony Lodge, held meetings in Botsford's tavern on the corner of Main and Thomson streets. Its charter was signed by Dewitt Clinton.

1927.

Chas. J. Bagley, W. M.   Henry Layman, Secretary

Hendrick Hudson Lodge, No. 189, I. O. O. F.

Instituted in Catskill Jan. 14, 1845. Its charter members:

William Bennett   B. O. Wait   Nathan Mack
James Johnson   Peter Baurhyte   William Adams
George Bell   Peter Hamblin   James H. Van Orden
                    A. D. O. Browere

The first death was that of John Lusk, in March, 1848.

1927.

L. Fred Rockerfeller, N. G.   Leroy Hover, Secretary

Athabasca Tribe, No. 251, I. O. R. M.

Organized thirty-three years ago.

On Past Sachem's night, 1926, four charter members were present: R. J. Stahl, P. D. Hitchcock, B. K. Van Valkenburgh and Charles Reinhart.

1927.

John Baker, Sachem   Albert Scott, Keeper of Records

Catskill Lodge, B. P. O. E.

John C. Welsh, Exalted Ruler   Wm. C. O'Brien, Secretary

Society of Sts. Cosmo and Damien.

Dominick DeSantis, President   Joseph DiPerna, Secretary

Bayard Taylor Unit, S. S. A.

Organized by Edwin Schaefer July, 1919.

Robert Henke jr., Magistrate   Harold D. Bush, Secretary

HISTORY OF GREENE COUNTY 183

Malaeska Lodge, Knights of Pythias.
Instituted April 16, 1873. Charter members:

J. F. Sylvester	A. D. Wilbur	F. P. Joesbury
William Joesbury	J. P. Baird	I. W. Van Gorden
E. K. Wilcox	William B. Gay	I. A. Penfield
B. F. Conklin	Wheeler Howard	Warren E. Egnor
George R. Olney	J. R. Burgett	David Mackey
Egbert Beardsley	Gottleib Fromer	C. A. Weed
	James B. Mitchell	

1927

Benn Hartmann, C. C.　　　Frank Snyder, Keeper of Records and Seal

Knights of Columbus.
Organized May 30, 1901.
First Grand Knight, Thomas J. McLaughlin.

P. D. Hitchcock, Grand Knight　　　James E. Wicks, Recorder
Wilfred Ford, Financial Secretary.

Rip Van Winkle Club.
This club celebrated its fortieth birthday in 1925.

George A. Deane, President　　　Lewis A. Freese, Secretary

Catskill Chamber of Commerce.
Herman C. Cowen, President　　　Mrs. Marie Butler, Secretary

Rotary Club.
Catskill Rotary Club owes its existence of three years to the efforts of P. Gardner Coffin, who was chief organizer.

1927

J. Lewis Malcolm, President　　　Willis P. Goldin, Secretary

Parent-Teacher Association.
In April, 1925, the Health Association which had existed for some time was merged in the Parent-Teacher Association with Mrs. Fred Fiero as president.

1927

Miss Alice Babcocck, President　　　Mrs. John L. Fray, Secretary

Republican Club.
Organized January, 1926.

1927

L. L. Parker, President　　　D. Harold Bush, Secretary

Twilight Baseball League.
Edwin J. Thomas, President　　　John J. Fitzsimmons, Secretary
Henry Place, Treasurer

CATSKILL FIRE DEPARTMENT.
The village fire department had its origin April 1, 1797, when an Act was passed "for the better extinguishing of fires in the village of Catskill, County of Albany." Trustees were empowered to appoint

firemen, not more than fourteen to each engine, giving certain exemptions for public service, and in Section 4 it was further enacted in brief as follows: Trustees, justices and constables were immediately to repair to the scene of the fire with staves and such other badges of authority as should be ordained by a majority of the trustees to be worn. They should assist in putting out fires and prevent goods from being stolen. (Catskill Packet).

1927

F. N. Wilson Hook & Ladder Co., No. 5.
Organized 1854.
Celebrated seventy-second annual dinner, 1926.

Leslie Wasson, President   Howard Rightmyer, Secretary

A. M. Osborn Hose Co. No. 2.
Reorganized and adopted its present name June 7, 1886.

John J. Fitzsimmons, President   John F. Cummings, Secretary

Wiley Hose Co., No. 1.
Henry F. Place, President   Roy H. Freer, Secretary

Citizens Hose Co., No. 5.
Edward M. Henderson, President   Gordon F. Wolfe, Secretary

Leeds Hose Company.

The Leeds Hose Company incorporated April 3, 1925, owes its beginning in 1923 to J. R. Person, who interested others in the project and was the means of raising the first money ($83) for the purpose of a fire truck. This was purchased Oct. 26, 1923, and the company turned out to their first fire at Mrs. E. R. Potter's tenant-house Dec. 2, 1923. A fire alarm was set up Dec. 30, 1924.

On Nov. 12, 1924, a lot was purchased of Marietta Harris, on Main street, for a hose house, and the plans of Otto Daucher accepted March 5, 1925. The building was completed during the year. Two additional chemical tanks were added to the equipment in 1926.

First Officers.

James R. Person, President   Arthur F. Kamm, Foreman
Lewis Wolfe, Secretary   Lawrence Wolfe, Assistant
Charles Bunce, Treasurer   James O'Connell, Second Assistant

Board of Directors.

Charles Weissel   Eugene L. Wolfe
J. Fred Elting   Harry C. Teich

1927

W. L. Van Vechten, President   Lewis Wolfe, Secretary

Howitzer Co., 10th Regiment, N. Y. N. G.
William Heath, Captain.

The deed for the land upon which the Armory was built was dated Sept. 1, 1888, and was given by William J. Hughes, Geo. W. Holdridge and Hannah Holdridge, who had secured the property. The Company was then known as the Sixteenth Separate Company

HISTORY OF GREENE COUNTY

and the officers at the time the Armory was built were: Arthur M. Murphy, Captain; Frank E. Van Gorden, First Lieutenant; Chas. E. Nichols, Second Lieutenant.

The Armory was built by Contractor Geo. W. Hildridge for $18,673, and Mr. Holdridge was awarded a bonus of $1,000 for excellent work, for which he had been strongly commended by the architect, I. G. Perry.

Catskill Post 110, American Legion.
Floyd Dumond, Commander   Nicholas Leone jr., Adjutant

Sullivan-Teator Post, Veterans of Foreign Wars.
Henry V. D. Smith, Commander   William Scott, Adjutant

John W. Watson Post, No. 514, G. A. R.
Organized 1884.

Watson Post was named after one of the sons of Catskill, Lieut. John W. Watson, youngest son of Judge Malbone Watson of that village. Lieut. Watson was killed in the battle of Nashville. He enlisted in the 5th Iowa Cavalry as a private in 1861, winning rapid promotion. Attached to the army of General Sherman, he was in many perilous engagements and showed great bravery. A more extended account of his life and service can be found at the G. A. R. rooms in the Court House.

Members, 1925.

Geo. W. Holdridge*   John H. Brandow
Edward Martin (deceased)*   J. B. Rouse, M. D.
W. W. Hull   William Brandow
John Young   Charles Trowbridge
Peter Overbagh   Edward Carpenter (deceased)
Charles Wilday   William Swartz
George Coons   Aaron Betts
George W. Winans (deceased) Erick Walters
William Caniff, Commander (deceased).   * Charter Member.

Commander Caniff received the appointment of Aide-de-camp on the staff of Commander D. J. McMillian, Dept. of New York State G. A. R (1925).

1926-27.
Geo. W. Holdridge, Commander.

William Hull of Catskill, who recently passed his eighty-sixth birthday (June 7th) was a member of Company D, 120th N. Y. S. Vol., under Captain Lansing Hollister of Coxsackie, which took part in the battle of Gettysburg July 2, 1863. He enlisted at Ashland, Greene Co., August 22, 1862, and a little less than a year later, in the late afternoon of July 2d, with General Sickles's corps advanced three-quarters of a mile beyond the main Union lines where the troops bore the brunt of the first charge.

"This," says Mr. Hull, "was owing to the fact that Sickles disobeyed instructions and left a strong position to lead his men to the front where they were without protection." When the order to fire came Hull shot with the rest but without result, as he saw nothing to shoot at, the company being drawn up at such an angle as to put the enemy on their left. A bullet went through his leg just above the knee, and it was with great difficulty he crawled to the rear, his only fear that of being made a prisoner. His captain was instantly killed, the second lieutenant lost his arm, and Stephen Hann of Prattsville was also killed and many others wounded. Most of Company D were from Greene county.

TOWN OF COXSACKIE.

Census 1920, Population 2,994
Census 1925, Population 3,477

OFFICERS.

Edward A. Webb	Supervisor	George M. Lamb	Assessor
F. P. Donovan	Town Clerk	Harvey A. Truesdell	Assessor
E. C. Hallenbeck	Justice Peace	Albert W. Pierce	Assessor
Wm. T. Haswell	Justice Peace	E. S. Anthony	School Director
Wm. R. Palmer	Justice Peace	A. C. Fairchild	School Director
Francis Worden	Justice Peace	John E. Cure	Constable
Isaac T. Boyce	Collector	John Q. Adams	Constable
A. C. King	Highway Supt.	Chas. H. Hill	Constable

Village Officers.

A. C. Fairchild	President	Wm. T. Haswell	Trustee
Wm. H. Salisbury	Treasurer	Arthur Spoor	Trustee
Wm. E. Brady	Clerk	Guerney J. Wilson	Trustee

Coxsackie National Bank.

Assets, $1,030,910.14   Capital stock, $100,000
Surplus and undivided profits, $121,347.44
Philip A. Goodwin, President   Henry A. Jordan, Cashier
O. L. Whiteman, Vice-President   W. H. Salisbury, Assistant Cashier

Post Offices.

Coxsackie .... Francis L. Worden, Postmaster
West Coxsackie .... George Hubbard, Postmaster
Climax .... August F. Lubbin, Postmaster
Urlton .... Harold G. Haines, Postmaster

Physicians.	Attorneys.	Druggists.
A. W. Van Slyke	Curtis & Warren	Jordan & Marsh
I. E. Van Hoesen	**Dentist.**	J. C. McClure
John L. Loutfian	Dr. W. I. Sax	Frank A. Yaguda

CHURCHES.

First Reformed Church.

Rev. M. G. Nies, Pastor.   Organized 1732

HISTORY OF GREENE COUNTY

Second Reformed Church.
Rev. Bruce Ballard, Pastor.

Christ's Episcopal Church.
Rev. Jerrold C. Potts, Pastor.

Methodist Episcopal Church.
Rev. Emmett E. Shew, Pastor.   Church built in 1917

St. Mary's Roman Catholic Church.
Rev. Thomas Phibbs, Pastor.   Church built in 1900.

Bethel A. M. E. Church.
Church built in 1856.

Coxsackie High School.
Robert Chaloner, Principal.
Class of 1927.

Neal Brandow	Mark Scully	Olga Karolake
Alice Truesdell	Naomi Barlow	Irving Van Dyck Sax
Louis Coment	Eugene Bronk	Vera Van Denburgh
	Morton Wilson	

Heermance Memorial Library.
Miss Margaret V. S. Wallace, Librarian.
Mrs. Leroy Spoor and Mrs. William Doherty, Assistants.
Trustees:
Dr. A. W. Van Slyke   O. L. Whiteman   Henry Salisbury
Henry A. Jordan   O. J. Greene

Ark Lodge, F. & A. M.
Instituted 1797.
George Cornwall, Master   Geo. W. Barber, Secretary

Coxsackie Lodge, I. O. O. F., No. 351.
Instituted 1907.
Grover Roberts, N. G.   W. H. Parslow, Secretary

Knights of Columbus.
Organized 1900.
Francis Dorlan, G. K.   Eugene Walther, Secretary

Steuben Society.

Rod and Rifle Club.
Organized 1927.
Geo. T. Morgan, President   Frank H. Wehrle, Secretary

Board of Trade.
George S. Marsh, President   Chas. D. Pen Dell, Secretary

Exchange Club.
George Sweet, President   E. C. Hall, Secretary

American Legion.
George Morgan, Commander.

HISTORY OF GREENE COUNTY

Village Improvement Society.
Opened Rest Room April 25, 1927.

Florence Perkins, President Mrs. H. L. Cooper, Rec. Secretary
Mrs. Marsh, Vice-President Miss M. Whitmore, Cor. Secretary
Mrs. G. I. Titus, Treasurer

Republican Club.
Lyman Black, President Chas. D. Pen Dell, Secretary

Veteran Fireman's Association.
Disbanded April 1927.

Of thirty-eight charter members five are still living (1927). E. C. Hallenbeck, Leland Smith, Matthew Moran, A. C. Thomas, Alonzo Burke.

Geo. H. Scott Hook & Ladder Co.
Chas. D. Pen Dell, President Wm. H. Parslow, Secretary

Coxsackie Hose Co.
Otto Mueller, Foreman Chas. H. Hill, Secretary

D. H. Hamilton Steamer Co.
Leo Longthon, Foreman William Latte, Secretary

TOWN OF DURHAM.

Census 1920, Population 1,211
Census 1925, Population 1,196

OFFICERS.

Wm. S. Borthwick......Supervisor	Ralph Ruland ....Assessor
Vernon Baldwin.........Town Clerk	Romaine Spencer ....Assessor
P. A. Scott ....Justice Peace	John E. Huyck................Assessor
J. S. G. Baldwin......Justice Peace	Webster Morse ......Overseer Poor
H. E. Utter..............Justice Peace	Wm. D. Hull ....School Director
E. L. Strong..........Justice Peace	N. G. Knowles ..School Director
Harold Turk ....Collector	Fred S. Anthony..........Constable
Judson Moss........Highway Supt.	

Election Districts.
Dist. No. 1—Located at Presbyterian Hall, Durham village.
Dist. No. 2—Located at Lawyer's Hall, Durham.

Post Offices.
Durham .... Joseph Baldwin, Postmaster
Cornwallville .... Addison Z. Smith, Postmaster
East Durham .... Grace O. Meloy, Postmistress
East Windham ....H. Anable Butts, Postmaster
Oak Hill .... Ernest E. Ford, Postmaster
South Durham .... W. Gates Van Orden, Postmaster
Sunside .... Lillian Bush, Postmistress
Rural Mail Carrier..Albert E. Smith

Route begins at Cornwallville post office, then via Edmont and Hedges farms to East Durham; thence Carter Bridge to Wright Street, Dean's Mills; thence to J. Albert Hallock's, Charles Jennings's, J. W. Mulberry's, Shady Glen, George Hull's, Elisha Parks's, Lewis Hill's, Arthur Strong's, Hervey Street, Hervey Street school house, to Boughton's corner via Gideon Palmer's, thence to Cornwallville.

Cornwallville Grain Threshers' Association.

Incorporated 1925, for purpose of threshing grain for farmers.
Allen Cunningham, President   Wm. C. Latta, Secretary-Treasurer

Schools.

Districts Nos. 10 and 14 contract. All are common school districts.

Physicians.

Duncan Sinclair, M. D.   M. Herbert Simmons, M. D.

Veterinary Surgeons.

Dr. G. Clark Dewitt, Oak Hill, N. Y.

Attorneys.

W. Mace Laraway, Oak Hill, N. Y.

Civil War Veterans.

Edgar L. Sherman, Cornwallville, N. Y.

Cornwallville Grange.

Clarence Jennings, Master   Mrs. A. Z. Smith, Secretary

TOWN OF GREENVILLE.

Census 1920, Population 1,362
Census 1925, Population 1,394

OFFICERS

Robert Van Houten ....Supervisor	Frank O'Hara ....Assessor
Egbert J. Abrams......Town Clerk	Leroy Schofield ....Assessor
A. J. Cunningham..Justice Peace	Millard Felter ....Assessor
J. W. Hallock...........Justice Peace	Jacob Cameron.........Overseer Poor
Elmer Story............ Justice Peace	C. P. McCabe ....School Director
Cornelius Bauman..Justice Peace	O. T. Losee .... School Director
Reuben Waldron ....Collector	Clarence Boomhower ....Constable
Stanley Ingalls....Highway Supt.	Albertus Becker .... Constable

Election Districts.

Dist. No. 1—In building formerly owned by David E. Powell, Greenville.

Dist. No. 2—Parks Hotel, Freehold.

Dist. No. 3—Rooms of A. J. Cunningham, Greenville.

HISTORY OF GREENE COUNTY

Post Offices.

Greenville Village (Third Class)............Homer Hook, Postmaster
Freehold Village (Third Class)..............Olin D. Beers, Postmaster
Norton Hill Village (Fourth Class)..........P. R. Stevens, Postmaster
Greenville Center (Fourth Class)............Mrs. Phelps, Postmistress
Gayhead (Fourth Class)......................Reuben Waldron, Postmaster
Surprise (Fourth Class).....................Robert Blenis, Postmaster

Rural Routes.

R. D. Route No. 1...................Thurman Vaughn, Carrier
R. D. Route No. 2...................Charles Newman, Carrier
      Terminal of Routes............Greenville

Physicians.

Charles P. McCabe, M. D.   W. A. Wasson, M. D.

Attorneys.

Harrison I. Gardner, Norton Hill, N. Y.

Nurses.

Mrs. Alice McAvoy, Greenville.

James M. Austin Lodge, 557, F. & A. M.

Its charter was obtained and its first meeting held in 1864.

John W. Hoffman, W. M.   E. Wackerhagen, Secretary
Electus Ramsdell, S. W.   David Turner, Treasurer
Humphrey Wilbur, J. W.   A. N. Bentley
James Stevens, S. D.   I. I. Van Allen
B. F. Hisert, J. D.   Luman Ramsdell
Platt Coonley, Tyler   J. E. Collins
                             David Griffin
                             1927.

W. P. Stevens, W. M.   Ralph M. Youmans, Secretary

Greenville Post, American Legion.

Organized Sept. 18, 1919.

Lynn D. Wessels, Commander   W. P. Stevens, Vice Commander

Royal Arcanum.

Organized November 11, 1894.
John Low, Regent.

Spanish War Veterans.

Harry Kirchner

CHURCHES.

Christ's Protestant Episcopal Church.

Rev. Harl E. Hood, Rector.
Organized April 4, 1825, at the house of Reuben Rundle.
Present church built in 1852.

HISTORY OF GREENE COUNTY

Presbyterian Church.
Rev. E. D. Van Dyck, Pastor.
Organized by Beriah Hotchkin, 1790.
First sermon of Hotchkin was preached April 5, 1789, in Benjamin Spees' barn. Church erected 1872.

Methodist Episcopal Church.
Rev. A. P. Lakeberg, Pastor.
Organized in 1825.
A church was built in 1825 at West Greenville, removed to Greenville in 1856. This church was burned and present one built in 1873.

Greenville High School.
C. J. Kearney, Principal.

TOWN OF HALCOTT.

Census 1920, Population 272
Census 1925, Population 268

OFFICERS.

Fred Bouton .... Supervisor	Sherman Ellis .... Collector
Marshall Bouton .... Town Clerk	Roswell Bouton .... Assessor
John Ballard .... Justice Peace	Earl W. Jenkins .... Assessor
Arthur Gordon .... Justice Peace	Hiram Avery .... Assessor
M. K. Morse .... Justice Peace	Robert Van Valkenburgh ....
Robert Van Valkenburgh	School Director
Justice Peace	Amos Avery .... Constable
John F. Van Valkenburgh	Sherman Ellis .... Constable
Highway Supt.	Garfield Reynolds .... Constable

Election District.
No. 1 in Grange Hall, Halcott Center.
No voting machines used.

Post Offices.
Halcott Center (Fourth Class) .... F. Thorn Moseman, Postmaster

CHURCHES.
Methodist Episcopal Church.

Rev. F. P. Venable, Pastor.
Dedicated December 29, 1849.

Stewards
J. P. Van Valkenburgh
Travis Faulkner
J. L. Van Valkenburgh
Mrs. L. Van Valkenburgh
Mrs. W. D. Griffin
Mrs. J. C. Johnson
Mrs. Effie Kelly
Mrs. B. A. Scudder

Trustees
Travis Faulkner
Fred Bouton
J. P. Van Valkenburgh
Myron Morse
Lorenzo Van Valkenburgh
J. C. Johnson
Mrs. Lemuel Kelly, Pres. L. A. S.
Mrs. A. C. Johnson, Director Sunday School Recreation

Halcott Center Creamery Company.
Milk Plant, principal place of business, Andes, N. Y.
John Schamback, President   Walter Ostrander, Secretary-Treasurer

Greene Valley Grange, No. 881.
Organized Oct. 4, 1899.

The Grange purchased the vacant Kaufman creamery and then traded buildings with the Halcott Center Co-operative Creamery Company. This trade was mutually advantageous. The former Co-operative Creamery was remodeled for a Grange Hall and in addition to the uses of the Grange has been used as a community hall.

Officials:

Lemuel Kelly, Master
James M. Whitney, Overseer
Esther Jane Jenkins, Lecturer
Earl Jenkins, Treasurer
Alexander Van Valkenburgh, Chaplain
Celestia H. Moore, Secretary

Wallace K. Crosby, Steward
Wilbur Whitney, Assistant
Maritta Peet, Assistant
Augusta Ballard, Pomona
Lena Ballard, Ceres
Gertrude Mead, Flora
Horace Peet, Gate Keeper

World War Veteran.
Chauncey E. Kelly

TOWN OF HUNTER.

Census 1920, Population 2,309
Census 1925, Population 2,925

OFFICERS.

J. Frank Lackey............Supervisor
Paul Fromer................Town Clerk
Bert F. Baker..............Justice Peace
Owen Glennon...............Justice Peace
George Griffin.............Justice Peace
Joseph Farrell.............Justice Peace
Harry F. Thorpe............Collector
Geo. E. Sweet..............Assessor
Harry R. Knight............Assessor
Richard F. Haines..........Assessor
Joseph Kissley.............Overseer Poor
Frank White................Overseer Poor
E. Delmar Smith............School Director
Helen T. Johnson...........School Director
J. E. Gillespie............Highway Superintendent

Village Officers.

Tannersville.

Samuel D. Scudder..........Mayor
R. Lee Rose................Trustee
Ralph Voss.................Trustee
Percy Wilson...............Clerk
Andrew J. Hill.............Treasurer
Wm. G. Bynder..............Police Justice
Frank North................Street Supt.
Fred Carn..................Collector

Hunter.

Edwin A. Ham...............Mayor
Frank Barkley..............Trustee
Fred Quick.................Trustee
William Ryan...............Clerk
Max Iskin..................Treasurer
Irving Boyarsky............Collector
Claude Lake................Police Justice
Abraham Gordon.............Street Supt.

HISTORY OF GREENE COUNTY

Hunter Chamber of Commerce.
Isidore Reiss, President   George J. Strenk, Secretary

Tannersville Chamber of Commerce.
J. Frank Lackey, President   Clara E. Lackey, Secretary
E. Delmar Smith, Treasurer

Mountains National Bank.
Capital Stock $50,000, Surplus $10,000, Undivided Profits $11,650.50
M. Lackey Jr., President   Sam Golding, Vice-President
S. D. Scudder, Cashier

TANNERSVILLE FIRE DEPARTMENT.
E. Delmar Smith, Chief   David E. Showers, Assistant

Jacob Fromer Hose Company.
M. Lackey Jr., President   Samuel Greene, Secretary
Ernest Haines, Foreman   Fred Wilson, Assistant Foreman

Citizens Hook & Ladder Company.
Andrew J. Hill, President   Louis Hyser Jr., Secretary
Gordon C. Campbell, Foreman   Thurber Kerr, Assistant Foreman

HUNTER FIRE DEPARTMENT.
Albert N. Taylor, Chief   James Jackson, Assistant

Hunter Hose Company.
August Strenk, President   Arthur L. Baldwin, Secretary
Walter J. Decker, Foreman   Geo. J. Strenk, Assistant Foreman

Tannersville Boy Scout Council.
J. Frank Lackey, President   Geo. B. Prosser, Secretary
George Woodworth, Scout Master

American Red Cross, Onteora Branch.
Greene County Chapter, Tannersville, N. Y.
Justine M. Watson, Chairman   Mrs. George D. Barron, Secretary
Miss Madeline Regan, Registered Nurse in charge.
Health Center, Tannersville Red Cross Emergency Hospital.

Bunt-Brewer Post, American Legion.
Carrol Campbell, Commander   George Prosser, Adjutant

Leo Squires Post, American Legion.
Vaille S. Baldwin, Commander   Leslie Diston, Adjutant

CHURCHES.
Roman Catholic.
Church of the Immaculate Conception................Haines Falls, N. Y.
St. Frances De Sales Church ....Elka Park, N. Y.
St. Mary's Roman Catholic Church ....Hunter, N. Y.
Rev. William H. Sheridan, Pastor

Protestant.
Presbyterian Church..Tannersville, N. Y.

Methodist Episcopal Church..Tannersville, N. Y.
Rev. H. H. Black, Pastor
Methodist Episcopal Church..Haines Falls, N. Y.
Methodist Episcopal Church..Platte Clove, N. Y.
Rev. L. C. Booth, Pastor
Methodist Episcopal Church..Hunter, N. Y.
Rev. C. B. Livingston, Pastor
St. John's Episcopal Church..Tannersville, N. Y.
Rev. Alonzo Wood, Rector.
All Souls Church..Onteora Park, Tannersville, N. Y.
Rev. J. B. Warner, Pastor.
Church of All Angels...................................Twilight Park, Haines Falls, N. Y.
Pulpit supplied.
Union Chapel..Twilight Park, Haines Falls, N. Y.
Rev. Wallace McMullon, Pastor.

Jewish.
Kal Israel Anshi..Hunter, N. Y.
Rabbi Hirsh Rapoport, Pastor.
Congregation Anshi Hashoran..Tannersville, N. Y.
Rabbi M. Horowitz, Pastor.

Onteora Lodge, No. 322, Knights of Pythias, Tannersville, N. Y.
Harry Gordon, Chancellor Commander   Ernest Cole, Keeper Records

Onteora Temple, No. 72, Pythian Sisters, Tannersville, N. Y.
Mabel Cole, M. E. C.   Marian H. Showers, M. of R. and C.

Mt. Tabor Lodge, No. 807, F. & A. M., Hunter, N. Y.
Walter G. Peterson, W. M.   Walter J. Decker, Secretary

Mt. Tabor Star Chapter, No. 284, O. E. S., Hunter, N. Y.
Anna MacDaniels, W. M.   Walter G. Peterson, W. P.
Carrie B. Lake, Secretary

Lockwood Lodge, No. 653, I. O. O. F., Hunter, N. Y.
Joseph Kissley, Noble Grand   George E. Sweet, Secretary

Daughters of Rebecca, No. 416, Hunter, N. Y.
Violet R. Baldwin, N. G.   George E. Sweet, Secretary

High Schools.
Tannersville High School..Tannersville, N. Y.
Gladys D. Pyer, Principal.
Hunter High School...Hunter, N. Y.
John S. Woods, Principal.

Attorneys at Law.
Paul Fromer   Milo Claude Moseman

Physicians.
Dr. Horace G. Baldwin   Dr. Maurice Axelrad   Dr. David Rodier

HISTORY OF GREENE COUNTY

Pharmacists and Druggists.

Lackey & Lord	Solomon Horowitz	Anson Johnson
Adolph Cohen	Regina H. Lackey	Charles Schuman
Rae Cohen	Howard C. Matthews	Hyman Angel

Dentists.
Dr. LeRoy G. Atwater

Civil Engineers.
Harding Showers   Morris S. Schapiro

Graduate Nurses.

Margaret F. Murray	Dorothy Peck	Edith Langraaf
Madeline Regan		Olive Crum

Post Masters.
Stanley D. Francis.. Tannersville   Frank G. Crosby.......... Lanesville
Horace G. Fromer............ Hunter   Mary Bunt..................... Elka Park
James H. Layman......... Haines Falls

Public Libraries.
Hunter Public Library.. Hunter, N. Y.
Mrs. Herman Krom, Librarian.
Haines Falls Public Library............................... Haines Falls, N. Y.
Mrs. Charles B. Legg, Librarian.

TOWN OF JEWETT.

Census 1920, Population 883
Census 1925, Population 861

OFFICERS.

Frank H. Haner.........	Supervisor	A. D. Morse	Assessor
Cyrus Carr	Town Clerk	Clayton Mead........	Overseer Poor
John Northrop	Justice Peace	Marvin Mulford......	Overseer Poor
Ralph Carr...............	Justice Peace	S. Clifford Hall....	School Director
Henry Distin.............	Justice Peace	J. Woodworth......	School Director
Benjamin Merwin..	Justice Peace	Percy Cook	Constable
John Merwin	Collector	Elmer Northrop	Constable
Merritt DeLong .	Highway Supt.	Wesley Gripman	Constable
William H. Ward............	Assessor	William Lawrence........	Constable
Frank C. Carr	Assessor	Arthur Barnum	Constable

One election district. Voting machine first used in 1919.

Post Offices.
Jewett Heights (Fourth Class)..................... William Rice, Postmaster
East Jewett (Fourth Class)............................ Herbert Edson, Postmaster

Rural Routes.
From Hunter to Windham .... Welcome Moore, Carrier
From Hunter to Lexington............................ Samuel Loucks, Carrier

Dentists.
Leroy Atwater, Jewett, N. Y.

HISTORY OF GREENE COUNTY

Methodist Episcopal Church, East Jewett.
Rev. H. H. Black, Pastor.

TOWN OF LEXINGTON.

Census 1920, Population 1,075
Census 1925, Population 899

OFFICERS.

Abram B. Roraback ....Supervisor
Robert S. Tuttle ....Town Clerk
Chris Riley...............Justice Peace
E. E. Dunham..........Justice Peace
Sidney L. Deyoe......Justice Peace
Romain L. Kirk......Justice Peace
Leslie Van Valkenburgh..Collector
W. E. Dunham......Highway Supt.
James Herdman ....Assessor
Robert H. Kirk.................Assessor
Everett A. Cross...............Assessor
Daniel C. Kirk.........Overseer Poor
Abram Truesdell....Overseer Poor
Edward Palmer....School Director
Edward Irwin ....Constable
W. S. Clawson...............Constable
Alden Hyatt .... Constable
R. Van Valkenburgh....Constable

Election Districts.

District No. 1.....................Lexington House, Lexington Village
District No. 2.........................Westkill House Pavilion, Westkill
No voting machines used.

Post Offices.

Lexington (Fourth Class).....................Eugene Bailey, Postmaster
Bushnellville (Fourth Class)..............Mary Kelly, Postmistress
Westkill (Fourth Class).....................Oliver L. Hare, Postmaster
Spruceton (Fourth Class) ....Bertha Riley, Postmaster
No R. F. D. Routes excepting one starting out of Prattsville, following the Prattsville and Lexington state road to Mosquito Point, thence the Little Westkill section to Prattsville.

Star Route, Lexington to Hunter (8 miles) Samuel Loucks, driver.

Star Route, Lexington to Shandaken (11½ miles) Alden Hyatt, driver.

Star Route, Westkill to Spruceton (5½ miles) Ferris Herdman, driver.

Physicians.

Alfred O. Persons, Lexington, N. Y.

Lexington Creamery Co. Inc.

Incorporated for the purpose of manufacturing cream, cheese, etc. Office and principal place of business, 363 Cherry St., New York city.

L. B. Samuels, President.

Civil War Veterans.

William Frayer, about eighty years of age, Lexington, N. Y.

HISTORY OF GREENE COUNTY

Highways.

The highway leading from the head of the Spruceton Valley and passing through the so-called Diamond Notch, leading to the Hunter town line near Lanesville, was abandoned Nov. 26, 1924, by order of the Town Board of Lexington.

TOWN OF NEW BALTIMORE.

Census 1920, Population 1,536
Census 1925, Population 1,554

OFFICERS.

Levit C. Powell	Supervisor	Herbert Travis	Assessor
Lyles Z. Nelson	Town Clerk	A. L. Kniffen	Assessor
Wyman Kniffen	Justice Peace	C. H. Burger	Collector
M. W. Smith	Justice Peace	I. G. Tompkins	Overseer Poor
A. L. Wheat	Justice Peace	Alfred Williams	Constable
C. J. Lisk	Justice Peace	William Fink	Constable
Charles Statts	Highway Supt.	Chas. H. Bronk	School Director
Jurdenette Carr	Assessor	E. C. Vanderpoel	School Director

Election Districts.

No. 1, Cornell Hall...New Baltimore Village
No. 2, Town Hall........Hannacroix No. 3.....................Hall at Medway
No voting machines used.

Post Offices.

New Baltimore (Fourth Class)................Platt S. Wheat, Postmaster
Hannacroix (Fourth Class)................Clarence Albright, Postmaster
Rural Route No. 1, from Hannacroix................Volney Titus, Carrier
To West Coxsackie ....Arthur Carr, Carrier
To Ravena ....E. C. Griffin, Carrier

Physician	Attorney
Percy G. Waller	Leland Winn

Nurses.

Laura Carey, C. N.   Ella McCann, C. N.   Bertha Hotaling, C. N.

Cornell Hook & Ladder Company.

Henry J. Baldwin, President   Levit C. Powell, Secretary

Social Friendship Lodge, No. 741, F. & A. M.

Instituted July 9, 1874, with 21 charter members:

Anthony H. Holmes	Benjamin Hotaling	Dewitt A. Fuller
John Colvin	Leonard Marshall	Philo H. Backus
James H. Chase	John A. Davis	Stephen Mead
George W. Smith	Jacob B. Holmes	Edwin S. Colburn
A. V. S. Vanderpoel	James B. Miller	Horace Rennie
A. J. Vanderpoel	Isaac Burns	Geo. H. Johnson
Ira Wilson	John H. Hotaling	Stephen Springstall

The first officers were: Anthony H. Holmes, W. M.; John Colvin, S. W.; James H. Chase, J. W.

John H. Hotaling is the only surviving charter member, and the late Byron Mansfield was secretary for twenty years.

1927.

Wyman C. Kniffen, W. M.   Arthur L. Kniffen, Secretary

A. O. Bliss Post, No. 305, G. A. R.

Organized Oct. 25, 1882. Its charter members:

John W. Wiggins, Commander	Frank Green, Q. R.
Robert Wilson, Vice President	Elias Van Steenburg, O. D.
Henry W. Mead, Adjutant	David Layton, O. G.
John Sullivan, Vice Adjutant	Chas. C. Lowery, Chaplain
Joseph Smith	Peter Van Hoesen
John F. Wright	James L. Warner
James S. Frazier	Norton Links
G. F. Hopper	Sylvanus P. Eaton

Richard H. Burlingham, U. S. Navy, is only Civil War veteran living

Echo Grange.

C. V. Baldwin, W. M.   Howard Forman, Secretary

Tuesday, June 25th, was opening night, when new home was dedicated.

CHURCHES.

Reformed (Dutch) Church.

Elders (1834)	Deacons (1834)
Tunis P. Van Slyke	William Mansfield
Stephen Parsons	Andrew Vanderpoel
Peter Matthews	Fountain H. Slater
1927.	1927.
Dale S. Baldwin (Clerk)	Clayton Albright
Orlando Cary	Dr. P. G. Waller
Paul O. Deitz	Platt S. Wheat
Bronk Van Slyke	Paul Van Slyke

Rev. Peter DeMeester, present pastor.

Dr. Percy G. Waller has served as treasurer for twenty-eight years.

Methodist Episcopal Church.

New Baltimore was a charge on the Coeymans circuit, and a Mr. Hilton was the first known class leader. Its church was built during 1855-56, under Rev. J. D. Macomber; building committee was Alanson Scott, William M. Scribner and William C. Hinman; its cost $1,400. The corner-stone of a second church was laid August 26, 1873; its cost $8,575.

Rev. N. J. Hess, present pastor.

Medway Christian Church.

Organized in 1807, present church built in 1861.

Rev. W. D. Rockwell, pastor.

First Baptist Church.

This church was organized in February 1869, the church dedicated October 1870. Before the church was built services were held in the schoolhouse and afterward in the village hall. The cost of the church and site was $4,000. The first pastor Rev. G. W. Slater.

Rev. A. Stockton, present pastor.

TOWN OF PRATTSVILLE.

Census 1920, Population 830
Census 1925, Population 817

OFFICERS.

Frank Rosecrans ....Supervisor	Charles Fredenburgh ....Assessor
Warren D. Becker........Town Clerk	Roscoe Decker..........Overseer Poor
Lyman Alberti..........Justice Peace	Mamie Peckham..School Director
Cyril Thorington......Justice Peace	A. A. Disbrow.......School Director
William Traver..........Justice Peace	Edmund W. Deyo............Constable
Vernon Chatfield....Justice Peace	Floyd Decker ....Constable
Chas. W. Becker.............Collector	Herbert D. Ives.............Constable
Jason Brandow....Highway Supt.	Franklyn Marquit ....Constable
Willis G. White...............Assessor	Charles W. Becker........Constable
Charles Shoemaker.........Assessor	

Post Offices.

Prattsville (Third Class).....................Austin E. Hummel, Postmaster
R. F. D. Route...B. S. Disbrow, Carrier

Reformed (Dutch) Church.

Established early in 1802 by Rev. Labaugh, who began preaching in houses and barns. He was followed by Rev. Cornelius D. Schermerhorn, under whom in 1804 a house of worship was erected.

Rev. J. D. Hopkins, present pastor.

Methodist Episcopal Church.

Connected with Durham circuit 1823-34. The church was built about 1834, on land given by Colonel Pratt. First pastor, Rev. Thomas S. Barrett.

Rev. Ralph S. Thorn, present pastor.

Protestant Episcopal Church.

Services were held before 1843; Rev. Thomas S. Judd the first rector in charge. The church was built by Nelson Finch and consecrated Sept. 25, 1846, by the Right Rev. William Heathcote Delancy. No present pastor.

Oasis Lodge, No. 119, F. & A. M.

Organized in 1847 by Mr. Willard of Troy, N. Y., and the following officers installed: C. K. Benham, W. M.; ———— Bouton, S. W.; ————Scanlon, J. W. Previous to this (1827) Aurora Lodge, F. & A. M., was instituted.

HISTORY OF GREENE COUNTY

Physicians.
Ichabod T. Sutton, M. D., Prattsville, N. Y.

Civil Engineers.
George H. Fifield   O. C. Hays   Chas. W. Bouton

Prattsville Milk & Cream Association.

Prattsville Library Association.

Booster Club.
E. W. Benson, President   Austin E. Hummel, Secretary

Rod and Gun Club.
Chas. W. Ives, President   Frank M. Layman, Secretary

TOWN OF WINDHAM.

Census 1920, Population 1,246
Census 1925, Population 1,336

OFFICERS.

Demont L. Chase	Supervisor	Henry Vining	Assessor
Grant F. Morse	Town Clerk	B. S. Schermerhorn	Overs'r Poor
Geo. L. Cook	Justice Peace	Sidney E. Payne	Overseer Poor
Thomas Cryne	Justice Peace	E. A. Brainerd	School Director
John Barlow	Justice Peace	G. W. Osborn Jr.	School Director
J. F. Moseman	Justice Peace	Charles Garvey	Constable
F. B. Thompson	Collector	Vance Fancher	Constable
Frank Butts	Highway Supt.	Howard Tompkins	Constable
Roscoe W. Howard	Assessor	Daniel Deyo	Constable
Julian Beers	Assessor	Harry Turk	Constable

Post Offices.
Windham (Third Class) .... James Richtmyer, Postmaster
Hensonville (Third Class) .... Walter J. Pelham, Postmaster
Maplecrest (Fourth Class) .... S. A. Moseman, Postmaster

R. F. D. Routes.

North Settlement; Old road, Brooksburgh. Starts and ends at Windham. Carrier, Donald F. Munson.

Star Route 7421; terminals, Windham and Hunter. Windham-Hunter road. Carrier, Welcome Moore.

Star Route 7422; terminals, Hensonville and Tannersville. Maplecrest-East Jewett road. Carrier, Clarence Tompkins.

Star Route 7415; terminals, Prattsville-Cairo on Mohican Trail. Carrier, Charles Alle.

Physicians.

H. H. Baker, Windham   Sidney L. Ford, Hensonville
Dr. W. E. Stevens, Dentist   Benjamin I. Talmadge, Lawyer
Wallace M. Gill, Veterinarian   H. T. Avery, Druggist

First National Bank of Windham.
Dr. S. L. Ford, President   Richard G. Munson, Cashier
S. O. Robinson, Vice President   Edward Miller, Assistant Cashier
F. A. Strong, Vice President
Resources, $459,355.11

Schools.
Seven common schools and one union free school (No. 3). No. 6 contracts with No. 3.

Windham High School.
Class of 1927.

Wesley Towner	Frank Ryan	Henrietta Rosecrans
Harvey Brockett	John Garraghan	Margaret Munson
Edward Phelps	William Davis	Mabel Schermerhorn
Glenn Beers	Elwood Hitchcock	Nina Moore
Katharine Strong	Arlie McGlashan	Viva Jordan
Irene Clark		Charles Holdridge

George Cook, Principal.

Mountain Lodge, No. 529, F. & A. M.

This lodge originated in 1804 under the name of Revival Lodge No. 117, which was instituted in the meeting-house in Batavia, when there were present officers of the Grand Lodge of the State of New York, among them Cadwalder Colden. At this time Samuel Gunn was designated Master, Thomas Benham, Senior Warden; George Robertson, Junior Warden. In 1807 this lodge organized under the title of Harmony Mark Master Lodge, and in 1863 reorganized under the present title.

1926.
Geo. W. Osborn Jr., W. M.   Benjamin I. Talmadge, Secretary

Gem City Lodge, I. O. O. F.
Harry Lammond, N. G.   Arthur Sherman, Secretary

FIRE COMPANIES

Windham Hose Company.
Harold B. Moore, President   Richard G. Munson, Secretary

Hensonville Hose Company.
Elbert O. Chase, President   Walter J. Pelham, Secretary

Hensonville Cornet Band.
Ernest Schoonmaker, President   George Radcliffe Jr., Secretary
John H. Hayes, Director

Elgin Creamery.

Benjamin I. Talmadge, President   Fred M. Goslee, Secretary

Windham Public Library.

Miss Margaret Osborn, President   R. M. MacNaught, Secretary
Miss Hattie Coe, Librarian.

CHURCHES.

First Presbyterian Church.

Organized before 1800. First church raised Dec. 31, 1800; enclosed the following year and completed in 1814. First pastor, Rev. Henry B. Stimson, 1802-26.

In 1831 the church was divided, the eastern division building a church 2½ miles east of the old one (1831), and the Center Presbyterian formed on the 29th of April, 1834, under the direction of Rev. David Porter, D. S. Present church dedicated Jan. 1, 1835. First pastor, Rev. Leonard B. Van Dyke, 1835-61.

Rev. John J. McClelland, present pastor.

Methodist Episcopal Church.

Part of Albany circuit in 1805; of Durham circuit in 1823.
Seth Crowell and Henry Stead were in charge 1805.
Rev. G. F. Wells, present pastor.

Hensonville M. E. Church.

Present church built in 1874; dedicated Feb. 17, 1875. Built through the efforts of Rev. Seney Martin. Pastor in charge, Rev. H. F. Odell. The bell was purchased by the Ladies' Aid Society.

Rev. Harry Lammond, present pastor.

Free Methodist Church of Big Hollow.

Organized June 24, 1871.   Present church built in 1875.
Rev. W. G. Peterson, present pastor.

Big Hollow (Maplecrest) Presbyterian Church.

Organized Dec. 10, 1822. First meeting-house burned Feb. 3, 1833; present church soon rebuilt. Erastus C. Peck assisted in building this church, hewing some of the timbers. He died in 1905, aged ninety-six years.

Rev. Harry Lamond, present pastor.

St. Theresa Roman Catholic Church.

Dedicated Monday, July 26, 1926, by the Rt. Rev. E. F. Gibbons of Albany. Dedication services preceded the Mass which was sung by the Rev. R. J. Roberts, Troy, N. Y. There were twenty-five priests present. The Bishop was assisted by the Rev. P. J. Dwyer of Philmont, and the Rev. C. J. King of Ravena, N. Y.

SCHOOL INSTRUCTORS

Dist. No. **Ashland**
1 Edna M. Hall
3 Wilma McMyne
4 Ada E. Smalling
5 Alice E. Dorn
6 Catherine Morse

Dist. No. **Athens**
1 Michael A. McCall, principal
Elizabeth C. Slattery
Isabelle C. Rainey
2 John Severence, principal
Ethel Torgesen
Marion Cooney
Mildred Strongman
Katharine E. Widmann
Gertrude Ellsworth
Frances P. Mangeot
Mrs. Marion B. Scudder
Anna M. Ford
M. Blanche Smith
Mrs. Helen J. Wood
3 Pauline Tompkins
4 Viva B. Clawson
5 Edrie Warner
6 Elizabeth Scott

Dist. No. **Cairo**
1 Charles Coutant, principal
Miss Crossley
Miss Davis
Miss Gurley
Mrs. Charles Coutant
Leonard DuBois
Helen Chadderdon
2 Emily M. Dorpfeld
3 Ethel Ruland
4 Albert Morrison
5 Ethel Bailey
6 Esther H. Knapp
7 Bessie Lee Jones
8 Harlan G. Wiltse
9 Lauren M. Barker
10 Isabelle D. Lane
11 Ruth Van Hoesen

Dist. No. **Catskill**
1 George H. Chadwick, principal
Florence Smith
Marguerite L. Young
Anna A. Eells
Adelaide Lewis
Dorothy Bennit
Lola F. Conklin
Mrs. Roy Coughtry
Anna M. Barlow
Susan C. Deakin
Florence T. White
Henrietta Lewis
Faith D. Avery
Beulah I. Timmerman
Elina C. Van Dyke
Mary C. Timmerman
Katharine G. Slattery
Bessie R. Muller
Olive P. Kennedy
Alice M. Dodge
H. May Ford
Edna Maguire, librarian
Teresa O'Shea, health nurse
H. Leon Sheppard,
        physical director
Eli Bartoo, agriculture
Grandview—
Alice L. Babcock, principal
Alice Ernst
Anna H. Smith
Mabel Hughes
Mae E. Van Valkenburgh
Pauline Davis
H. May Ford
2 Mrs. Verona A. Beare
3 Alice E. Jones, principal
Virginia Blakelock
4 Ruth Steele
5 Jessie Hevner
6 Lettie P. Holmes
7 Ensey Bailey
8 Bessie C. Van Arsdal
9 Hazel Crocoll
10 Arthur C. Lewis, principal
Ferdina Timmerman

Dist. No. **Catskill**
11 Julia M. Vedder
12 Mary O'Brien, principal
    Eva A. Dunn
13 George P. Holmes
15 John W. McMenamy, principal
    Frederick D. Johnson
    Marion Middleton
    Florence E. Cole
    Elizabeth Worth

Dist. No. **Coxsackie**
1 Robert Chaloner, principal
    Mrs. Rebecca Bogardus
    Esther Barnes
    Mae Fitzgerald
    Mildred Campbell
    Rose M. Seenman
    Ellen Smith
    Mrs. Alice Case
    Edith J. VanDenburgh
    Mrs. Mary Waters
    Mrs. Dudley Lyall
    Mrs. Robbins
    Ella O'Brien
    Mrs. Nellie Lewis
    Viola Sabedra
    Miss Olmsted
    Miss Hickey
    Mrs. Jessie Smith
    Catherine Hotaling
    Josephine Cohan
2 Gertrude Tryon
3 Mrs. Alma Simpson
4 Mrs. Bertha Hallenbeck
5 Mrs. Frank K. Swartwout
6 Jennie A. Whitbeck
7 Mrs. Beulah K. Roe
8 Mrs. Dorothy L. Brooks
9 Mrs. Wilema V. Conrad

Dist. No. **Durham**
2 Hannah Wheat
3 Gertrude Murta
4 Mrs. Lloyd Tompkins
5 Elizabeth Eldred
6 Olin Haskin
7 William A. Fox
8 Mary D. Wade

Dist. No.
10 Effie Bates
11 Ruby F. Rundell
12 Henrietta Morse
14 Contracts
15 Mary A. Foster
16 Esther Van Tassel

Dist. No. **Greenville**
1 Harriet Spalding
2 Edna Story
3 Harriet Wickse
4 C. F. Kearney, principal
    Viola Light
    Cecelia Bliss
    Alice Stevens
    Mary Mabie
    Charlotte Story
    Helen Salley
    Scott Ellis
5 Alice Chesbro
6 Eva Evans
7 F. May Shaw
8 Irene Worth
9 Contracts
10 Gladys Beylegaard
11 Dorothy Irish
12 Howard Story
13 Contracts
14 Ruth Corley
15 Contracts

Dist. No. **Halcott**
1 Mrs. Leora Kittle
2 Mary V. Griffin
3 Ethel Sanford
4 Marjorie H. Todd

Dist. No. **Hunter**
2 John S. Woods, principal
    Helen L. Hann
    Marion McCambridge
    Mary V. Howard
    Ada L. Purdy
    Mrs. Ruth L. Strenk
    Mrs. Cecile Woods
3 Doris Decker
4 Gladys P. Dyer, principal
    Mary Gormley
    Agatha Flick

Dist. No.   **Hunter**
4 James Flahive
   Leon M. Peters
   Muriel Prediger
   Mrs. Jessie Showers
   Annie Glennon
6 Jennie Downs
7 Mrs. Miriam E. Lester
8 Stewart W. Tuttle, principal
   Mrs. Anna Tuttle
   Anne E. Stock
   Mariana Gorham
9 Vera McLean
10 E. Delmar Smith

Dist. No.   **Jewett**
1 Ernest F. Cole, principal
   Vesta L. Tompkins
2 Lucile E. Woods
3 Mrs. Hazel Wilson
4 Mrs. Dema Crosby
5 Mrs. Elva T. Lacy
6 Nelson Griffith
7 Mrs. Belle Cruikshank
8 Mrs. Gladys Peck

Dist. No.   **Lexington**
3 Margaret Dunham
4 Beulah M. Jennette
5 Mrs Alice Stiles
6 Mrs. Olive Shoemaker
7 Mrs. Blanche Van Valkenburgh
8 Mary Bergin
9 Mrs. Iva O. Hand
10 Mrs. Ruth West
11 Mrs. Gladys Van Valkenburgh
12 Mrs. Elsie W. Ellis
13 Mrs. E. Van Valkenburgh

Dist. No.   **New Baltimore**
1 Anna White
2 Susie Cary
4 Jessie Boyd
5 Florence Wood
7 Lydia Smith
8 Lelita Mahler
9 Contracts
10 Caroline D. Shear
11 Grace Gibbs
12 May B. Blake
14 Hazel C. Bailey

Dist. No.   **Prattsville**
1 Mary MacCoubrey
2 Fred Russell, principal
   Hazel V. Gregory
   Mrs. Dora E. Petherbridge
3 Mrs. Mary E. Peckham
4 Mrs. Katharine Bishop
5 Mrs. Alta L. Hapeman
6 Mrs. Nina L. Griffin

Dist. No.   **Windham**
1 Dorothy Chase
2 Edythe Vining
3 George L. Cook, principal
   Shirley D. MacNaught
   Mildred Miller
   Irone Michael
   Abner Woodworth
   Raymond Moseman
   Harriet Campbell
   Alice Stevens
4 Mary L. Dunham
6 Contracts
7 Alice Brandow
8 Ellen MacGlashan

INDEX

Towns

Ashland—Town of	13
Village of	16
Athens—Town of	19
Village of	24
Cairo—Town of	29
Village of	30
Acra	32
Sandy Plains	33
South Cairo	32
Round Top	33
Purling	31
Woodstock	30
Catskill—Town of	37
Village of	42
Old Katskill	39
Leeds	49
Jefferson	51
Imboght	53
Kiskatom	55
Palenville	57
Cauterskill	59
Coxsackie—Town of	64
Village of	65
Upper Landing	67
Jacksonville	68
Coeymans Patent	71
Morin Patent	70
Houghtaling Pat't	68
Roseboom Patent	68
Durham—Town of	74
Village of	78
Oak Hill	77
Cornwallville	79
South Durham	81
East Windham	81
Greenville—Town of	85
Village of	86
Freehold	87
Gayhead	88
Halcott—Town of	89
Halcott Center	91
Hunter—Town of	92
Village of	93
Tannersville	95
Haines Falls	96
The Cloves	96
Jewett—Town of	101
Jewett Heights	103
Jewett Center	103
Lexington—Town of	105
Village of	107
West Kill	108
Beach Ridge	108
Bushnellville	108
New Baltimore—Town of	110
Village of	110
Prattsville—Town of	114
Village of	115
Red Falls	119
Windham—Town of	120
Village of	120
Hensonville	122
Maplecrest	124
Mitchell Hollow	125
Brookline	126
Union Society	126

HISTORY OF GREENE COUNTY

Pioneers		Obituaries	
Abeel, David	60	Botsford, Henry T.	150
Allerton, Jonathan	35	Bronson, Corwin B.	129
Austin, Moses	82	Butts, Romaine	155
Barker, James	36	Cole, Osborn A.	160
Baldwins, the	83	Conklin, George, M. D.	150
Benham, Dr. Thomas	18	Curtis, Harrie McKelvie	149
Bogardus, Jacob	89	Ford, Edwin L., M. D.	156
Brandow, Godfrey	88	Jennings, Dr. Dean W.	133
Bronk, Leonard	71	Kerr, Ira B.	140
Chase, Zephaniah	104	Mackey, Elmore	130
Edwards, Col. William	100	Mansfield, Byron	158
Henson, John*	123	Martin, Christopher A.	153
Maben, John	109	Stevens, Orrin C.	151
Newton, John	109	Voss, Charles	154
Miller, Jonathan	112		
Morss, Burton G.	119	**Chronology**	
Stimson, George	127	1925, 1926, 1927	129-160
Stimson, Henry	18		
Strong, Elisha	18	**Directory**	
Van Slyke, Cornelius Anton-		Officials; organizations	161-202
issen	113	School Teachers	203-205

* William, not John, was a soldier of the Revolution.

www.ingramcontent.com/pod-product-compliance
Lightning Source LLC
Chambersburg PA
CBHW050148170426
43197CB00011B/2004